Up in the Air

BETTY RIEGEL

**SIMON &
SCHUSTER**

London · New York · Sydney · Toronto · New Delhi

A CBS COMPANY

First published in Great Britain by Simon & Schuster UK Ltd, 2013
A CBS COMPANY

3 5 7 9 10 8 6 4 2

Simon & Schuster UK Ltd
1st Floor
222 Gray's Inn Road
London WC1X 8HB

www.simonandschuster.co.uk

Simon & Schuster Australia, Sydney
Simon & Schuster India, New Delhi

A CIP catalogue record for this book
is available from the British Library

ISBN: 978-1-47111-225-6
eBook ISBN: 978-1-47111-227-0

Typeset in the UK by M Rules
Printed and bound by CPI Group (UK) Ltd, Croydon, CR0 4YY

Contents

This book is dedicated to my parents, Ruby and Sidney Eden: without their unselfishness and encouragement, much of my magical life would not have happened. To my lifelong Pan Am 'sisters' – my friends Brenda, Mimi, Sandra, Hazel, Joyce, Angie andAngela – who have helped contribute so many mutual memories and to my friend Dawn who was with me from the beginning. Finally, to Pan Am – my wonderful mentor – who offered me such a spectacular opportunity for which I will be forever grateful.

Prologue

As the turbo engines fired up and started to roar, I closed my eyes and gripped my seat with a mixture of nerves and excitement. Then came the huge surge of power and noise as we hurtled down the runway, followed by an incredible feeling of weightlessness as the plane's wheels lifted off the ground and we soared into the sky like an elegant bird.

I peered out of the window. Everything looked so different from up here. I could see the smoke from coal fires snaking out of the chimneys of the houses, the tiny cars on the road and a steam train chugging along, probably packed full of people on their way to work. I took one last glance at the familiar suburbs and the frosty green fields of the English countryside before we disappeared up into the clouds, as I knew it would be a long time before I saw them again.

It was 2 February 1961, an ordinary Thursday to most of the people down there on the ground, but to me it signalled the start of an incredible adventure. Today was the day I knew my life was about to change forever.

'Welcome aboard this Pan Am flight to New York,' said a voice over the PA system.

'New York!' said Paula, the girl setting next to me, her eyes shining with excitement. 'Can you believe it, Betty? We're on a jet plane and we're off to the Big Apple.'

In all honesty, I couldn't. New York to me was a magical, mystical place I had only ever seen in films, and Pan Am planes were something movie stars and prime ministers jetted around the world on. Not me, ordinary Betty Eden, who grew up in a council house in Walthamstow and whose annual family holiday was two weeks in Margate.

'None of it seems real,' I said, smiling.

And the reason I was here on this trip of a lifetime? I was one of seventeen young British women who had been selected to train as a stewardess for Pan American, the world's premier and most sophisticated airline. Thousands had applied, but I was one of the few they had chosen. I could still barely believe it now, even though we were on our way to New York for an intensive six-week course.

In the 1960s every little girl dreamt of being a Pan Am stewardess. Every woman wanted to be one and every man wanted to be seen with one on his arm. Now that was going to be me. It truly was the job of my dreams, but it had come at a price. I'd had to leave my parents, Ruby and Sidney, my brother, Geoff, and my high-school boyfriend, Ernie, behind, while I was about to begin a new life thousands of miles away from home.

But looking around the first-class cabin gave me a taste of the amazing things to come.

'It really is a different world up here,' I sighed, staring at all the passengers dressed in their Sunday best. It was like being in a five-star hotel at 37,000 ft. There were fresh flowers, china plates, heavy silver cutlery, crystal glasses and expensive linens.

Champagne corks popped, handsome men in suits strolled to the cocktail bar for Manhattans and wealthy women in elegant hats and gloves smoked cigarettes while enjoying a game of Gin Rummy.

It was also the perfect opportunity to study the Pan Am stewardesses at work. They all looked so classy and elegant in their glamorous blue uniforms, and they seemed to do everything with such style and panache, whether it was remembering every single passenger's name or preparing and serving a seven-course gourmet meal.

'That will be us soon,' whispered Paula.

'I know,' I said. 'I can't wait.'

While most of my peers at home were getting married and having children, I was about to embark on a wonderful career that would pay me to travel around the world in five-star luxury. I couldn't believe my luck, and there was one thing that I was absolutely sure of as I embarked on this amazing adventure: I was going to have the time of my life.

Chapter One

A World at War

The loud wailing noise disturbed me from my deep, blissful sleep. I felt Mum's familiar, warm body start to stir next to me and then swiftly spring into action.

'Come on, Betty,' I heard her say. 'It's time.'

I didn't need telling twice. I knew the drill by now.

In a split second, I was wide awake and leaping out of bed to put on my coat and shoes. Mum made sure we always slept in our clothes, so we were ready to go. While she grabbed a couple of blankets, I hunted for my beloved Teddy and Golly and tucked them safely under my arm. Then she took me tightly by the hand and we rushed down the stairs and out of the front door into the freezing-cold night.

'Run, Betty, run,' Mum yelled, not letting go of my hand for a second as we bolted through the pitch-black terraced streets. Even over the incessant wail of the air-raid siren, I could already hear the low, menacing throb of the German planes in the sky above us, and I knew any second now the bombs would start falling.

I put my head down and ran as fast as my little legs could carry me. I didn't dare look up, as the only time I had, I'd seen a plane alight directly above us in the night sky. I had been both fascinated and terrified by the sight of that burning orange fireball spiralling through the darkness.

Soon we were safely inside the Nissen shelter at the bottom of our street. Mum and I curled up on one of the wooden benches along the sides and tried desperately to get some sleep. But it was always hard to block out the unmistakable shrieking of the bombs in the distance as they decimated our neighbourhood.

The year was 1942, and this was normal life for me. This was war.

I was born on 27 March 1939, six months before the Second World War broke out. So, growing up, all I knew was wartime. For the first six years of my life, it was just my mum, Ruby, and me. My dad, Sidney, worked at a timber site for a company called Goldman and Son, where he had gone straight from school. When I was six months old, he was called up for national service and conscripted to the Black Cat regiment of the Royal Artillery, who were stationed on Salisbury Plain.

I knew Mum missed him terribly. She and Dad had met when they were fourteen and he was the local paper boy, and they had been together ever since. Before the war, they had never even spent more than a day apart, and he was her world. Mum had a tiny black and white photograph of Dad looking very handsome and smart in his brown uniform, which he had sent home to her, and she always carried it with her in her handbag. One afternoon I remember walking into the kitchen and catching her looking wistfully at it.

'Oh, Betty,' she sighed, 'I miss your daddy so much.'

Although I was only little, I could tell she was feeling sad, so

I leant down and gave the photo a little kiss. Mum smiled and did exactly the same.

'Don't worry,' she told me. 'Daddy will be home soon and then we'll be able to give him proper kisses.'

Every night before we went to sleep, we would say our prayers together. 'Dear God, please bring my daddy home safely' was always the last thing I said before I shut my eyes. Afterwards, Mum would lie down with me and stroke my hair until I fell asleep.

So, with Dad away at war for the first six years of my life, it was just Mum and me, and we were such a tight little unit. We lived in a three-bedroom council terrace in Walthamstow, a small town in the Home Counties, an hour outside London, that is now known as Waltham Forest.

One of my first memories is of Mum setting up all her cans of food on a table in the scullery, so I could play shops while she did the washing in a big tub she called 'the boiler'. She would ladle cold water into it, which was heated up by a gas flame underneath, then she would put the clothes in and stir them for ages with a long wooden stick to get them clean. Then she'd run them all through a mangle before putting them on the line. One lot of water had to do several loads, and she always sang away as she worked. Vera Lynn was the forces' sweetheart and the mascot of families like us, left to hold the fort at home, and Mum loved her songs, like 'White Cliffs of Dover' and 'You'll Never Walk Alone'. But her favourite was always 'We'll Meet Again'. Singing was Mum's therapy, and as she sung the words of that song, her eyes would well up with tears and I always knew she was thinking of Dad.

'Oh, Mummy, please sing the funny ones,' I would beg her. Then I would collapse into fits of giggles as she burst into a rendition of 'My Old Man Said Follow the Van'.

Her nickname for me was 'Tink', as she said I was a little tinker who was always getting into mischief. Like the time we both went for a nap one Sunday afternoon and I woke up before Mum. As she was still asleep and I wasn't able to dress myself yet, I managed to unlock the front door and walked down the street completely naked, with my clothes under my arm, until I found a neighbour I could ask to help me. Poor Mum was horrified when she woke up to find I was gone!

She wasn't best pleased when I ate all her bananas either. They were extremely rare during the war, and when you did see them, they were very expensive. One day Mum had managed to get hold of a bunch. I had never seen one before and I couldn't wait to taste this funny-looking fruit. When her back was turned for a second, I reached up to the fruit bowl, took all the bananas, then ran and hid under the table and ate a couple of them as fast as I could. Mum was so cross when she found me crouched under there, surrounded by a pile of banana skins, and the ones I hadn't eaten were ruined because they were so bruised.

'It wasn't me, Mummy, it was Dang Dang that did it,' I told her, blaming it on my imaginary friend who lived behind a chair in the living room.

But most of the time I was like Mum's little shadow, helping her do all the chores around the house. Our Saturday morning job, and one of my favourites, was giving the green and purple checked lino in the living room a good clean. Mum would be on her hands and knees, smearing polish over the floor, and I would be crouched behind her, on my hands and knees too, shining it up with a cloth.

If I wasn't helping, I was tap dancing. Sometimes when Mum was cooking, she would lay a piece of plywood down on the floor so I could hear the clip-clop of my shoes while she sang a song for me to dance along to.

But most of my earliest memories are connected to the war. It was at night that you really felt it most. It would start at dusk, when you had to put up your mandatory blackouts at the windows. Wardens would walk around the streets, and if they saw even a little crack of light through the glass, they would knock on your door and you would get a telling off or a fine. People were not allowed to go out at night unless it was absolutely essential, so everywhere was deserted and it was pitch-black, as the street lights were turned off so they couldn't help to guide enemy aircraft.

I always slept with Mum in her bed. I loved her bedroom, especially her rosewood dressing table with the crocheted doilies and the cut-glass dressing-table set that Dad had bought her on her twenty-first birthday. Sometimes she would let me sit there, and if I was very careful, I was allowed to touch the precious glass candlesticks and the beautiful little sparkling bowls with lids.

We always went to bed fully dressed because every night, without fail, the air-raid siren would go off to warn us that the bombing was due to start. There was an Anderson shelter at the bottom of our garden, as the government had given them out for free to people who earned less than £5 a week, but Mum hated it.

'It's too lonely in there,' she told me.

Looking back, I don't blame her. It was made out of curved pieces of corrugated iron and it had an earth floor, so it was always cold, dank and damp, and the walls would stream with condensation. It was only 6 ft by 4 ft, so it was cramped too, and it had a horrible musty, earthy smell that would cling to your clothes.

Even though it was further to run to, when the air-raid siren would sound, we would head to the larger Nissen shelter at the end of our street. It was a long brick hut with a corrugated-iron roof and rows of benches around the sides, and there were often thirty or forty people crowded in there. There was no lights or a toilet, but a couple of neighbours would bring gas lanterns and there was a makeshift bucket just in case you got desperate.

Despite the horrors that were going on outside, there was a friendly, communal atmosphere inside the shelter. Some people chatted quietly, but most curled up on a bench, like Mum and me, and tried to get some sleep. Mum still laughs today when she tells the story about how we were at the shops one morning when a chap walked in and I loudly announced: 'Look, Mummy, there's the man you slept with last night!' She hurriedly had to explain that I was referring to the fact that the gentleman had been on the next bench to us in the air-raid shelter.

We would have to stay in the shelter until we heard the long continuous tone of the all-clear siren, which normally didn't come until the next morning, when it was light. Then we'd emerge, blinking in the harsh daylight like moles, to face the devastation of the previous night's bombing. As we walked through the dusty streets littered with rubble, you would see a gap where a building used to be or a house that looked like it had been sliced in half. The wallpaper would still be on the walls and you could see the furniture inside, just as it had been left, but the entire front would have been blown off, so it looked like a dolls' house.

The closer we'd get to our terrace, the harder we would pray that our home was still standing. Our neighbours' houses were sometimes damaged, but thankfully ours never took a direct hit.

These were the days before television, but we would go home and listen to the news on the radio in the front room. It was a huge, dark-wood thing with Bakelite buttons that rested on a four-legged stand. Central London was the worst hit and we would see terrible pictures in the newspapers. It was total devastation and people were forced to sleep in the Tube stations. One of the few buildings that were untouched was St Paul's, which Mum told me the Germans never bombed because they used it as a landmark.

Death and destruction became a way of life. Thankfully none of our family was killed in the war, but everyone would dread seeing a messenger boy cycling into their street, as a telegram only meant one thing – bad news. Everywhere we went, we would see people wearing black armbands, a symbol to show they were mourning a loved one lost in the war.

I remember hearing some neighbours talking to Mum in hushed tones one day about how our milkman, Fred Wilkins, had been shot and killed by a low-flying German aircraft as he did his rounds.

Mum and I had our own close shave too. One afternoon I was playing with my doll in the front room when I looked out of the window and saw a metal cylinder floating through the sky attached to a parachute.

'Mummy!' I shouted. 'Look at that!'

When Mum ran to the window, her face drained of colour.

'Oh my goodness!' she gasped.

We both watched and waited with bated breath as this mysterious thing floated down and landed in the middle of our street. But when nothing happened, I was puzzled.

'What is it, Mummy?' I asked.

'It's a bomb,' she said, giving me a hug. 'But it's OK, it didn't detonate. It's obviously not our time to go.'

Sending down bombs on parachutes into residential areas was a common technique the Germans used. It should have blown us all sky–high, but by some miracle it hadn't gone off. Mum and I were even more amazed a few minutes later, when some neighbours came running out of their houses with scissors and started to cut the parachute up.

'Silly women,' Mum sighed. 'What on earth are they doing?'

We found out later that they didn't want to waste the lovely green silk the parachute was made of, so they were going to use it to make underwear. But the bomb could have gone off at any point! I was fascinated, but Mum made me keep away from the window until the Home Guard had taken it away.

But, as a little girl growing up in wartime, all of this seemed completely normal to me. Bombs fell, houses burnt, people were shot. That was just life, as far as I was concerned, and I didn't know any different. The other big fear was of a gas attack, and everyone had to carry around regulation gas masks in a wooden box. I had a red rubber Mickey Mouse one. We had to practise taking it on and off, but even that was a game to me.

When I was with Mum, I never felt scared and, luckily, I was too young to realise the seriousness of the situation. It's only when I look back now that I realise how brave Mum was and how hard it must have been for her, especially when I was a baby. She must have been so scared and she missed Dad terribly, but I never once saw her break down and she always put on a brave face for me. Thousands of children, especially those from larger families, were evacuated out to the country, but Mum was determined to keep us together.

'I can protect you better than any stranger,' she told me, and she refused to let me go, even though the majority of children in our neighbourhood did. As an adult, I've heard so many horror stories from people who were evacuated during the war, about how homesick they were or how badly they were treated by the people who took them in, and I'm so grateful to Mum for insisting that I stayed with her.

But she was keen to get us both away from the city and the bombs, so when I was four, Mum's older sister, Alice, invited us to go and stay with her and her husband, Len Brookman, and their two-year-old daughter, Peggy, in Hatfield, Hertfordshire.

'I don't like the thought of the two of you being in that house all by yourselves, with bombs going off and no man around to take care of you,' Alice told Mum.

Mum was one of four sisters and they were all very close. However, the one sticking point was that Mum wasn't keen on Alice's husband, Len. He was a volunteer fireman, which meant he was exempt from being conscripted, so he would be around if we went to stay. Len was a real disciplinarian who liked to throw his weight around and believed his word was law.

'That man likes the sound of his own voice,' Mum always used to tell me, and poor Aunt Alice lived in his shadow. He never laid a finger on her, but he was a real bully and he had a terrible temper.

Mum used to tell the story of how Len had tried to date her when they were teenagers, but she'd given him short shrift. 'He wouldn't have had an easy life if he'd married me,' she joked.

So, thinking we would be safer in the country, Mum reluctantly agreed to go and stay with them.

Unfortunately, it wasn't much of an escape, as a few weeks after we got there, the Germans started to bomb airfields across the UK, and there was a big one at Hatfield.

But I liked being in the country, and Aunt Alice and Uncle Len had a nice three-bedroom semi, with chickens in their garden. I loved collecting the eggs and walking in the fields behind the house, picking daisies and buttercups. They had a metal Morrison shelter in their dining room that also doubled up as a table, so when the air-raid siren went off, we would all crawl under there, which I thought was great fun.

While we were living there, I started at the local nursery school, which was at the bottom of the street. Every day I walked there all by myself. But I still liked to live up to my 'Tinker' nickname every now and again, and one morning I decided I didn't want to go to school. Instead, I walked to the local bakery and bought myself a doughnut with the thrupenny bit Mum had given me for my milk. I was sat on the bakery steps tucking into it when Uncle Len cycled past and saw me. He marched me straight to school and, boy, was I in big trouble when I got home later that day!

Uncle Len and his strict ways were the reason our stay in Hatfield came to an abrupt end. One night we were all having dinner together. I was full, but Len wouldn't let me leave the table.

'You're not going anywhere until you eat every last scrap on that plate,' he told me.

I'd had my mutton chop, but I couldn't stomach another mouthful of sludgy, grey boiled potato or tinned peas.

'I can't, Uncle Len,' I said. 'I feel sick.'

'You're lucky to have food at all, young lady,' he said. 'Now eat it up.'

I forced a spoonful into my mouth, but it made me gag and I started to cry.

'Don't turn on the waterworks with me, girl,' he said. 'Eat your dinner.'

I could see it was upsetting Mum that I was getting distressed, and she tried to take bits of food off my plate and eat them when Len wasn't looking.

'Let her be, Len,' Mum told him. 'She's had enough.'

But he wouldn't back down and I was astonished when I saw

that Mum had tears trickling down her face. I'd never seen her cry before and that made me howl even more.

'Stop blubbing, for God's sake, and finish your food,' he shouted.

I could see Aunt Alice was getting agitated too.

'Please just let her go, Len,' she begged. 'You're upsetting the poor child.'

But Len didn't take kindly to being told what to do. 'You stay where you are, young lady,' he roared at me. 'While you're living in my house, you will abide by my rules.'

That was the final straw for Mum. She pushed back her chair with a screech, stood up and said, 'That's quite enough, Len.'

She picked me up and carried me upstairs, where she quickly threw all of our things into a suitcase.

'Don't worry, Tink,' she told me. 'We're going home.'

Aunt Alice came running upstairs and started sobbing when she saw us packing. 'You can't leave now, Ruby!' she cried. 'Not at this hour. It's pitch-black out there, and what if the air-raid siren goes off?'

But Mum's mind was made up. 'I'm sorry, Alice, but I can't just sit there and let him treat my daughter like that,' she told her. 'We're going back to London.'

Despite Alice's protestations, Mum said goodbye to her and we marched out, hand in hand, into the dark night. Thankfully Uncle Len had made himself scarce, so we didn't have to see him. It was freezing cold and we had to get a train and a bus, which took hours. At one point we were stopped by a policeman.

'What are you doing out at this time of night, madam? It's highly dangerous,' he said.

'I just want to get my daughter back to London,' Mum told him tearfully.

It was well after midnight by the time we walked through our front door, but we were both relieved to be home. A few days later a letter arrived from Alice:

'I'm sorry about Len's behaviour. You know what he's like. But I don't want to let it come between us.'

Mum knew Len would never apologise in a million years, as he was so stubborn and didn't believe he had done anything wrong. 'Alice, you're my sister and of course I will always love you, but I couldn't bear to spend another minute under the same roof as that despicable man,' she wrote back.

After that we still saw Aunt Alice and Uncle Len, and Mum was always polite to him for Alice's sake, but there was no love lost between them. I don't think she ever told Dad what had happened, as she knew he would have been furious that someone had been mean to 'his girls' as he called us. She learnt to button her lip and kept her true feelings hidden from then on, as she didn't want to cause a rift in the family.

Mum was my protector and there was only one time during the war that I remember being truly frightened. Sometimes there were daytime air raids, and one Sunday morning Mum and I were in the Anderson shelter at the bottom of our garden. It was half full of water as usual, so we had to perch on the ledge around the sides. We were shelling peas for Sunday dinner to help pass the time when suddenly we heard the sound of heavy boots coming up the path.

Mum froze, and it was the first time I had ever seen her look scared. Even though I didn't know why, I was automatically frightened because I could tell she was.

'What is it, Mummy?' I whispered.

'Shhh,' she said, holding me close.

We both sat deadly still, listening to the clump, clump, clump of the boots as they came closer and closer towards us up the garden path. My heart was racing when the door of the shelter finally creaked open …

'There you are, girls!' said a cheery voice.

It was my Uncle Jim, my mum's only brother, who was in the Home Guard.

'Jim,' Mum sighed, 'you nearly gave me a heart attack! I thought you were a German soldier who'd parachuted down onto our street.'

'I just thought I would come and check on you ladies and make sure you're managing,' he told us.

'How kind of you,' Mum said, and I could hear the relief in her voice.

Life must have been one long struggle for Mum, especially when it came to making ends meet. Dad sent money home, but it was very little and everything was rationed. Then, three years into the war, tragedy struck. During a military exercise, Dad badly injured his leg in a motorbike crash and he spent a year in hospital in North Yorkshire. He was in a lot of pain but, looking back now, the accident was a blessing as it probably saved his life. While he was recuperating, the rest of his regiment were sent to Italy, where most of them were killed in action.

Afterwards, he went back to help train the troops on Salisbury Plain. Over the six years he was away, Mum was only allowed to visit him once. She always talks about going to see him and walking past a fence and hearing someone bellowing out orders to the soldiers. She couldn't believe it when she got to the other side and saw that the man with the loud, scary voice was her mild-mannered, gentle husband.

I only saw Dad once before I turned six. I opened the door one day and this strange man was stood there. He was tall and skinny, but he looked very handsome in his brown uniform.

'Betty, it's your dad,' he said.

I was excited to see him, but mainly because one of the American soldiers stationed at his base, a man called Rocky from New Jersey, had given him a tin of peaches to bring home for me. Fruit was scarce in those days, so it was a real treat. Dad sat in the living room polishing the brass buttons on his uniform, while Mum and I tucked into those peaches straight from the can, the sweet, sticky juice trickling down our chins.

Even though we didn't see Dad, he wrote to Mum all the time, and she would read his letters out to me. 'Please give my Tink all my love and tell her Daddy will be home soon.' I've still got one of those letters, and it's one of my most treasured possessions.

On 8 May 1945, life as I knew it changed forever. It was all very exciting, as Mum and I sat around the radio and listened to the special broadcast from Downing Street, where the Prime Minister, Winston Churchill, announced that the war was finally over.

'That means Daddy's coming home!' Mum said, beaming.

Neighbours ran out of their houses onto our street, cheering and laughing, and it was like a festival atmosphere. We heard on the news that people had packed into Trafalgar Square and all the way up the Mall to Buckingham Palace, where King George and Queen Elizabeth appeared on the balcony to greet the cheering crowds.

There were street parties everywhere. Everyone made food and all the women set up tables in the road. There were red, white and blue streamers and balloons, and posters were stuck on lamp posts, with a big picture of a German soldier on them and the words 'We've beaten this one.'

A few days later I was playing in our yard when Mum came out to see me, a huge smile on her face.

'Betty, I've got a surprise for you,' she said, leading me into the kitchen. My mind was suddenly filled with ideas of a whip and top or even a puppy, so I was shocked to see a man in a brown uniform stood there.

'Daddy's home!' said Mum.

Even though Dad was quite a skinny man, he seemed so big to me, and it felt like he took up the whole room. He wrapped his arms around Mum and me and squeezed us so tight, I could hardly breathe.

'My girls,' he sighed. 'It's so good to be home.'

It felt strange hugging this man whom I hardly knew, but I could see how happy Mum was and I knew how much she had missed him. Tears of joy and relief ran down her face.

Mum's eldest sister, Flo, and her husband, Ted, lived down in Margate and their son, Ron, was a tail gunner in the air force. Thankfully he had come home safely too, so a few days later we went down to their house for a big demob party.

The whole family got together for a week of celebrations. The food and drink flowed and everyone was singing and dancing. I thought it was wonderful, especially as every night I got to sleep in a bed with my cousins Peggy and Jill. It was such a happy time after all the stresses and strains of the war.

I will always remember Dad hoisting me up on his shoulders and saying, 'There will never be another war, Betty.'

But then the celebrations were over and normal life resumed. To me, 'normal' meant going to bed fully clothed, spending the night in air-raid shelters and constantly ducking bombs, but suddenly the war had ended and everything that I had ever known in my life had changed.

I could see Mum was pleased to have Dad home, but really he was a stranger to me. Mum had always told me what a kind, gentle person he was, but my only experience of men had taught me they were to be feared, like German soldiers or strict Uncle Len, and in all honesty, I was anxious about what it would be like having this man living in our house. It was strange seeing his razor in the bathroom and getting used to the strong smell of the Ringer's A1 tobacco that he smoked. I would stand there for ages, completely fascinated, watching him roll a cigarette with fingers that were stained yellow from all the nicotine.

Then there was the non-stop whistling that now echoed around our house. Dad whistled from the minute he got up to the minute he went to sleep, but at least it meant I always knew where he was in the house.

But the thing that horrified me the most was when I realised he wanted to sleep in the same bed as Mum.

'But, Daddy, where will *I* sleep?' I asked him.

'In your bedroom,' he said.

I was really put out, as I'd had Mum all to myself for six years. Suddenly everything in my little world was different, and I wasn't best pleased that I now had to share my lovely mother with someone else.

'We're the lucky ones, Tink,' Dad told me. 'We're all safe and back together.'

I knew he was right. We were in the minority in that we hadn't lost a single loved one in the war. So many children's fathers, brothers and uncles were never coming home. Killed in action or missing, presumed dead. So many families had been ripped apart and would never be the same again.

Dad must have known how I was feeling, as he did his best to make sure I was never left out. One day we were walking down the street to the butcher's. Mum and I would always stroll along hand in hand when we were doing the shopping, but now it was her and Dad with their fingers entwined, while I trailed sulkily behind them. Dad must have noticed I was dragging my feet because suddenly he turned around to me.

'Come on, Tink,' he said, letting go of Mum's hand and holding out his own. 'You go in the middle.'

Well, my scowl soon disappeared! I thought it was lovely, Mum on one side, Dad on the other, holding my hands and swinging me up in the air as we walked. That's when I first realised the benefit of having two parents. I had always enjoyed being in the spotlight, and now I had two people to lavish me with attention and give me a round of applause when I tap danced.

Every day I discovered new things about my dad. Mum had always told me how good he was at DIY, and he had a little shed in our garden which had remained untouched during the war years. A couple of weeks after he came home, he disappeared into it each day for a few hours.

'What on earth are you doing in there, Sid?' Mum kept asking him.

'Ah, you'll see,' he said, giving me a cheeky wink.

A week later he emerged clutching a beautiful handmade wooden sledge with a rope handle.

'This is for you, Tink,' he said, 'to say thank you for looking after your mother so well while I was away.'

'Oh, Sidney,' Mum laughed, 'it's only May. The poor girl's going to have to wait months to use it.'

But I didn't care. 'It's lovely, Daddy,' I said.

Besides Teddy, that sledge was my most treasured possession, and I kept it beside my bed. Every night before I went to sleep, I would stare at it and then close my eyes and pray for snow. But as it was almost summer, I was always in for a disappointment in the morning, and it was a good seven months before I got to use it.

The other thing that I learnt about Dad was that he loved his books. Like Mum, he'd left school at fourteen, but he liked reading about nature and geography and he was obsessed with maps. He had never been out of the UK, but he was fascinated by all the countries in the world.

'Come and sit with me,' he would say, tapping his knee.

I would perch on his lap and he would tell me about the beautiful mahogany wood found in South-East Asia and the giant trees that grew in California that were over 3000 years old.

'They're called sequoia trees, and one of them is so big it has a road running through the bottom of its trunk, so you can drive through it,' he said. 'Imagine that, Tink. Wouldn't that be fun?'

'Where's California, Daddy?' I asked.

'Let's get out the map and I'll show you,' he said.

Then he would carefully point out all the different places he had been telling me about, while I listened, completely fascinated.

Slowly I got used to Dad being around, and I soon realised what a wonderful man he was. He had been home a month when he got a job at a Forestry Commission site on the River Lea in Hertfordshire, and sometimes he would take me to work with him. We didn't have a car, so we would have to leave when it was dark in the morning and get a bus and a train. Dad would get me set up with a rod, some worms and a bucket and I would fish in the river while he worked. I loved it, although I never managed to catch a single thing! Then, at lunchtime, we would sit on the riverbank and eat the cheese and pickle sandwiches Mum had made us and chat about all the birds and wildlife we could see around us.

One Sunday, Dad insisted that we got our tea from the cockle and winkle cart that pulled up into our street.

'I'll show you how to take the hat off a winkle,' he told me.

I was a bit apprehensive as he demonstrated how to peel the top off with a pin, then stab it, pull it out of its shell and dip it in vinegar. But I grew to love this little ritual and it soon became our weekly teatime treat, which we would eat with brown bread and butter.

There was even more change when, a few months after the war ended, Mum told me she was expecting a baby. My nose was definitely put out of joint when I was sent to stay with some friends of the family, Bob and Margaret Saggers, for two weeks while Mum went to Thorpe Coombe Maternity hospital to give birth to my brother Geoffrey. They were an elderly couple with no children and, by all accounts, I was very naughty while I was there. I remember thinking that my parents were sending me away and I was being replaced by the new baby.

Poor Geoffrey didn't stand a chance with a bossy older sister like me around. I wanted to be his second mother and I was determined to help Mum do everything, from pushing his huge navy-blue pram to the shops to changing his terry-towelling nappies. He was a lovely, quiet little boy with a mop of blond hair, who liked playing with his Dinky toys and had a fascination with washing his hands.

Growing up, we had very little money, but we never felt poor. Mum made sure we were always well fed, clean and nicely presented. After she had left school she'd trained as a seamstress, and she made most of our clothes on her Singer sewing machine. 'Make do and mend' was a popular slogan during the war, but that applied to our household all of the time. As we couldn't afford to replace them, clothes were repaired, socks were darned and zips fixed.

Every year we went down to Margate for our annual fortnight's summer holiday, where we would stay with Auntie Flo and Uncle Ted. Well, I say 'summer', but sometimes it was so cold and rainy, Dad and Ted would be sat in their deck chairs on the sand wearing raincoats, while Mum, Geoffrey and I huddled by a wind break. One summer, when I was ten, Mum made a cover-up to keep me warm on the beach. She had sewn two old white towels together to create a poncho and stitched some cord around the edges.

I thought it was lovely and felt like the bee's knees when I put it on. One afternoon I had been sent to get some ice creams and was proudly strolling across the sand in my new cover-up, when I saw a sign outside the bandstand that said: 'swimwear competition'.

'Hmm, that sounds interesting,' I thought to myself, so I popped in to have a look.

I was so proud of my new poncho that I decided to enter, even though I was the youngest person there and most of the other entrants were teenage girls trying to look glamourous in their swimsuits.

Much to the other contestants' disgust, I ended up winning first prize for Mum's home-made creation and was thrilled when I was presented with a beautiful black vanity case. I was still basking in my glory when suddenly I remembered the ice creams I was supposed to be getting and I realised I'd already been gone an hour by then. So I ended up staggering across the sand with an armful of melting cones and this lovely new case.

'Where on earth have you been?' asked Mum. 'And what have you got there?'

They all laughed when I told them it was my prize for winning the swimwear contest.

'We never know what you're going to do next, Tink,' chuckled Dad.

I always loved those holidays. My cousins, Jill and Peggy, and I would watch Punch and Judy shows on the pier or go for donkey rides, while the adults tucked into cockles and mussels from the beach stand. Auntie Flo was an avid knitter and she knitted the three of us matching red woollen swimsuits. Can you imagine how itchy and uncomfortable they were? Especially when we went into the sea and they got all wet and sandy. I remember Dad teaching me how to swim by holding me by the crossover on the back of the swimsuit, and I would be shivering violently because the water was so cold.

It was down in Margate, after the war, that I watched television for the first time. Uncle Ted and Auntie Flo were the first members of our family to get a television set, and none of us had ever seen anything like it. It came on at 8 p.m. every night for two hours, and there was great excitement as we all sat in a line on straight-backed dining chairs half an hour beforehand, watching a test pattern and listening to 'Greensleeves'.

But there were no luxuries like television sets for us at home, and life was a constant struggle for Mum and Dad, especially at times like Christmas. They always made sure we had a pillow-case full of presents, but they were little things like satsumas, nuts, a board game or a baby doll, and we never had a tree as they were too expensive. But you don't miss what you've never had and Geoffrey and I made colourful paper chains instead and strung them up around the house.

Mum couldn't afford to go to the hairdresser's and she didn't have many clothes, but she always took great pride in her appearance. She usually had her hair pulled back neatly with a ribbon and she always wore lipstick and powdered her face with a puff.

Both my parents were from large, working-class families in Hackney. Mum's father worked at a power station and Dad's was a shoemaker. Despite her modest upbringing, Mum always insisted on good grammar and made sure Geoffrey and I spoke properly. She didn't like the Cockney accent and, when I was a teenager, she was horrified when my cousin Jill tried to fix me up with a Cockney friend of hers.

'You can't go out with him,' Mum told me. 'He's a Fink and Fort.' That was her nickname for Cockneys, which made fun of the way they pronounced 'think' and 'thought'.

Growing up, Mum encouraged me to hold myself properly and walk with my head up and shoulders back. She was also very keen on manners.

'Good manners don't cost anything,' she'd say.

She taught me how to set the table nicely for tea, and how to leave my knife and fork together in the middle of the plate when I had finished, and showed me which cutlery to use for which part of the meal. Lord only knows where she got it from, but she's always been bit of a perfectionist. Even now, at the ripe old age of ninety-eight, she will tell me: 'You're not wearing that colour dress with those shoes, are you?'

Dad would tease Mum about her high standards, but I know he wanted the best for me too, and he was very proud when I passed my eleven plus, which meant I could go to South West Essex Grammar School.

Mum's great pride in her appearance rubbed off on me, and when I was sixteen, we were out shopping one day when someone handed us a flyer for the Walthamstow Carnival Queen competition. The summer carnival was a big deal in our area in those days, and the queen and her attendants would get to ride on the back of an American convertible car through the town.

'Oh, Mum,' I said, 'I'd really love to enter.'

So I chose my best dress, one that Mum had bought me from Walthamstow High Street for £4. It was a pink A-line with thin straps, and the front of the top was shaped so it looked like the petals of a tulip. I convinced my friend, Kathleen Smith, who lived on our street, to come with me to the auditions a few weeks later at Leytonstone Baths.

It was very exciting, as the MC was a famous American comedian called Alan King, and a small crowd of people had come to watch. There were twenty other girls there, and we were all given a number and had to parade up and down in front of the judges. I felt very nervous as we waited on stage for ages to hear the results.

'I'm proud to announce that this year's Walthamstow Carnival Queen is ... number fifteen, Kathleen Smith!'

Kathleen squealed with excitement as she was presented with her crown. Even though I was one of the two runners-up and would still ride on the float at the carnival, I was a little bit put out that I hadn't won. I didn't tell anyone though, and put on a brave face.

The actual carnival was very exciting. We all got to wear white satin strapless dresses and ride through the town waving at people from our car. Afterwards, we went to a reception hosted by the local paper, the *Walthamstow Guardian*. There were all sorts of dignitaries there, like the mayor, and I was introduced to a man who was on the board of Hunting-Clan, a small British airline that had started after the war.

'You're a lovely young lady,' he said. 'Have you ever thought about a career as a stewardess?'

'I haven't,' I said, 'but I'd love to travel and I bet that would be very exciting.'

Perhaps a seed was sown in my mind that day, but little did I know that in a few years' time that conversation was going to change the course of my life forever.

Chapter Two

Working Girl

A clear, turquoise sea sparkled in the sunlight. A woman in a halterneck swimsuit laughed as she walked across golden sand, arm in arm with a handsome, bronzed man. I closed my eyes and imagined the feeling of warm sun on my legs and hearing people babble away in a language I didn't understand.

'What have you got there then, Betty?' said a voice, interrupting my perfect daydream.

It was the office post boy, doing his afternoon rounds with the trolley.

'Oh, they're just holiday brochures,' I sighed, packing them away. 'I'm trying to decide where to go.'

'What do you want to go abroad for, love?' he said. 'There's nothing wrong with good old Clacton.'

It was 1955 and I was sixteen and had just left school and started my first job working as a shorthand typist at an advertising agency called Mather & Crowther in London. I worked for the big boss's PA and was the office 'do everything' girl.

As far as the office hierarchy went, you couldn't get much lower than me. But I thought it was exciting to work in London, even though it took me over an hour to get there each day from Walthamstow by steam train, tube and bus. My parents were very pleased I had gone into such a respectable profession as secretarial work. Mum had taken me on a shopping trip to Walthamstow Market to celebrate, where we'd bought a smart tweed suit so I would have something to wear to the office.

There were certain expectations for a working-class girl in the 1950s, and one of them was that you left school at sixteen and got a job. There was never any mention of university, even for 'clever girls' like me who had passed their eleven plus and gone to grammar school. You had to go out to work to bring in some money to help your parents until you got married and had children.

My new job paid £4 a week, and out of that I gave Mum and Dad ten shillings for my bed and board. It wasn't much, but it felt good to have my own money and be able to earn my keep. It also meant I could start saving up for the one thing I'd dreamt of for so long: my first holiday abroad.

Ever since Dad and I had spent hours poring over his maps after he'd come back from the war, and he had told me about all these fascinating countries, I had become more and more determined to see all these places for myself one day. I loved geography at school, and that had only fuelled my ambition to see the world. Our annual summer holiday was always two weeks in Margate, so the idea of getting on a boat or plane and going somewhere hot, where people spoke a different language and ate exotic food, seemed wonderful to me.

In the 1950s people rarely went abroad, but the package holiday, where a travel agent organised your transport, transfers and accommodation, had just been introduced and was becoming more popular. On my lunch hour I would wander up the Strand to Swan's Travel Agency and pick up some brochures. Then I'd bring them back to my desk and drool over them. I liked the look of Italy and Spain the most, with their beautiful old buildings and golden beaches.

Every month I saved as much of my wage as I could, but I knew it was going to be years until I could afford it.

'Never mind, Tink,' Dad told me. 'I'm sure it will be worth the wait.'

He viewed my burning ambition to travel with mild amusement. I was surprised that he had no desire to go abroad. After all, he'd been the one who had first told me about all these incredible places. I would often ask him why he didn't want to travel overseas and his usual response was: 'There's a lot of England that I haven't seen yet.'

Mum thought it was all as exciting as I did.

'Look at this, Mum,' I said, showing her some photographs in a brochure about Italy. 'This is the Amalfi coast.'

She oohed and aahed over the pictures of the dramatic coastline and the hotel that had a lift built into the cliff to take you down to the beach.

'Look at that beautiful old church in the square,' she said. 'And Spain's supposed to be nice too. I've heard you can buy lovely leather handbags there for as cheap as chips. I wish I could have done that at your age, but people didn't go abroad then. We just didn't have the money.'

This made me even more determined to go on one of these new package holidays.

I liked working at Mather & Crowther, but after a year, I realised there wasn't going to be much opportunity to progress and I started to get itchy feet. So I found a job in the typing pool at a magazine publisher called Link House Publications.

As well as getting a pay rise to £6 a week, this was definitely a step up the career ladder. On my first day I was shown around by Miss Wiggins, the office supervisor. She was a spinster in her late fifties and wore sensible shoes and old-fashioned dresses and cardigans. She gave me a stern look over the top of her wire spectacles.

'You will sit here, Miss Eden,' she said, whipping the cover off a Remington typewriter. 'I sit over there, so I can keep an eye on all you young ladies, and I won't stand for any nonsense.'

It felt a bit like being back at school again. There were twenty girls sat in five rows, with Miss Wiggins in a glass office at the front, where she would give us the evil eye if we talked too much. But the noise was deafening, as we all clattered away on our typewriters, so there wasn't much opportunity to chat.

Miss Wiggins ruled the typing pool with an iron rod. She watched our every move and no one would ever dare be late. Every so often, she would call us in to go and take dictation from one of the big bosses.

There was a strict hierarchy, and managers had their own dining room, toilets and lifts, separate from us lowly typists. The work was ever so dull – mostly we had to type hundreds of copies of the same letter – but the girls were very friendly. Half of them were married and the rest were single or dating, like me.

I told them about my boyfriend, Ernest Taylor, and how we had been going out for the past year, ever since we'd met at school.

'He's a very nice fellow and my parents love him,' I said.

Ernie, as I called him, was a bit on the chunky side and he had blond hair and a thin moustache. After we'd left school, he'd got a job with Rothschild Bank in the City. He was gentlemanly and kind and took me to the pictures to see films like

South Pacific, or he would come round for tea with Mum and Dad. It was all very innocent. We would hold hands and sometimes Ernie would steal a kiss when the lights went down at the cinema.

'You know I think the world of you, Betty,' he would tell me.

Ernie was from a much more well-to-do family than mine. His father was in banking, but he was divorced from Ernie's mother, Irene, which caused a few raised eyebrows from my parents. No one we knew was divorced, and it was still seen as being a bit of a scandal in the 1950s.

Ernie was an only child and lived with his mother in Essex. I'd only met her for the first time a few weeks before, when he had invited me round to have tea with her. I felt a bit nervous as we pulled up outside the large semi-detached house. I knew they were wealthy but the place was huge compared with my pokey terrace.

'Don't worry, Betty,' Ernie said, squeezing my hand. 'I'm sure Mum will love you as much as I do.'

His mother answered the door in a fancy flowery dress, a hat and gloves. She looked like she was going for an afternoon at the Ritz rather than having a cup of tea at home with me. But the first thing I noticed, apart from her clothes, were her terrible brown, wonky teeth.

'Ah, you must be Betty,' she said, in a very posh voice, holding out her gloved hand. 'Come through to the parlour.'

'Nice to meet you, Mrs Taylor,' I said, shaking her hand.

She ushered me into a room at the front of the house which was so pristine, I could tell it was only ever used for visitors. As we all sat around on uncomfortable high-backed armchairs, I felt like I was at a job interview.

'Now, Betty, do you like Lapsang Souchong or Darjeeling?' she asked.

She could have been talking gibberish for all the sense she was making to me.

'Just a pot of PG will be fine, Mother,' said Ernie, coming to my rescue when he saw my puzzled face.

For the next hour, all Mrs Taylor did was fire questions at me about my family. What did my parents do, what had their parents done, where did we go on holiday? I felt like I was being interrogated, and it was a relief to get out of there.

'Don't mind Mother,' Ernie told me when we'd left. 'She means well.'

But I wasn't so sure. I came away feeling like I wasn't good enough for 'my Ernie', as she called him.

When Ernie and I had been dating a year, Mum and Dad decided it was time for them to meet his mother too.

'Things are obviously serious between you and Ernest,' said Dad.

'He's my best friend,' I told him.

We were far too young to think about marriage, and we'd never even talked about it, but Mum and Dad felt it was only polite to invite Mrs Taylor round. She was completely over-dressed, as usual, and I'd already warned Mum and Dad about her airs and graces.

Mum, bless her, was very proud of her little house and she always kept it neat and tidy, but I could see Mrs Taylor looking around and I felt like she was turning her nose up at us. I couldn't take any more of her disapproving glances, so I went to help Mum and Dad in the kitchen.

'Well, she might be all la-di-da and worth a bob or two, but she's got a terrible set of gnashers,' whispered Dad.

'Oh, Sidney,' Mum scolded, but I couldn't help but laugh.

After that, I always got the impression that she didn't think I was good enough for her precious Ernest. To be honest, I didn't warm to her, and I tried to avoid going round to Ernie's when-ever possible. She was always very cold and businesslike with me, and I never saw her show any emotion.

Thankfully Ernie was a kind, sweet, funny man, nothing like his overbearing mother, whose face never cracked a smile. Now that Geoffrey and I were older, Mum had got a job making underwear for Marks & Spencer from home. All the girls in the typing pool were in hysterics when I told them how Ernie had come round one day when we weren't in, so he had decorated the living room with bras to help pass the time.

'Mum and I were in fits,' I said. 'He'd hooked them together and draped them all over the place, like Christmas decorations.'

'Your Ernie sounds like a real hoot,' said Wendy.

Wendy Sullivan and Dawn Harper were two of my closest friends in the typing pool. Wendy was a rather plump girl with a plain face and long, poker-straight hair that she pulled up into a tight knot. But she was very giggly and great fun to be around. Dawn was very sophisticated and attractive. She was always very well dressed in tailored black suits and she wore blue eye shadow.

At 5 p.m. on the dot everyone would get up, cover their type-writers, put on their coats and gloves and head off. By five past the place was deserted. We all travelled into London from different areas, so we didn't socialise much after work, although sometimes a lady called Gladys, who worked in the post room and had a daughter who was my age, would invite Dawn, Wendy and me round to her house in north London. Rock and Roll was just becoming popular, and we would put Buddy Holly or Bill Haley records on and practise our dancing. Wendy and I would giggle away as we twirled each other around the front room to 'Rock Around the Clock'.

It was there that I first tried smoking. Wendy was always

puffing away on a Woodbine, while Dawn preferred French cigarettes, which she smoked in a long, sophisticated holder.

'Why don't you have a try of one of my fags, Betty?' Wendy
asked one day.

Smoking was so fashionable and I don't know why I hadn't
tried it before. Perhaps it was the strong smell of tobacco in our
house from Dad's cigarettes that had always put me off.

'Go on then,' I said.

But as soon as I took a couple of puffs, my throat started to
burn and all I could do was cough.

'I don't get why everyone does this,' I croaked.

In March 1957 I turned eighteen, but the real milestone for me
came the summer after that. By then I had finally achieved my
goal and had saved up £30, which was enough to pay for my
first holiday abroad. I booked a week in a hotel in Riccione on
the Adriatic coast of Italy and persuaded my cousins Jill and
Patty to come with me, even though they were a bit nervous.

'It's so far away,' said Jill. 'We won't understand what anyone
is saying.'

'Don't worry, I'll look after you,' I told them. 'It will be an
adventure.'

We couldn't afford to fly, so it took us a whole day to get
there. The ferry crossing was dreadfully choppy and we all felt
as sick as dogs. In France we got on a train and travelled for
hours through the night. We couldn't afford a carriage and the
seats were rock-hard and uncomfortable, so we didn't sleep a
wink. But I thought it was all part of the fun and I was mes-
merised by the beautiful scenery as we travelled through the
Alps and northern Italy.

Riccione was a lovely, quaint little town, with lots of old buildings. Every day we would wander through the local markets,

looking at leather bags and sandals, then we would spend hours lying on the beach.

It was very fashionable to have a tan in those days – in fact, it was a sign of wealth, as it meant you had been abroad – so we lay out in the sun for hours on end. Our poor, pale, English complexions had never known such heat and there was no such thing as sun lotion back then. By the end of the first day we all had such terrible sunburns, we looked like lobsters.

But I loved every minute of it, and as soon as we got home, I started saving up for next year's trip. This time, Patty, my friend Wendy from the typing pool and I went to Benidorm for a week. The flight there was very exciting, and I loved stepping off the plane in Alicante and feeling the warm air hit my face and hearing the cicadas chirping in the distance.

Benidorm was just a little fishing village in those days; there were none of the skyscrapers there are today. It was more like a working port than a beach resort, and the sand was a dirty brown colour and the water was murky and grey, not at all like it had looked in the brochures. But we didn't let that put us off.

Every day we lay out in the sun next to the fishing boats and at night we put on our cotton sundresses and went out to sample the local restaurants. We couldn't speak Spanish and the locals didn't speak any English, so we communicated with hand gestures. It was always a surprise when our dinner arrived, as most of the time we hadn't got a clue what we had ordered!

I loved trying all the local cuisine, like paella and huge prawns, but Patty and Wendy were a bit less adventurous. One night Patty ordered squid by mistake.

When she saw all those rubbery heads and tentacles piled up on her plate in a pool of black squid ink, she looked like she was going to pass out.

'There's no way I'm eating that,' she said.

Wendy and I thought it was hysterical, although we weren't game enough to try it either.

Afterwards we went to an open-air café which was playing Spanish music. It was still unusual to see tourists and all the local fishermen swarmed around us.

'Hay-lo beautiful Engleesh laydee,' one of them said, whisking me into his arms. 'I teach you Paso Doble.'

We had a great time being swung around the dance floor by the Spanish boys. But, much to my distress, all too soon our latest adventure was over and it was time to go back home to reality.

I had been at Link House for three years when I was summoned into Miss Wiggins' office one day.

'I have some good news,' she said. 'The advertising manager, Mr Goodwin, would like you to be his secretary.'

It would mean I would have to leave the typing pool and sit in his office instead. I would miss the girls, but I was very pleased to have been promoted.

Mr Goodwin was a skinny, mousy kind of a man with a thin moustache. He was very quiet and he told me he didn't like us to talk about our personal lives. He was married and thankfully he wasn't the kind for making passes, like some of the other managers I had heard about. His only bad habit was cigarettes and his office was always shrouded in clouds of thick smoke.

I shared a desk with his personal assistant, Deidre. She was the most glamourous woman I had ever met, with her long, curled blonde hair and cherry-red lips. She had an enviable figure and wore feminine dresses with nipped-in waits and full skirts. I was even more impressed when she told me she was dating an Egyptian fellow called Ibrahim who had won the Mr Universe 1958 contest.

Every day Mr Goodwin would disappear for lunch and

would stroll back a couple of hours later twirling his black umbrella.

'I can smell alcohol on his breath,' I'd whisper to Deidre.

'All the big bosses always have a liquid lunch,' she said. That was considered the norm in those days.

Mr Goodwin was the advertising manager for five magazines and one of them, called *Health and Efficiency*, caught my attention straight away. I was shocked to find out it was a naturist magazine and it was known as the 'nudist bible'. After the Second World War, naturism had suddenly become very fashionable and lots of nudist colonies, which were known as 'sun clubs', were opening up around the UK.

'I've never seen anything like it,' I told Mum that night. 'It's all a bit racy.'

'What on earth possesses people to want to take their clothes off and parade around like that?' she said.

There was normally a naked woman on the cover and there were some very revealing adverts. Sometimes I had to deal with readers' enquiries too.

One afternoon the operator put through a call.

'Is that the naturist magazine?' said a man's voice. 'It's a full moon tonight and I want you to know that I'm sitting here with no clothes on!'

I felt my cheeks burn red and I was so shocked, I almost dropped the receiver.

'Um ... er ... h-h-hold the line please, sir, and I'll put you through to my boss,' I said politely, my hands shaking.

Another of the publications that I dealt with was *Prediction* magazine, which really intrigued me. As a child, I had dabbled with a Ouija board and I'd always been interested in the supernatural. But what really captured my imagination was an article I read about palm reading. I loved the idea that you could tell someone's future by looking at the lines on their hand, so I ended up buying a book and teaching myself how to do it. Over the years, it became my party trick, but it got me into trouble a few times when, without thinking, I would tell people in front of their spouses that they were going to be married more than once, which never went down too well.

I was still working at Link House, aged nineteen, when I went to a badminton night for ex-pupils of my old high school, South West Essex. While I was there, I got talking to a girl called Dallas Swales, who had been in the year above me.

'I like working,' I told her. 'But the thing I love most is to travel.'

She told me about a summer job she'd had working as a stewardess for a small airline called Silver City, who flew across the Channel.

'It sounds wonderful,' I said. 'I would love to do that.'

'Well, why don't you?' said Dallas. 'They're always looking for girls to help them out over the summer. You should apply.'

Suddenly I remembered the man from Hunting-Clan airline whom I'd got talking to at the Walthamstow Carnival reception all those years ago. He had thought I would make a good stewardess.

'Do you think I should give it a try?' I asked Wendy at work the following day.

But she just looked at me like I was mad.

'Ordinary girls like you and me don't do fancy jobs like that,' she said. 'Anyway, you've already got a good job here.'

Maybe I was fooling myself, but I couldn't get the thought out of my mind, so I wrote to Silver City and they sent me an application form and said they would write to me with details of a recruiting day they had coming up.

Two months later, I got a letter giving me a date for an

interview at an office in Kensington. I didn't tell a soul I was going and I went in my lunch hour, as I didn't want Mr Goodwin to know I was thinking of leaving.

But it was a horrible, rainy day and I had a stinking cold. By the time I'd got across London, I felt dreadful and looked like a drowned rat. Wearily, I plonked myself down next to another girl in the waiting area and we eventually started chatting. When she told me she was a trained nurse and spoke six languages, my heart sank.

'Who am I kidding?' I thought. 'Wendy was right. I'm a secretary who lives in a terrace house. They're not going to hire me.'

Not only that, I looked like Rudolph, with my red, streaming nose, sniffling into a hankie.

'It was nice to have met you, but I don't think I'm going to stay,' I told the girl, getting up to leave.

'But you can't go now,' she said. 'They've already seen you.'

I supposed she was right – it would look a bit rude just to walk off – so I decided to stay and get the ordeal over and done with as quickly as possible.

The interviews were being conducted by the chief pilot and stewardess of Silver City.

'Tell us a bit about yourself,' the man said.

So I described my job at Link House and told them about my holidays abroad. Then they quizzed me about what amenities one might find in the bathroom of a five-star hotel. I had never stayed in a five-star hotel in my life, but I had seen pictures of plenty of them in the brochures that I spent my lunch hour flicking through.

'There would probably be nice towels,' I said. 'And scented soap and perhaps a shower cap.'

The chief stewardess explained that it was just a summer job, the wage was £7 a week and we would have to work six days, with one day off. Suddenly I remembered that I was due to be a bridesmaid for my cousin Len Simpkins and his fiancée Jean. I knew there would be real ructions in the family if I didn't go to the wedding.

'I'm sorry, but I have promised to be my cousin's bridesmaid one Saturday in July,' I told them. 'So if I did get the job, I'd need to take that day off.'

The chief pilot shook his head. 'Saturday is often our busiest day,' he said. 'If you did get the job, then I'm afraid you would have to choose between working for us and being a bridesmaid.'

They said they would write to me if I was successful, but I didn't have a very good feeling about it. I could have kicked myself for mentioning Len's wedding. It didn't look good, asking for a day off before you had even been offered a job.

Two weeks passed and I didn't hear anything, so I assumed it was bad news. But then, a week later, a letter from Silver City arrived. I couldn't believe it when I read that I had been accepted for the summer and, to my delight, there was a handwritten note at the bottom saying that I could have the day off to be a bridesmaid. I was thrilled, not to mention relieved that I could still go to Len's wedding.

'You must be mad,' Len said when I told him. 'I'd turn it down if I were you.'

He thought I was crazy to give up a permanent office job that paid £14 a week for a temporary summer job that only paid £7 and gave me one day off.

'But I don't care about the money,' I told him. 'This is what I want to do.'

Mum and Dad seemed equally surprised that I was giving up my steady job in a respectable profession, but they could see how pleased I was and I think they were as excited as I was about the fact that I was going to be a stewardess on a plane. At the time, it was seen as the ultimate job for a young woman, and everyone thought stewardesses were the height of glamour and sophistication. Dad seemed particularly proud and he went round telling everyone: 'Did you know our little Tink's going to be a stewardess? Getting on a jet will be like catching a bus for her.'

If they were worried, they didn't show it. So I handed in my notice at Link House.

Silver City was based at Lydd Airfield in Hampshire, which meant that I would have to leave home for the first time. I knew Mum and Dad would be sad to see me go, and I was going to miss them terribly.

'It's only for the summer,' I told them. 'I'll come back on my day off.'

It was only going to be for a couple of months, so I just took a small suitcase of clothes. As I stood on the front doorstep, Dad handed me an envelope.

'This is for you, Tink,' he told me.

He explained that ever since I'd started working, they had put the ten shillings I'd been giving them each week for my bed and board into a savings account.

'We wanted you to have a little nest egg when you left home,' Mum explained.

'Thank you,' I said, my eyes filling with tears.

I was touched. It meant so much to me, especially as I knew they could have done with that money themselves.

I caught the train down to my new home – a room at a boarding house run by a woman called Mrs Hinkley. She was a kind, grandmotherly old lady, with snow-white hair and a big, fat ginger cat called Tiddles. Silver City had sent me a list of boarding houses, and there was another trainee staying there for the summer. Dawn Hester was a tiny, pretty little thing with short, dark hair. She was a couple of years older than me and had been living in Manchester, where she had worked for an airline called British European Airways.

Dawn and I hit it off straight away. I looked up to her, as she was used to living away from home, and I was in awe of the fact that she already had experience of working for an airline. Unlike me, she knew how to cook for herself too, and I was amazed on our first night there when she made me a curry. It was totally different to the traditional dinners Mum made, but I loved it.

I was nervous on our first day at work, as we got the bus into Lydd. There were six of us girls that had been taken on for the summer, and I was thrilled when we were given our uniforms – a navy-blue pencil skirt, tailored jacket with lapels and a military-style hat.

We did a week's training, to learn about the safety procedures and what we would be expected to do. I soon realised the job wasn't in the slightest bit glamorous and was going to be extremely hard work. Every day we would fly across the Channel to Le Touquet in France and back six times, on a Bristol Freighter plane, which was known as an air ferry. It carried fourteen passengers plus three cars in the nose, and flew at an altitude of only 1000 ft.

'It never gets above cloud level,' the chief stewardess, Jill, warned us. 'So it's very noisy and bumpy.'

There was only ever one stewardess on board in the cabin, and the pilot and co-pilot were up high at the front of the plane, so you could only contact them through an intercom. There were no meals or drinks and our main duty was to spend the twenty-minute journey selling duty free to the passengers.

When training was over, Jill asked for volunteers to transfer to Manston Airport, where Silver City had opened a new base.

'I'll go,' I said straight away.

I already knew that area because it was near Margate, where Auntie Flo and Uncle Ted lived, and I liked the idea of being close to them. Dawn volunteered to come too, as well as two other girls called Mary and Anne, so we all found a two-bedroom house to rent.

It was a semi-detached and there was a separate living room, dining room and a small kitchen, as well as a little overgrown garden. It came already furnished, although the decor was tired and everything was covered in a thick fug of dust, from the gaudy patterned lamps to the chipped dark-wood sideboard and the dining chairs with wobbly legs.

'It looks like my grandmother's house,' laughed Dawn.

'It's a bit shabby,' I agreed, 'but it's cosy.'

Dawn and I shared a room and we had a single bed each.

On our first day we got picked up by Reg in the Silver City crew shuttle, and he took us to the airfield at Manston. Reg was a chirpy fellow and he looked very smart in his navy-blue uniform and peaked cap.

'Morning, ladies,' he said as we climbed into the van, bleary-eyed.

I was a bit apprehensive about my first flight. There was hardly any room in the cabin, so we would be working alone.

When all the passengers were in and I had closed the doors, it was time to get going. But as soon as the B170 took off, I realised this wasn't going to be fun.

'It's like travelling in a washing machine,' I thought, as we rattled and lurched all over the sky.

As soon as I bent down to get the duty free out of the locker under the seats, I felt horribly sick.

'It will pass,' I told myself.

But as the plane bounced along and my stomach lurched with it, I realised I was about to vomit.

'What am I going to do?' I thought, panicking.

There was no toilet on board, but I couldn't bear the idea of being ill in front of the passengers. So, grabbing a handful of sick bags, I dashed into the hold where the cars were and promptly threw up.

I spent the rest of the journey running backwards and forwards between serving duty free in the cabin and crouching down by the cars in the hold being sick. Thankfully I don't think the passengers could hear me over the terrible din of the engines.

By the time we landed back in Manston on the return journey, there was a pile of bulging sick bags in the hold and I was a wreck. I was weak at the knees, pale as a ghost and had double vision from throwing up so much. Much to my embarrassment, when the cleaner came on board, I had to tell her about the unpleasant surprise waiting for her.

'I'm dreadfully sorry,' I sighed. 'It won't happen again.'

I hoped that as I got used to the rough crossings, it would get better. But it didn't. Every flight that week was the same, and I spent the whole time being ill. The poor cleaner got used to it and always made sure there were plenty of sick bags on my shift.

By the end of my first week at Silver City, I was in a terrible state. I practically crawled down the steps of the plane.

'That's it,' I told Dawn. 'I don't think I can take any more. I'm just not cut out for this job.'

All of the other girls had been OK. I marched into the operations room, determined to hand in my notice to Jill. But, much to my annoyance, I couldn't find her anywhere. After a few weeks of the same thing happening, I realised that she always saw me coming and went and hid so I couldn't resign!

But if there was one quality I had in spades, it was persistence.

After a long day of throwing up, I would stagger home in an awful state. But then I'd have a boiled egg and some toast and a good night's sleep, and in the morning I would feel fine again.

Thankfully, after a month, the terrible nausea started to subside. I still spent a lot of the time feeling queasy, but I learnt little tricks, like focusing on the horizon and not having anything acidic like orange juice before a flight. I think the cleaner was as grateful as I was!

Once I had stopped being so sick, I really started to enjoy my job, especially chatting to the passengers, who were mainly holidaymakers going to France and the continent.

One day there was a woman who had never been on a plane before, and she was absolutely petrified of flying. All day long this poor lady had been too frightened to get on any of the flights, and she'd been at the airport for hours. Before each flight, I sat with her and her husband in the café at Manston and gave her a pep talk.

'It will be fine,' I told her. 'You can do this. It's only twenty minutes.'

I was so proud of myself when, finally, on her fourth attempt of the day, she agreed to walk out onto the tarmac with me towards the aircraft.

'You're doing so well,' I told her as she climbed up the steps and sat down next to her husband.

But as the propellers whirred into action, she let out a bloodcurdling scream and jumped up out of her seat.

'I can't do it,' she yelled, trying to wrench open the plane doors.

I quickly radioed up to the pilot and asked him to turn off the engines and unlock the doors. The second they opened, she made a run for it across the tarmac, leaving her embarrassed husband still in his seat.

'Well, she'll have to get the boat across on her own,' he grumbled. 'I'm staying here.'

Being a stewardess was hard work, but the weeks flew by. As the end of the summer drew near, I knew I would have to start looking for a new job. I assumed I'd have to go back to secretarial work, but the thought of typing boring letters all day filled me with dread.

But one day Jill took Dawn and me into the office.

'We'd like to offer you both a full-time position,' she said.

She explained that Silver City had just started operating charter flights to Europe and they needed stewardesses to work on those. I was ecstatic. We had to have training on how to work on the new aircraft, which were called DC-3 Dakotas. Like the car planes, there was only one stewardess on board and up to thirty passengers, and we would have to serve them a cold meal tray as well as selling the usual duty free.

Even though Dawn and I were now permanent staff, we didn't get a pay rise and it was always a struggle to make ends meet. After the rent and bills had been paid, we hardly had any money left for food, so we would take leftover oranges and bananas and unopened packs of crackers from the meal trays to have for our dinner, but I often went to bed with my stomach rumbling from hunger.

Sometimes good old Auntie Flo would come to our rescue.

'Come round and I'll give you girls a good feed,' she would tell me.

I would take Dawn with me, and we'd gobble down huge portions of sausages and mash or steak and kidney pie, without pausing for breath.

There was definitely no spare money for nights out and, besides, we only ever had one day off a week. This was normally a week day, as weekends were always the busiest time for flights. So, as the summer passed, I didn't make it home that often, as during the week my parents and Ernie would be working.

One of the Silver City pilots, Captain John Wrigley, lived near London, and if he was driving back, I would sometimes hitch a lift with him to go and see Mum and Dad. One Saturday evening we were heading back when Captain Wrigley decided to break up the journey at a pub.

'What's your tipple, Betty?' he asked.

I scanned all of the bottles behind the bar, but I hadn't got a clue what to ask for. Mum and Dad hardly drank, so I never had either. Growing up, our social life was very much centred around our family and going to a relative's house. Sometimes Ernie would take me to the local pub and he would have a pint of bitter, but I'd always have a bottle of juice.

'I'll have a grapefruit juice please,' I told Captain Wrigley.

'Go on, have a proper drink,' he laughed.

'OK then, skipper,' I said. 'I'll have a sweet Martini.'

It was the first alcoholic drink that came into my mind. When it arrived, it was a bright red colour and looked just like cordial, and I took several big gulps, not realising it was just pure Vermouth. It tasted so strong it brought tears to my eyes, but I quite liked the nice warm glow it left in my throat. A few minutes later my glass was empty, and I started to feel quite dizzy.

'Everything's looking a bit blurry,' I mumbled to Captain Wrigley. 'I think I'd better sit down.'

He thought it was hilarious as he helped me to a nearby chair.

'I don't think you're cut out to be a drinker, Betty,' he told me.

Neither did I. One large Martini later and the room was spinning. When we got back in the car, I fell asleep straight away. When I woke up, we were driving through London, and

I had dribble running down my chin and the most terrible headache.

'I'm dreadfully sorry, skipper,' I told Captain Wrigley. 'I really don't think that Martini agreed with me.'

'Don't worry, Betty,' he said. 'I think you needed that nap.'

I still felt awful when I staggered through my parents' front door.

'Are you OK, dear?' asked Mum. 'I've never seen you look so pale.'

I'd learnt my lesson, and after that I always stayed well away from alcohol.

Flying might not have given me much time off or money to have a social life, but I loved it. I flew to Majorca, Frankfurt and Pisa, although I didn't see anything much of these places, as we always flew straight back to the UK. But unlike most girls of my age in the 1950s, I felt like I had a career rather than just a job and, most importantly, I was on my way to achieving my ambition to travel the world.

Chapter Three

The Chosen One

A figure in a winceyette nightgown dashed into the bedroom and pulled open the curtains.

'What is it, Dawn?' I muttered sleepily as I blinked in the harsh daylight. 'It's practically the middle of the night.'

My friend and roommate Dawn Hester had something in her hand and was waving it around like a woman possessed.

'Oh, Betty,' she shrieked, bouncing on my single bed. 'You've got to have a look at this.'

She thrust a copy of yesterday's *Daily Mail* into my hand and I began to read what had whipped her up into such a frenzy this early in the morning.

Pan American Airlines is coming to London to recruit potential stewardesses. The company, who says it likes the 'well-scrubbed look' of English girls, is looking for young, single ladies aged between twenty-one and twenty-seven, of good moral character, with good posture and appearance and weighing between 7 st 12 lb and 9 st 8 lb.

'Please tell me you'll come with me,' Dawn pleaded.

I must admit, as I read the article, my heart started to race with excitement.

It was December 1960 and Dawn and I had been working for Silver City for the past eight months and were still living in our rented house in Margate. While I loved my job, I would have described it more as bloomin' hard work rather than glamorous. We still didn't make enough money to be able to ever go out or even feed ourselves properly, and we relied on Auntie Flo's generous dinners and the leftovers from the cold meal trays we served on the flights to get us through the week.

It was a world away from Pan American, the world's number one airline and the epitome of glitz, glamour and sophistication. Everyone who was anyone flew with them, from royalty and world leaders like President Eisenhower and British Prime Minister Harold Macmillan, to Hollywood stars like Marilyn Monroe, Ava Gardner and Frank Sinatra.

Pan Am had just launched the Boeing 707, the world's first commercial jet, and it was the start of what had been christened 'the jet age'. Everyone wanted to be part of the jet set, flying on a fast plane to exotic places.

I closed my eyes and imagined strolling down the aisle of a jet wearing that iconic pale-blue uniform, serving Manhattans to presidents and lighting the Marlboros of movie stars.

In the real world, I knew the chances of little Betty Eden from Walthamstow getting a job with the world's number one airline were slim, but what was the harm in going to take a look? Besides, it would be a fun day out.

'Go on then,' I told Dawn. 'It will be an adventure.'

She was grinning like a Cheshire cat as she called the number listed and booked us both a slot. As we both had jobs already, this was just a bit of a giggle, and I was keen to find out more about Pan Am too. A couple of months previously I'd been on a Silver City charter flight that was grounded at Frankfurt due to bad weather when I had noticed a Pan Am Boeing 707 parked on the tarmac. In those days, anyone could go to the airport for a look around, and the new 707 always attracted huge crowds. People would queue up for hours for a chance to go on board and have a look inside, and I couldn't resist going over myself to have a peek.

'Wow,' I'd gasped, my mouth gaping in awe. 'I've never seen anything like it.'

The plane was huge and it was so new and modern. First class looked so luxurious, with its lounge bar and beautiful fresh flower displays everywhere.

I couldn't resist sitting down in one of the huge, grey-leather reclining seats.

'Ooh lovely,' I'd sighed, as my legs dangled on the padded footrest. 'I could get used to this.'

But what had stuck in my mind the most were the stewardesses. In the 1960s Pan Am stewardesses were in the same league as models and rock stars. Every little girl wanted to be one and every red-blooded male wanted to be seen with one on his arm. They had all seemed so sophisticated, but nice too, and had looked so glamorous in their smart blue uniforms, pillbox hats and pristine white gloves. It was in a completely different league from Silver City.

Dawn and I couldn't wait for our big adventure. We both requested 2 December 1960 off work, and we spent the weeks before discussing the most important matter in hand ...

'What are we going to wear?' I wailed.

Our meagre salary of £7 a week meant I didn't have many clothes to choose from, just a few suits and dresses left over from when I worked in the typing pool. In the end, I picked my best dress – a pale, powder–blue, double-knit number with big pockets. Like most of my clothes that hadn't been made by Mum, it had been bought from a stall at Walthamstow market.

'Classic and not too flashy,' said Dawn, nodding approvingly.

'But it's so plain,' I sighed.

I'd wear it with my navy court shoes and my Silver City navy-blue trench, which was the smartest coat I owned. My hair was always as straight as string, so the night before I set it in some rollers.

Finally the big day arrived, and Dawn and I were up at 5 a.m., like two giggling children on Christmas Day. It was still pitch-black outside as we smeared on Nivea cream and applied our make-up. We chatted away excitedly as we caught the 7 a.m. steam train to King's Cross. A two-hour bus journey later, we finally arrived at the Ariel Hotel at London Airport, which was what Heathrow was called in those days, where the Pan Am interviews were being held. We pushed open the doors of the conference room and gasped.

'Oh my goodness,' said Dawn.

It was mayhem. Everywhere we looked there were queues of young women, chattering and laughing, and the noise was deaf-ening. Being a stewardess for Pan Am was one of the most desirable jobs in the world at the time, so I wasn't surprised to see how crowded it was. But I was shocked when someone in front of us turned around and whispered, 'There are a thousand girls here, you know.'

None of us had any idea about how many trainees they were recruiting, but it didn't take a genius to work out that our chances were slim.

'Oh well,' said Dawn, sounding as crestfallen as I felt. 'Let's just enjoy the experience.'

I was fascinated as I looked around the room. There were girls of all shapes and sizes and from all walks of life. Pan Am's only stop-off in the UK was in London, so some of them must have travelled miles. I could hear many cut-glass accents, from girls who had obviously been privately educated at some of the country's top schools, but there were also more down-to-earth young ladies with broad Scouse or Brummie twangs.

It was interesting to see all the different outfits people were wearing and what they had deemed would attract the attention of a Pan Am recruiter. A lot of the girls were dressed in smart business attire, like Dawn and I, but some looked more like they were going to a dance, in their tight sweaters and over-the-top make-up.

Dawn and I joined the first queue to fill out an application form. Then we waited in another line to be weighed and measured. It sounds very un-politically correct now, but I wasn't surprised. This was the world's premier airline, and I knew from the newspaper advert that it had strict criteria about appearance.

Unlike some of the chunkier girls, I wasn't worried about being weighed. Luckily, at 5 ft 4 in and 8st 6lb I had always been slender, like my dad, and I didn't have to watch my weight – if only I could say the same now!

Everyone was politely pretending not to look as each girl stepped on the scales, but in truth we were all having a sneaky peek out of the corner of our eyes. There was a bigger girl in the queue in front of us, and when it was her turn, the supervisor looked at the dial and shook his head.

'I'm sorry,' he said. 'You're way over.'

She burst into tears, and I felt really sorry for her. It must have been so humiliating, having to leave at such an early stage in the process, and in front of all of those people too.

Thankfully Dawn and I made the cut, and the next step was an interview. There were so many girls to get through, we had to wait hours until it was our turn. I wasn't in the slightest bit nervous. I think there's a certain confidence that you have when you already have a job. Also I never in a million years thought that I had a chance of making it through, so Dawn and I were treating it all like a game.

A middle-aged man and a woman were doing the interviews. They weren't in uniform, but they told me they were supervisors and they seemed quite friendly. They were the first Americans I had ever met and I was fascinated by their accents.

'So, tell me something about yourself,' the man asked.

'Well, I have always wanted to travel and see the world,' I told them. 'I used to be a secretary and now I'm working as a stewardess for Silver City.'

I saw them give each other a look and the man rolled his eyes.

'Silver City?' he said. 'I've never heard of it. It must be a paltry little airline.'

'How condescending!' I thought.

If he was deliberately trying to yank my chain, it was working.

'Do you mind?' I said. 'It's a wonderful little airline. It's very professional and I'll have you know everyone there works very hard indeed.'

Suddenly the room fell deadly silent, and I could have kicked myself. That was it – I had definitely gone and blown it with my little rant.

There was a long pause, then the woman finally said, 'Well, Miss Eden, you're certainly very loyal and passionate about your employers, which is good to see.'

'I like your attitude, young lady,' the man chuckled.

They both started to laugh and I ended up laughing too –
mainly out of relief, I hasten to add!

Much to my surprise, instead of being shown the door as
I expected, I was told to wait in the next room, as I was
through to the next and final stage – an interview with the
board.

Dawn had made it through too.

'Betty, I think we're doing rather well,' she whispered. 'It's so
exciting, isn't it?'

I looked around. The room was no longer packed with thousands or even hundreds of girls. There were around thirty of us
sat there.

Suddenly it hit me that she could be right. Our fun day out
had turned into something potentially life-changing, and that's
when I felt the first flicker of nerves in the pit of my stomach.
Things had just got serious, but there was no time to panic, as
I was called in for my interview.

There were five of them sat behind a long table – three
women and two men.

One of them, a very polished lady with beautiful skin, introduced herself as Lee Trujillo and said she was a supervisor in
New York.

'Before you sit down, Miss Eden, could you walk to the other
side of the room and back for us?' she said.

It felt odd, having five people looking me up and down and
watching my every move. I knew they were checking my posture and looking at my figure, and as I did my little catwalk, I
thought of Mum and how she had always told me: 'Head up,
shoulders back.'

Then it was time for them to give me a grilling.

'Do you speak any languages?' one of them asked.

'I learnt French for five years in high school, but I'm a bit rusty,' I said.

They got me to translate a paragraph for them, which thankfully I just about managed.

'Are you single?' was the next question.

I told them about my boyfriend, Ernie, but said I had no plans to settle down.

In those days, most airlines made you leave your stewardess job once you got married. Even if you weren't married, some airlines still made you retire at the age of thirty-two, and they would never employ divorced or separated ladies. So, in 1960, being a stewardess was definitely only seen as a profession for young, single women.

Then Miss Trujillo told me a bit more about the job. She explained that if I was selected, I would have to go to New York for six weeks of intensive training, where I'd live in a dormitory with other girls and I'd learn things like safety, deportment and how to prepare and serve the gourmet meals.

'You will have to take exams every week and it's very hard work,' she said. 'But then, if you pass, you get to fly around the world and visit all sorts of incredible places.'

At last I'd get to visit all those countries I had learnt about at school and with Dad, and the more she told me, the more I wanted the job more than anything in the world.

'It really does sound wonderful,' I told them. 'It would be a dream come true.'

'Thank you for your time,' said Lee, shaking my hand. 'You will be hearing from us within the week.'

'Well, how do you think you did?' Dawn asked when I got back fifteen minutes later.

'I can't really believe it, but I think it went OK,' I told her.

But poor Dawn was convinced hers hadn't gone that well.

'You will be fine,' I said, linking my arm through hers. 'Imagine us both going to New York.'

It was so exciting.

As soon as I got back home to Margate, I phoned Mum and Dad and told them all about it.

'That sounds lovely, dear,' said Mum.

'Wow, New York,' sighed Dad. 'Wouldn't that be an adventure, Tink?'

In reality, I don't think they thought I was going to get a job with Pan Am in a million years, although they never would have said that to me.

Then I went round to see Auntie Flo and Uncle Ted.

'If I get picked, I'll have to go and live in America,' I told them.

'What do you want to go there for?' Uncle Ted said, wrinkling up his nose. 'It's full of Americans.'

Manston had been a US airforce base during the Second World War, so their only experience of Americans had been the GIs who had come over during the war and seduced all the local girls. You were considered racy and a bit of a good-time girl if you had gone out with an American and, growing up, I had always been told to stay away from them.

Over the next few days, Pan Am was all Dawn and I could think and talk about. Every night after work, we rushed home to check the post, but days passed and nothing arrived.

Finally, exactly a week after the interview, we got home one evening to find identical crisp white envelopes with the distinctive blue ball logo on them lying next to each other on the mat.

'Pan Am!' I gasped, my heart thumping.

'Oh goodness, Betty,' said Dawn.

I felt sick with nerves as I ripped it open, while Dawn did

exactly the same thing next to me. I could barely read what it said, I was trembling so much.

'Dear Miss Eden, we are very pleased to inform you that you are one of the seventeen British girls who have been selected to become Pan Am's fifth international class. You will be expected in New York in eight weeks to begin your stewardess training.'

'I don't believe it, Dawn!' I gasped. 'I did it!'

I looked at her face and she looked at mine.

And that's when I knew Dawn hadn't got in.

'I didn't make it, Betty,' she said, tears filling her eyes.

'Oh, Dawn, I'm so sorry,' I said.

I'd wanted to jump up and down and scream the place down with happiness, but now I felt terrible. Dawn was my friend and I didn't want to go to America without her. I could tell she was upset, but she was so lovely about it.

'I'm so happy for you, Betty,' she told me. 'Please don't feel guilty.'

I was completely astounded that my Pan Am dream had suddenly become a reality. It was unbelievable to think I was one of only seventeen girls chosen out of the thousand interviewed that day at the airport; it just didn't seem real. Girls like me, who hadn't gone to well-known private schools or had wealthy parents didn't get picked to do a job like this, did they? I kept having to check the letter, just to make sure I hadn't read it wrong. But it was there in black and white.

I felt overwhelmed and apprehensive about leaving my family, but so happy at the same time. I called Mum and Dad to tell them the news.

'You'll never guess what,' I gasped. 'I'm going to New York.'

The line suddenly went silent.

'Oh, Betty!' Mum exclaimed. 'Oh my goodness!'

'Sidney!' I heard her shouting to Dad, who must have been in the other room. 'Our Betty's got the job with Pan Am.'

'But when do you go, dear?' she asked.

'The letter said eight weeks,' I told her.

I could tell she was taken aback, but then she put Dad on the line.

'America,' he sighed. 'I can't believe it. It's so far away.'

'Please be happy for me,' I told him. 'This is the job of my dreams, Dad.'

'Of course we are,' he said. 'Your mother and I are so proud of you. It's just a bit sudden, that's all.'

'We'll all get used to the idea,' I said.

I could tell he and Mum were shocked by the news, but I also knew they were genuinely happy for me, as they knew how much I had wanted this.

At the time, I took it for granted, and it's only looking back now that I realise what unselfish, wonderful parents I had. On one hand, I know they were so proud of me and what I had achieved, and they could see how pleased I was. But on the other, I'm sure they were absolutely devastated by the news and didn't want me to leave. They had never been abroad, never mind to America, and at any point they could have begged me not to go, but they never did.

But I knew there was one person who was not going to take the news quite so well, and that was my boyfriend, Ernie. He was my best friend and although we had never been intimate, we would 'pet', which was nothing more than holding hands and kissing.

I did love Ernie, but I felt I was too young to settle down, which was unusual for the time. A lot of my school friends and many girls from the typing pool were already married by the age of twenty, but there were too many things I wanted to see and do first. Ernie and I had never discussed getting married or engaged

When I had moved to Margate to start the job with Silver City, Ernie and I had started to drift apart. I worked six days out of seven, so we hardly had a chance to see each other. But neither of us had officially broken it off and I was dreading ringing him to tell him the news. Finally I bit the bullet and picked up the phone.

'America?' he said, sounding shocked. 'But I won't get to see you much if you're over there.'

'I've never been, Ernie,' I told him. 'I just want to go over there and have a look around and see a few places, then I'll come back.'

I was shocked by how upset Ernie sounded and I could tell it was a real blow to him. Although we had never talked about getting married, I realised that maybe he had thought that one day we would, and I felt really guilty about that.

'I care deeply for you, Ernie, and I don't want to hurt you, but this is something I really want to do,' I told him.

'What about us, Betty?' he said. 'What am I supposed to do?'

'Well, we can write to each other,' I told him. 'Then one day I'll come home and we can see what happens.'

I had always dreamt of travelling the world and now, through Pan Am, my dream was about to come true. Maybe I was ahead of my time, but I wasn't prepared to give that up. I loved Ernie, I really did, but in all honesty my desire to see the world and have a career as a stewardess was so strong, I knew I had to do this, even if it meant leaving him behind.

But with only a few weeks left before I had to leave the UK, there was a lot to sort out. In a way, it was a blessing, as it didn't give me time to think about the enormity of the situation. Along with my acceptance letter, there was an application form for a visa, which I had to fill in and take to the American Embassy, where I would also have to have a physical examination.

So, a couple of weeks later, I got the train up to London and went to the embassy in Grosvenor Square. Once I had queued up with the paperwork, I was directed to a small dressing room.

'Skirt and stockings off,' a woman told me. 'You can leave your coat and shoes on. Then get in line for your physical.'

'Good grief,' I thought.

It was a freezing-cold winter's day and the idea of standing in line with a bunch of strangers in my knickers wasn't very appealing. But I did what I was told and whipped off my nylons, suspender belt and skirt and joined the line of other shivering people. Thankfully I was wearing my trench coat, so it was long enough to preserve my modesty, but some poor people who had short jackets on just had to stand there in their undergarments. I didn't know where to look!

Finally it was my turn. A doctor checked my eyes and then got me to lie down on a couch. But as he examined my legs, he shook his head.

'Hm, that's not ideal if you're flying,' he said. 'It could be a real problem.'

'What is it?' I asked, sitting bolt upright.

He pointed to a tiny blue vein on my inner left knee, which I had never even noticed before.

'It could mean that you are susceptible to varicose veins, which is dangerous if you're flying all the time and on your feet for hours on end,' he explained.

Another doctor was summoned to examine me and suddenly I started to get very anxious. I hadn't given the physical a second thought; I'd just taken it for granted that I would pass. But now, because of this miniscule mark on my knee, my job with Pan Am and my whole new life were in jeopardy.

I tried not to panic. 'I'm sure it's nothing,' I told them. 'We don't have a history of varicose veins in my family. It's never bothered me before. In fact, you can hardly see it, can you?'

But I was really worried. It felt like the longest twenty minutes of my life, as a gaggle of doctors poked and prodded me. Finally, after inspecting what felt like every inch of my body, they gave their verdict.

'We will pass you,' the doctor said. 'But please keep a close eye on your legs, young lady.'

'Oh, thank you so much,' I sighed.

I quickly got dressed and dashed out of the embassy before they could change their minds.

But there was yet another hurdle in my path. The letter from Pan Am had stated that I needed to bring $300 with me to New York, which was the equivalent of around £100, a huge amount of money in those days. My flight was paid for and I would be living in a dormitory rent-free, but I wouldn't get paid for the first couple of weeks, so I would need the cash for food and other living expenses.

It was a real worry. I didn't have any savings and I knew Mum and Dad didn't have that kind of money, so I didn't want to ask them. I would be mortified if I had to go to Pan Am and explain that I couldn't come up with it.

One day Auntie Flo came round to see me while I was packing up my things in Margate.

'Your mother saw the letter from Pan Am about the money you need to take to America, and she told me about it,' she said. 'Don't worry, dear, Uncle Ted and I will find it for you.'

I was so relieved, I threw my arms around her.

'Thank you so much,' I said tearfully. 'As soon as I get paid, I promise I will pay you back.'

I was so grateful to them.

Now, finally, I could start to prepare for my new life. I handed my notice in at Silver City and said goodbye to the girls.

'We're going to miss you,' Jill, the chief stewardess, told me. 'When you come home, you can have your job back anytime you want.'

'Thank you,' I said.

I knew I would miss Dawn too, and I still felt terrible that she wasn't coming with me.

'Good luck,' she said, giving me a hug. 'Not that you'll need it. You are going to be great.'

I didn't want anyone to make a fuss, so I didn't have a leaving party. There was no big goodbye with Ernest either.

'I'll be coming home,' I told him. 'I bet I will be flying through London all the time.'

He gave me a kiss and a hug, but his glum face betrayed how he really felt.

As the days passed, I tried not to think about leaving Mum, Dad and Geoffrey back in the UK. My family was so important to me and the thought of being so far away from them devastated me. But I knew this was the opportunity of a lifetime and I had to take it.

'I'm not going to America for good,' I constantly told Mum and Dad. 'I'm just going to have a look around and see a few places, then I'll be back.'

Looking back now, I know I told myself that so I didn't think of the implications. I could never have made the decision to leave my family permanently. My plan was to do the training, have a look around New York, fly as many of the routes as I could and then eventually come home.

I was only allowed to take two suitcases with me, so I just packed clothes. There was no room for any knick-knacks. The night before I left, Mum made me my favourite dinner of steak and kidney pie and mashed potato. As the familiar, comforting smell of Mum's cooking filled the house, I breathed it in for the last time. That night I hardly slept a wink; I couldn't stop thinking about what I was doing and how my life was going to be so different.

The next morning I put on my nicest outfit – a nubbly suit which was black with red, turquoise and orange flecks, with a Chanel-style boxy jacket and a pencil skirt and heels. I felt a strange mixture of nerves and excitement as I looked around my bedroom for the last time.

'Are you ready, Tink?' said Dad.

He and Mum drove me to London Airport in his green Morris Minor. As usual, Mum chatted away, while Dad was quiet. He was the strong, silent type and was always the deep thinker. I kept looking at his face and wondering what was going through his mind. I had never doubted my decision, but I was dreading saying goodbye.

As I walked over to the Pan Am desk to check in, I tried to steel myself.

'Don't cry, Betty,' I told myself. 'You'll be coming home soon.'

I knew that if I cried, Mum and Dad would too, and I wasn't sure I could cope with that. It was easier to pretend I was going on holiday.

Dad put his arms around me.

'Keep in touch, darling,' he said. 'Look after yourself. We're going to miss you.'

'Write to us, dear,' said Mum, her voice quivering.

It wasn't until many years later that Mum told me that when they said goodbye that day, they honestly thought that they would never see me again. Thinking about how they must have felt still breaks my heart. America seemed so far away to them and such a strange, unknown place that they didn't think I would ever come back.

I know they must have been in pieces on the way home. I'm sure there were lots of tears, but God love them for putting on a brave face for me at the airport.

'Goodbye,' I said, swallowing the big lump in my throat. 'I promise I will see you soon.'

Then, without daring to look back, I walked through the doors to the airplane to begin my adventure.

Chapter Four

New York, New York

The 2nd of February 1961. A date that will stay ingrained in my mind forever, as it was the day I arrived in New York for the very first time.

The flight over there was an adventure in itself, and I couldn't believe it when I got on the plane to find that I was in first class. I had never felt so special and pampered, and it was the perfect start to my new life with Pan Am.

An even bigger surprise was seeing a familiar face sat in the seat next to me.

'Paula!' I gasped.

Paula Arnold had worked for Silver City as an administration assistant in the operations department. I didn't know her well, but it was so nice to see someone I recognised and it took my mind off thinking about Mum and Dad driving home to Walthamstow without me.

'I didn't know you had applied to Pan Am,' I said.

'I'm not sure why, but I kept it hush hush,' she told me.

Unlike me, who had been so proud I had told every man and

his dog about my new job, Paula had not told a soul at Silver City that she was going over to America. She explained that her boyfriend, Don, was a salmon fisherman in Alaska and as soon as the training course was over, she was hoping to get a transfer to Seattle to be near him.

As well as Paula and me, there were six other British girls on the same flight, all heading over to New York for training. It wasn't difficult to spot us, as we all stuck out like sore thumbs. The rest of first class was made up of wealthy businessmen in suits, then there was us – excitable young women, dressed in our smartest clothes, chatting and laughing away. The others looked as thrilled as I felt as we settled into our luxurious leather seats.

It was going to take eight hours to get there. It was the longest flight I had ever been on in my life, and I was determined to savour every single minute. I could barely believe it, as I tucked into caviar and lobster thermidor, and I ate every scrap of food on my fine bone china plate.

'I could get used to this,' I joked to Paula, as I had a little sip of Dom Perignon Champagne. I had never tasted anything like it before and I giggled as the bubbles exploded up my nose.

'If only Mum could see me now,' I thought sadly. I knew she would have loved everything about this.

I was tired, but I was way too excited to sleep, and soon there were other things to think about. As the captain announced that we were coming in to land, I was literally glued to the window. I felt a shiver of excitement run through me as we passed over Manhattan and I got a bird's-eye view of the magnificent skyline for the first time. It didn't seem real to me somehow; it looked like something from a film.

The ground was thick with two feet of snow as we landed at Idlewild Airport, which was what JFK Airport was called in those days. I put on my faux-fur hat and wrapped my brown A-line winter coat around me, but I was still shivering as I walked out of the airport lugging my two suitcases along. I'd saved up for months when I was working at Link House to buy that coat from a little shop on Walthamstow High Street. It was a bit worn now, so I'd stitched a little fake-fur collar onto it, to try to make it a bit more sophisticated. After all, I was going to be wearing it in New York!

A man in a Pan Am uniform was waiting for us and we were all ushered onto a bus, which would take us to our dormitory.

'You girls are headed to Forest Hills,' he explained. 'It's a nice, quiet little suburb close to the airport where you will be doing most of your training.'

'I can't believe they've stuck us out in the suburbs,' I heard one of the girls behind me say.

'I'd rather hoped we would be in Manhattan,' said Paula, obviously disappointed.

If truth be told, I had too. When I thought of New York, I immediately pictured the Statue of Liberty and skyscrapers, not the quiet suburbs, but in reality I knew that it would have taken too long to travel to class every day.

'We can get the bus into the city,' I told Paula. 'I bet it's not far.'

I'm sure, looking back now, that the powers that be had deliberately chosen a sleepy suburb. I bet they thought the city would hold too many temptations for young women in a strange country, many of whom would be living away from home for the first time.

I looked out of the window, taking everything in with wide-eyed excitement, as the bus struggled through the snow. At first glance, the suburbs didn't seem that different from Walthamstow, with their shops and red-brick terraced houses. Our 'dorm' turned out to be an ordinary-looking four-storey block of apartments, which were all owned by Pan Am. A short woman in her fifties, with curled red hair, was waiting outside for us.

'Good morning, ladies, and welcome to America,' she said in a thunderous voice. 'I trust you had a good flight? I am your house mother Miss Bohanna.'

When I'd found out we would have a 'house mother', my mind had conjured up an image of a kindly little old lady with grey hair, wearing old-fashioned clothes. But even though Miss Bohanna was no spring chicken, there was nothing frumpy or grandmotherly about her. She was very slim and looked stylish in her pencil skirt, sweater and high heels, and from her perfectly applied make-up, it was clear that she still took great pride in her appearance.

She may have been small, but she had the most powerful, booming voice that I had ever heard. And, as we soon found out, she certainly liked to use it.

'I live in an apartment on the ground floor, so I can keep an eye on you girls,' she told us. 'Let me warn you now, nothing gets past me.'

She explained that there would be four of us in each two-bedroom apartment. I was sharing a room with Paula, and there were two other girls in with us – Hazel Hepworth and Sandra Burdett.

'Come, come, girls,' Miss Bohanna said, clapping her hands. 'Follow me.'

Miss Bohanna was small, spritely and moved like a whippet, and the four of us had trouble keeping up with her as she scurried across the lobby to get the lift to the top floor. We all trooped after her down the long corridor, dragging our cases along behind us.

'So,' she said, turning the key in the lock and pushing open the wooden door. 'This is your new home.'

The Pan Am planes might have been the height of luxury, but the dorms certainly were not. Our apartment was spartan and bare, with basic wooden furniture. It had an open-plan kitchen, a small bathroom with a shower over the bath and two single beds in each bedroom, with mattresses as thin as paper.

'Oh, it's not very homely,' Paula said to me, not realising Miss Bohanna was right behind her.

'What did you expect, dear?' she said brusquely. 'The Waldorf Astoria?'

'Oh no, Miss Bohanna,' Paula said, her cheeks burning red. 'I just meant there aren't any knick-knacks or pictures or anything.'

'Knick-knacks?' said Miss Bohanna. 'I'll pass that on to the Pan Am executives. Does anybody have any other complaints?'

'No, Miss Bohanna,' we all mumbled.

'Fine,' she said. 'Well, that's all for now, girls. I'll leave you to get settled in.'

As the door closed, we all breathed a sigh of relief.

'I wouldn't want to get on the wrong side of her,' said Hazel.

'She's a bit of a dragon,' sighed Paula. 'I think it's too late for me. My card's already marked.'

I walked around the apartment, taking it all in. It was very plain, with its painted walls and tiled floors. There was nothing cosy about it, and it was entirely different from the house Dawn and I had shared in Margate, which had been stuffed to the gills with dusty ornaments and chintzy furniture.

'Well, it will do,' I said. 'We're not here for long, and besides, we're in New York!'

'I know,' said Sandra. 'I can't wait to go and explore the Big Apple.'

We were only going to be staying there for six weeks, while we did our training, so I had no complaints. I was busy unpacking when there was a loud rap on the door.

'Uh-oh,' said Hazel. 'Miss Bohanna's back.'

We all dashed into the living room and practically stood to attention as she walked in. Although we eventually found out her name was Dorothy and we nicknamed her Dottie behind her back, we wouldn't have dared address her as anything but Miss Bohanna to her face. A spinster whose family originally came from Ireland, she had been hired as a stewardess by Pan Am in the 1930s and had worked her way up to becoming a purser, the person in charge of the cabin, before her retirement. I could imagine that she was very good at her job, as she certainly let us know who was boss from day one.

'Sit, girls,' she told us. 'I'd like a quick word. It's my job to keep tabs on you young ladies, and let me tell you that a lot is required of you It's important that you work hard and keep out of mischief. You will be in class all day and then at night you will have to study for the next day's test.

'So forget those thoughts about sneaking off into Manhattan or staying out until all hours. The last girl who tried that was out of here on her way to the airport so fast, her feet hardly touched the ground.'

She paused dramatically and then focused her steely gaze on us.

'Remember,' she said, 'you are all replaceable.'

I gulped with fear.

'In the past, some trainees have been sent home for not taking things seriously enough, and I wouldn't want that to happen to any of you. Whatever you may have heard, Pan Am isn't about glamour or serving fancy drinks to handsome men. On the contrary, as you'll soon find out, it's about darn hard work.'

Sandra leaned over to me.

'That's a shame,' she whispered. 'I was only in it for the handsome men.'

Dottie must have heard us giggling.

'Is there something urgent you want to share with the rest of the group, young lady?' she asked Sandra.

'Oh … er … no, Miss Bohanna,' Sandra said meekly, her cheeks burning red.

'Good. Well, I'll leave you to unpack,' she said and, with a sniff of disapproval, she was gone.

Her words were enough to strike the fear of God into all of us.

'Imagine the shame of being thrown off the course and being sent back to England?' said Hazel.

'I know,' said Sandra. 'My mother would have my guts for garters.'

Just the idea of it made me feel sick to my stomach.

We all knew how lucky we were to have been given this amazing opportunity and none of us intended to mess it up. For each one of us, there were another hundred girls who would have bitten our hands off for the job, and we knew that for the next six weeks, we couldn't put a foot wrong.

Of course all of the trainees on our course were female; the airlines didn't hire male stewards in the 1960s. The passengers who could afford air travel at that time were mainly wealthy men and they wanted young, single, attractive women to serve them in the cabin.

Our intake was made up of seventeen of us Brits and three Japanese girls, who were all from Honolulu, Hawaii. I had never met anyone Japanese before and I was intrigued, so I wandered down the corridor to say hello. Much to my amusement, all three of them were on their hands and knees, scrubbing the apartment from top to bottom, because they didn't think it was clean enough.

'Hello there, I'm Harumi, but you can call me Mimi,' said one of them. 'And this is Joyce and Florence.'

Florence and Joyce, who we called Jo, had been born in Hawaii, but Mimi was first-generation Japanese. They seemed so exotic to me, with the way they took their shoes off inside and wore funny little socks that had a separate bit for their big toes.

'What are those things on your feet?' I asked.

'They're called tabis,' said Florence. 'They're very common in Japan.'

I was also fascinated by all the strange-looking food they were unpacking. When I went round to their apartment the next morning, they were having breakfast, and I watched in amazement as Mimi scooped some rice into a bowl, cracked a raw egg over it and sprinkled some seaweed on the top.

'That's a bit different from bacon and eggs,' I said.

'You should try it sometime,' laughed Mimi.

They seemed very gentle and sweet, and I instantly warmed to them.

'Those Japanese girls are very quiet,' said Sandra.

'I'm not surprised,' I told her. 'I feel a bit sorry for them, as they're completely outnumbered by us noisy Brits.'

The following day the final nine girls flew in from the UK and we all got to know each other before our training started. We were all from completely different backgrounds and walks of life, and I found it fascinating.

I told everyone about Mum and Dad and Ernie.

'Oh, he sounds nice,' said Hazel.

'He is,' I told her. 'He wasn't best pleased about me coming over here though.'

'I know what you mean,' said Angie. 'One of the reasons I wanted to get away from England was because of a man, and he wasn't too happy about it either.'

Angie Vaughn from Birmingham was an ex-model and she

was stunningly beautiful, with a voluptuous hour-glass figure. She had short, chestnut-brown hair that was perfectly curled and set, which she later dyed a peroxide blonde, like Marilyn Monroe. All our eyes were as wide as saucers as she told us, in her Brummie accent, about the older man she had been dating.

'He was my mentor,' she said. 'He helped me get into modelling, but then he got too clingy. He was insanely jealous too.'

When she showed us a photograph of him, we were even more shocked.

'He's ancient,' whispered Paula. 'He's at least thirty.'

'Well, I've come to America to be closer to my sweetheart,' said another girl in a very plummy accent. 'He's an American serviceman stationed in Arizona.'

Her name was Angela Kirby and she was the only one out of all of us who had gone to college. She'd been at RADA to study drama and was an actress. I could tell she was quite well-off by her posh accent.

'I met him when he was stationed in Suffolk and he used to come into my parents' public house,' she said. 'He's very handsome and his name's Charlie Blue Eyes.'

'Why's he called that then?' asked a girl called Janet, and we all laughed.

Janet Brown was the joker of the group. She was a very down-to-earth lass and the kind of person who called a spade a spade. Her dad was a bricklayer and she was one of seven children. She had a great sense of humour, but she was a little on the plump side, and I suspected she was going to struggle to keep her weight down to the required limit.

I felt like I had led a bit of a sheltered life compared to some of the other girls.

Hazel told us how she had been a dancer with a famous

troupe called the Bluebells. She was very fit and elegant, with short, brown, curly hair and chubby cheeks.

'That sounds so glamorous,' I said.

'I suppose it was,' she told us. 'I performed with them in Paris and we were even on television.'

She was very outgoing and chatty and, as an only child, I suspected she had been spoilt by her parents.

'I'm from near London too, Betty,' said Sandra.

She was from Kingston-upon-Thames, but had worked at her ex-boyfriend's family's Italian restaurant in Soho. Every night after it closed, they would go to the International Club in Soho.

'I've never been to a nightclub before,' I said. 'What was it like?'

'I know people probably think they're seedy places full of gangsters and shady characters, but it was wonderful, Betty,' she told me. 'We'd meet all sorts of interesting people, like jazz musicians and chaps from Europe.'

I knew London well from when I worked there, and I loved to walk down the Embankment and the Strand on my lunch hour. But I'd never had enough money to go out in central London, and I knew my parents thought nightclubs were a bit racy and would have had a blue fit if I'd gone to one.

'Gosh, the girls all seem so sophisticated,' I said to Paula that night.

'Well, they might be, but you're the only one out of all of us who has any experience of being a stewardess,' she said.

It did put me at a bit of an advantage, and the other girls had been keen to hear all about where I'd been and the type of planes I'd flown in.

The Japanese girls were a lot more shy and reserved than the English girls, but I had a lot more in common with Mimi than

I had realised. One afternoon we got talking about our families and she told me how her dad was a doctor who was sent to Korea as part of the Japanese expansion that had helped to trigger the Second World War. It was strange to think that her father and mine had both fought in the same war, but had been on opposing sides, so in effect I was now friends with the enemy.

I must admit, it felt a bit uncomfortable, and we never really spoke about it much after that. Later on in my career, I became friends with a German girl called Brigitta, whose father had been a Luftwaffe pilot during the war. I remember going round to her house for dinner and seeing a photo of him in his uni-form on her dining-room wall, and I couldn't help but think that he could have been one of the pilots dropping the bombs down on our neighbourhood.

Dottie was right when she told us all one day: 'Pan Am brings the world together, and anyone who wears that blue uniform is now a sister.' It didn't matter about our nationalities or back-grounds or what had come before this moment, now we were all on the same side. In fact, some of my closest friends today are still my Pan Am 'sisters'.

Overall, it was a friendly bunch, and we all got close very quickly. It was only natural, I suppose. We were all in the same boat – in a foreign country, thousands of miles away from home and our families – so from day one, we were joined at the hip.

With one exception. There was a girl called Nancy Turner that nobody took to, as she seemed a bit moody and stand-offish. She didn't say much and never got involved when we were all talking. Angie shared a room with her and she took her under her wing, which I thought was very kind of her.

'I don't care for that Nancy,' said Paula that night.

'No, I think she's a bit flighty,' I agreed.

It wasn't until a few weeks after training had ended that we found out why. Nancy had moved into an apartment with Angie, but one day she was working on a flight to London and had never come back, leaving Angie to pay a huge telephone bill of hundreds of dollars that she had racked up. It turned out that when she'd first come to New York, she had found out that she was pregnant by her English boyfriend, so she had gone back to the UK to be with him. It was a real scandal in those days to be an unmarried mother, and all of us girls were terribly shocked.

'It explains why she was so stand-offish, I suppose,' I said. 'She was probably sick with worry.'

If truth be told, I felt a bit sorry for her. We all assumed she would be forced to have a shotgun wedding before the baby was born.

Now that everyone had arrived, Dottie called a meeting to lay down the dorm rules. We were all chit-chatting away when she walked in.

'Ladies!' she boomed. 'A little hush please.'

We soon simmered down.

'I expect your rooms to be kept clean and tidy,' she explained. 'The windows must remain closed at all times, as we have just had a very sophisticated modern system called central heating installed in all of the apartments.'

'Yes, Miss Bohanna,' we all chorused.

'And one more thing,' she said looking at us all over her glasses with her beady blue eyes. 'Under no circumstances are there to be any overnight guests of any variety. Am I making myself crystal clear?'

'Yes, Miss Bohanna,' we repeated.

By now we were all terrified of getting on the wrong side of Dottie.

'It's worse than living in a convent,' joked Janet.

'I bet she lets herself into the apartments to check up on us when we're not here,' said Angela.

I knew it wouldn't be long before one of us faced the wrath of Dottie for the first time. But I didn't expect it to be me.

One afternoon it was suffocatingly hot and stuffy in our apartment, so despite the cold and the snow, I opened up our dorm window just a tiny crack, to let in some fresh air. Literally a few minutes later, there was a frantic banging on the door. I opened it to find a furious Dottie standing there, her face as red as her hair.

'Young lady, did you not listen to a word I said about not opening the windows?' she said, marching over to it and slamming it shut. 'You are wasting the heat.'

'I'm sorry, Miss Bohanna,' I said.

'Well, you certainly will be if you open that window again,' she muttered before storming out.

Needless to say, I didn't dare do it again.

I wasn't the only one to get on the wrong side of Dottie. When we'd first arrived, she'd told us that she had a spare key to every apartment and we had all joked that she let herself into each dorm when we were out, just to check up on us. Sure enough, when the Japanese girls came home one evening, there was a note stuck to the ashtray on their coffee table. 'It is common decency to keep your apartment in a respectable state. Please dispose of all ash appropriately in the future.'

Like many of the girls, Jo smoked, and although she had tipped out the ashtray that morning there had been a tiny speck left behind. It was obviously enough to be spotted by Dottie's keen eyes, and she had made her feelings well and truly known. From that point on, we made sure our apartments were spotless and not a thing was out of place when we left on a morning.

We had a few days to settle in before our training started and all of us girls couldn't wait to explore New York. We found out that we could catch a bus at the end of the street and it would take about an hour to get into Manhattan.

First, I had to make do with a trip to the corner shop, but even that felt like an adventure. Our local store, opposite the dorm, was a Jewish deli, so there were all sorts of things we had never heard of, like Manischewitz wine and matzo crackers. We gazed around in awe at all these exotic delicacies.

'Look at this,' I said to Paula. 'It's macaroni cheese in a packet.'

'Amazing,' she gasped.

I had never seen anything like it in my life. You just added water to a powdery mix and you had a meal. I was even more stunned when I saw the instant mashed potato in a packet. We had never even heard of convenience foods in the UK in the early1960s.

'I can't wait to tell my mother about this,' I said. 'She'll think I'm pulling her leg.'

The little Polish man who ran the deli thought it was hilarious.

'You British gals have sure got cute accents,' he told us.

That was the one thing that immediately struck me about New York: it was a melting pot of so many different cultures. Growing up in Walthamstow in the 1950s, I had never seen anyone Chinese, Indian or black. In fact, the most diverse group of people that lived on our street was a Catholic family. That was as multicultural as it got in those days for me! But walking around New York, even in the suburbs, you saw a rainbow of nationalities wherever you went, and it felt like the whole world was there. It was a real eye-opener for a naive young woman like me, who wasn't used to anything other than white English faces, and it felt like I was seeing the real world for the first time.

I was beside myself with excitement on our first weekend there, when Paula, Janet, Sandra, Hazel and I got the bus into Manhattan. Growing up, I had seen images of it when I went to the Walthamstow Odeon on a Saturday morning. Before the cartoons started, they would show the British Pathé newsreel, which consisted of black and white footage, with a plummy-voiced narrator telling you the world news, and there were often snippets about New York. I had seen pictures of the big buildings and all the people bustling around, and it always looked so fast-paced and exciting. Now I couldn't believe I was about to see it for myself.

Dottie insisted on coming to see us before we left. 'If you are determined to go into the city unaccompanied, there are a couple of things you need to know,' she said. 'My advice to you, girls, is that if you want to stay safe, avoid the subway at all costs and do not make eye contact with anyone, as there are some unsavoury individuals out there who would love nothing more than to take advantage of unchaperoned young ladies.'

'Yes, Miss Bohanna,' we said impatiently, eager to begin our adventure.

We practically ran to the bus stop, we were so excited to be going into Manhattan. But it took us over an hour to get there, as we seemed to stop at every single suburb on the way. Finally we pulled up into the Midtown bus terminal. It was a bitterly cold, foggy morning and we all wiped a little circle of condensation off the window, desperate to catch our first glimpse of the city.

'Look at the crowds,' gasped Janet. 'I've never seen so many people.'

Even though I had worked in London for years, it seemed busier and much more hectic.

'My goodness,' I said. 'Everyone seems to be in such a hurry.'

'Look up at the buildings, girls,' said Hazel.

We all looked upwards and couldn't believe our eyes. I'd never seen such towering skyscrapers, and they seemed to go on for miles.

'I'll have a crick in my neck by the end of the day,' laughed Sandra.

I couldn't wait to get off the bus and start to explore. We all linked arms as we walked down 42nd Street. Janet screamed as she stepped out in front of a taxi and it gave her a loud toot, and we all laughed.

The roads were so wide and several lanes of traffic had come to a standstill.

The noise, with the constant beeping from the cars and taxis, was deafening.

'It's so loud,' said Paula.

'Eurgh, and smelly too,' I said, pressing my handkerchief over my nose. It was that unpleasant, mysterious whiff that floats up through grates in a city's streets – you're never quite sure exactly what it is, and you don't really want to know either.

But despite the noise and the smells, the whole place felt really magical. The fog soon cleared to reveal a crisp, clear winter's morning and the buildings almost seemed to glitter in the sunlight. We just walked and walked for miles, taking it all in.

'Let's head to Broadway,' said Hazel.

'Well, I don't know about anyone else, but there's no way I can afford to see a show,' replied Janet.

'We can just go and have a look and soak up the atmosphere,' I suggested.

None of us had been paid yet and all I had was the money Auntie Flo had given me, which I needed for food. So we walked to Times Square and saw all the billboards and the bright lights.

But my favourite part of all was wandering around Midtown, where all the fancy stores were. I loved watching the wealthy ladies rushing by, their arms weighed down by huge bags and hat boxes. They were so well groomed, with their perfectly set, bouffant hair and glossy red nails and matching lipstick

'Look at her,' I whispered to Hazel as I noticed a woman going past. She had a fashionable little hat perched on her head, with a veil that came over her face, dark gloves and a long mink coat. Around her neck you could just see the sparkle of a diamond necklace.

'I bet they're real,' said Hazel.

We pressed our noses up against a window of Saks Fifth Avenue and just stared at the lavish displays.

'Well, it's a bit different to Marks and Sparks,' said Janet.

I had never seen anything like it in my life, and I loved everything about the huge department stores like Saks, Macy's and Bergdorf Goodman. They were like ornate palaces and were so vast that they literally took up several streets. Their interiors were just as elaborate. As I pushed open the door at Macy's, it felt like I was walking into a magical world full of wealth and promise. It was the world's biggest department store at the time and it was decorated in a lavish art deco style with marble columns.

I liked the way my heels click-clacked on the polished wood floors, and the air smelt of cigarette smoke and fancy French perfume. There were sparkling glass counters where well-dressed assistants stood waiting to serve you and elegant dining rooms where ladies that lunched nibbled on dainty sandwiches with the crusts cut off.

'There are fifteen floors,' gasped Sandra. 'We could get lost for days in this place.'

It had everything from fancy handbags and clothes to a meat

counter, a bakery and a pet department. But best of all was what we discovered when we got to the top of the first-floor escalator.

'Oh my giddy aunt,' said Janet. 'It's a perfume fountain.'

'A what?' I gasped.

None of us truly believed it until Hazel dipped her finger in and gave it a good sniff.

'Good heavens, she's right!' she said. 'That's not water in there, it's Chanel.'

'A Chanel fountain!' whooped Janet.

'Only in New York,' I laughed.

It was the most incredible thing I had ever seen. I took my handkerchief out of my coat pocket, dipped it into the fountain and doused myself in the expensive scent. Perfume was a luxury I had never been able to afford, so it felt wonderful. We all must have reeked to high heaven by the time we left the store!

In the month before we had arrived, on 20 January 1961, John F. Kennedy had been sworn in as the youngest ever president of the United States. The 43-year-old's glamorous wife, Jacqueline, was the country's most popular fashion icon and all of the women in Manhattan seemed to want to emulate her style, with pillbox hats and short, boxy jackets with oversize buttons. They all looked so bright and colourful in their Jackie Kennedy-inspired suits in pastel colours and shift dresses in swirling Pucci or paisley prints.

'My clothes just seem so plain and dull in comparison,' I sighed to Hazel as we perused some glass cabinets full of scarves. 'Everything I own is either navy, brown or tweed, not even sophisticated black.'

'What would madam like today?' asked a well-dressed shop assistant walking towards us.

'I'd like it all,' I sighed.

But sadly I couldn't afford any of it. There was no way on earth any of us girls could buy anything from the likes of Macy's or Saks. So instead we went to Lerner's, which was a bit more downmarket, and I treated myself to a little pink and white checked blouse with a frill on the front for $3.

'I feel like the cat's whiskers,' I said, admiring myself in the changing-room mirrors. 'I shall call this my New York blouse.'

After our window shopping, we decided to get the ferry to the Statue of Liberty. It was absolutely freezing on the New York Bay in the icy wind, and we were all horrified when we floated straight past the famous landmark.

'We're on the wrong boat,' laughed Sandra.

We ended up on Staten Island and had to go back again to get another ferry out to the Statue of Liberty. But it was all part of the fun and none of us could really believe we were there. Afterwards we bought postcards from a little stand and I couldn't wait to write home and tell Mum and Dad all about it.

Because Manhattan was home to so many different nationalities, there was a whole array of cuisines that came with them. There was Little Italy and Chinatown, although that felt a bit too 'foreign' to us girls and we were a bit scared to wander down there alone. Every street was full of restaurants and delis, although sadly we couldn't afford to eat in any of them. But on the way back to the bus station, we spotted something called an Automat machine. It consisted of rows of around twelve little glass boxes built into the wall and there was food inside each one – everything from a hamburger or a pie to a grilled cheese sandwich.

'Heavens above,' said Hazel. 'Look at this.'

We all watched in amazement as she put a few cents in the slot and pressed a button and we screamed in delight when she lifted a hamburger out.

'Dinner is served,' laughed Hazel. 'And it's hot too.'

'I can't wait to tell my dad about this,' I said. 'He'll never believe it.'

We'd never seen anything like it in the UK and I thought it was incredible that you could get hot food out of a hole in the wall. There were shrieks of excitement as we all put a coin in and out popped our dinner!

Everyone except Janet. I could see her looking longingly at us as we hungrily devoured our greasy burgers.

'Go on, Janet,' I said. 'Put a dime in the slot.'

'I really shouldn't,' she sighed. 'I bet they'll weigh us on the first day and I'm already worried I'm over my limit.'

'You've got to eat something,' said Paula.

'OK,' she sighed. 'Maybe I will, and then I just won't eat at all tomorrow.'

I could see that poor Janet was going to struggle with her weight, and she was forever on a diet, although this mostly consisted of her starving herself for a few days before each weigh-in.

Dinner over, we were all so exhausted from so many hours of walking, we decided the only option was to get the subway back to the bus station.

'But what about what Dottie said?' asked Paula, looking a little worried.

'Come on, it will be fine,' said Hazel. 'It can't be that bad.'

I must admit though, I did feel a little nervous, and as we walked down the stairs to the subway, I grabbed Sandra's arm. When we got on the train I made sure I kept my head down, so as not to make eye contact with any dubious people.

That is until Hazel let out on ear-piercing scream.

'What on earth was that?' she yelled. 'Something's just run over my foot.'

We all looked down at the floor and there, scurrying around, was the biggest beetle I had ever seen in my life.

'Eurgh, what the heck is that?' squealed Janet.

'It's a cockroach, ma'am,' a man sitting near us told us. 'The subway's full of 'em.'

We were all terrified.

'I'm petrified of creepy crawlies,' said Paula. 'I'm not coming anywhere near these grotty trains again.'

Finally we made it to the bus station, but it was well after 10 p.m. by the time we pulled up into Forest Hills. We all crept through the front door of the dorm, trying to stifle our giggles.

'Shh, don't let Dottie hear us,' whispered Hazel as we tiptoed past her apartment on the ground floor.

'She'd be disgusted we stayed out so late without a chaperone,' said Sandra.

'And don't tell her about the subway,' whispered Janet.

As soon as the lift doors closed, we all burst out laughing. By the time we got back to our apartment, I was totally exhausted. We'd walked for miles and I had big, painful blisters on the back of each of my ankles, but I had a stylish new blouse, I smelt of Chanel No. 5 and I'd seen the most amazing things.

'It sounds silly, but I still don't really believe that I'm in New York,' I said as Paula and I got into our nightdresses. 'All day I've felt like pinching myself. It just didn't seem real.'

'I know what you mean,' said Paula. 'It seems like a jolly long way from home.'

I was shattered, but I knew there was one more thing I had to do before I fell asleep. I got out the postcard that I had bought at the Statue of Liberty and started to write to my parents. It was too expensive to phone them, so I hadn't had any contact with them since I'd arrived.

'Dear Mum and Dad, I'm here! New York is terrific. We went

sightseeing today and saw the Empire State Building and the Statue of Liberty. It's just like you see in the films. The girls are all friendly and we start our training soon.'

Up until now, it had all felt a bit like a holiday, exploring this wonderful city and getting to know the girls. But now the real hard work was about to begin and I was very nervous. Was I really up to the job of being a Pan Am stewardess or would I be on the next plane home, like Dottie had warned us?

Chapter Five

A Lady in Training

Thrashing and kicking as hard as I could, I fought desperately to keep my head above the freezing-cold water. But I was exhausted and my sopping-wet clothes felt like lead weights, dragging me deeper and deeper down to the bottom.

'You can do this, Betty,' I told myself, desperately trying to swim back up to the surface, where I could see the shadowy outline of the life rafts.

Finally, with one last frantic push for survival, I emerged through the water, coughing and spluttering. I took several deep, painful breaths, savouring the feeling of relief as oxygen filled my lungs again. Then, using every last bit of strength I had left in my body, I heaved myself onto the life raft and collapsed in a shivering heap.

'Well done, Betty,' said our trainer, Al West, throwing me a towel. 'You've passed.'

Safety training was the least enjoyable but perhaps the most necessary part of our six-week Pan Am stewardess course. We would come to the Young Women's Christian Association swimming pool to practise our ditching drills for hours on end. We would have to jump into the freezing-cold water fully clothed, swim several lengths and then climb onto the life rafts. I'm not a strong swimmer, and I hated every single exhausting minute of it. By the end of the session, I was always close to tears, so now it was such a relief that I had finally managed to pass.

I had taken comfort in the fact that I was not the only one who had found it hard. Some of the girls, like Janet Brown, were really frightened of the water. While I had managed to get myself on the life raft, she was still flailing around in the deep end.

'Look at poor old Janet,' said Angela.

She was really struggling and we were worried she was about to go under, so we paddled the raft over to her.

'Do you need a hand?' I shouted.

'Just leave me alone,' Janet snapped back.

But she was thrashing around so much, she accidentally managed to inflate the life jacket she was wearing. She was trying to swim, but it was so big and bulky, she wasn't going very far. Much to her disgust, Angela and I couldn't stop ourselves from crying with laughter as we watched her swim round and round in circles, with a very annoyed look on her face.

Really, we all knew it was no laughing matter. We had to pass this part of the training, otherwise we would fail the whole course. Thankfully, after some extra tuition at the pool and a few more attempts, Janet and a couple of the other girls managed to scrape through.

I'd known we were going to be put through the mill, but our Pan Am training was proving to be extremely hard work. There was so much to learn and the days were long and tiring. Every morning, at 7.30 a.m., we caught a bus from outside our dorms in Forest Hills to the classroom at Idlewild Airport. We always had to make sure we were smartly dressed in business suits, as you never knew who was going to call into the classroom to meet the latest trainees, and we were constantly on our best behaviour.

On our first day we sat at our desks, clutching our pencils and notebooks, eager to get started. There was an ashtray in front of us, in case we wanted a cigarette during the lessons, and although most of the girls were smokers, I wasn't. We all sat up to attention when a man in a suit walked in. He was in his fifties, with a grey crew cut, and was very smiley. He took off his jacket, sat on the desk and lit up a cigarette.

'Hello, ladies,' he said. 'I'm Alan West, but you can call me Al.'

'He looks like Bing Crosby,' whispered Hazel.

He explained that he was a supervisor in San Francisco, but had been sent to New York to be our lead trainer. It didn't take long for us to tell that Al relished being the king in this court full of women. Well, what red-blooded male wouldn't enjoy all these young girls hanging on to his every word? He loved regaling us with legendary Pan Am stories, like the one about the sea plane that couldn't land in San Francisco Bay because of terrible fog so had to land in the Sacramento River and then spent hours taxiing back down to the city.

He immediately took a particular liking to Hazel, because she was very outgoing and always had her hand up asking questions, but we all knew he was married and it never went further than a bit of harmless flirting.

Despite his easygoing demeanour, Al had high standards, and he expected a lot from us.

'Every morning you will be tested on what you learnt the day before – and remember, you're being observed at all times,' he told us.

He gave us a schedule which explained what we would be studying each week, anything from world geography to learning how to deliver a baby using a chair and a doll. Thank goodness I never had to do that during my career, as I'm not sure that a chair bears that many similarities to a woman's body! We even learnt how to tie off the umbilical cord using scissors and string.

Al taught us about different parts of the world and warned us that we had to be very health and safety conscious.

'Do not, under any circumstances, drink the water anywhere outside of the United States, and always brush your teeth with Coca Cola,' he told us.

We all looked at each other, completely confused. Surely he didn't mean we couldn't drink the water in the UK? In the end, Sandra put her hand up.

'Excuse me, sir,' she said, 'but surely it's safe to drink the water in England?'

Much to our amazement, Al shook his head.

'Nope, not even in England,' he said.

All of us seventeen Brits were up in arms about this, as we had obviously been drinking tap water all our lives and had come out unscathed. None of us batted an eyelid about brush- ing our teeth in Coke though.

As I said earlier, my least favourite part of the course was the safety training. We all knew flying had its risks, especially in the early 1960s, when passenger planes were still so new, but I hated dwelling on the negative side of things. As well as the ditching drills and practising how to inflate the evacuation slides, we had to learn to use fire extinguishers by putting out a fire in a wastepaper basket, which I always found terrifying.

'When people say that when it's your turn to go, there's noth- ing you can do about it, don't believe it, because we have proof that with good training you can survive,' Al told us.

To back up his point, he showed us the silent film of the Pan Am plane which, by some miracle, had managed to land safely in the Pacific without any engines.

In October 1956, on a flight from Honolulu to San Francisco when the engines failed, Captain Richard Ogg had managed to ditch the Boeing 377 Stratocruiser into the Pacific Ocean, saving the lives of all thirty-one of his passengers. There had even been a book published and a film made about it, and most airlines at the time used this footage to show their pilots the perfect example of an emergency landing.

'The only casualties were the forty-four cases of live canaries that drowned in the hold when the plane eventually sank and Captain Ogg's glasses, which he sat on in the lifeboat,' Al told us.

Stratocruisers were Pan Am's earliest airplanes and were like luxurious flying hotels. On board, there were two levels connected by a spiral staircase, with a lounge on the ground floor and twenty-eight private bedrooms with full-size beds and room service on the upper floor. Later on in my career, I heard many salacious stories from the stewardesses that worked on the Stratocruisers about bed-hopping amongst passengers, and apparently it wasn't unusual for two passengers to get friendly and one would invite the other back to their room. Often royalty would travel on them, and my friend Brenda tells the story of a maharajah of an Indian state and his wife. When they retired to their private state rooms, all of the stewardesses took it in turns to try on her beautiful mink coat that was hanging in the first-class cloakroom.

A part of the course that provided a bit of light relief was the make-up classes. One afternoon a week, we were assigned to the Merle Norman make-up school in Manhattan. Merle Norman was a huge American cosmetic company that was stocked by all the top department stores.

At our first session, I thought it was wonderful when we were shown into a room lined with huge mirrors, all with bright movie-star lights around them, where one of Merle Norman's glamorous advisors taught us about skincare and make-up. She chose Hazel as her guinea pig and we all tried not to laugh as she painted her face with a bubblegum-pink face pack.

'Ow, it really stings,' Hazel yelped.

Then we all had to practise doing the same thing. It was hilarious, sitting in front of these big mirrors, all with matching bright-pink packs on, trying to keep our faces straight so they wouldn't crack. Then, when it had finally dried like cement, we had great fun peeling it off to reveal our bright-red cheeks.

I loved these expensive lotions and potions, and it all seemed so luxurious to me. Like Mum did, I just used soap and water to scrub my face, or if I was feeling fancy, some Pond's cold cream followed by a quick smear of Nivea.

Pan Am had strict regulations about our appearance, and that extended to our make-up. We all had to wear identical blue eye shadow to match our uniforms, the same pink nail polish and a Revlon lipstick in a shade called Persian Melon. Even though the pale, peachy colour made some of the girls look like corpses, they had to have written permission if they wanted to use a different colour. All of our make-up had to be very conservative and was to be applied sparingly, as we were told we had to look natural and wholesome.

We were permitted to wear one ring and small earrings, but we couldn't wear necklaces or bracelets, and no one was allowed to have hair any longer than collar length. There was great excitement, three weeks into our training, when we were taken into Manhattan for an appointment at the world-famous salon at Bergdorf Goodman on Fifth Avenue.

'Welcome to Coiffures Americana, girls,' said Lee Trujillo, who had interviewed me in London for Pan Am and was now one of the trainers on our course.

'It sounds so sophisticated and French,' whispered Hazel.

'I'm sure I read in a magazine that this is where Jackie Kennedy gets her hair cut,' I said.

As we walked in, we all gave a collective gasp. This place was more like a stately home than a hairdresser's. The walls were covered with pink flocked wallpaper, huge blue antique chandeliers twinkled from the ceiling and the floor was covered in cream marble tiles that looked like something out of a French chateau. There was a team of women in matching pink uniforms waiting to greet us.

'Can I take your coat to the cloakroom, madam?' one asked me.

'Oh ... er ... yes please,' I said.

'Would you like morning coffee, madam?' asked another.

'That would be lovely,' I said.

We each had a stylist assigned to us and, as there were hardly any female hairdressers in those days, they were all men. Mine was called Kenneth and was dressed very fashionably in a tight black polo neck and slim-fitting trousers.

I was led to a line of blue padded-leather chairs, where my hair was washed over a basin, then I was taken back to Kenneth. I'd never had so much time and attention focused on my hair before. It was carefully cut before Kenneth tightly wound it into rollers and secured each one with a pin, then applied a freezing-cold setting lotion.

'An assistant will take you to the drying room, Miss Eden,' he said.

I was led into another beautifully decorated room, with a long line of chairs, each with a large drying bonnet that was pulled over your head. Normally you had to sit under there for an hour, or until you got so unbearably hot you had to wave frantically to your hairdresser to come and get you out before you started to smoke. But Coiffures Americana had state-of-the-art drying bonnets that each had their own dial control, which you could turn down if you felt like your hair was burning. I was sat next to Sandra, but you could hardly hear anything under the plastic bubbles, so we flicked through *Vogue* instead of chatting.

Half an hour later, I was ushered back to see Kenneth in the styling room, where he removed the rollers, brushed them out and did a bit of teasing and back-combing.

'There,' he said. 'Just beautiful.'

My hair was much bigger and bouffier than anything I had ever had done in England, but he had managed to get a soft wave in my poker-straight locks and had framed my face with a few pin curls.

'It's lovely,' I said. 'Thank you so much.'

Afterwards, we all crowded excitedly around the big mirrors in the reception area to admire our new hairdos. It was soon apparent that, under instruction from our supervisor, we all had variations of the same style.

'Oh, you've got a flip,' I said to Sandra. 'I love it.'

This was where the hair flicked out at the bottom rather than under, like mine, a style which had been made very fashionable at the time by Jackie Kennedy.

I felt so stylish with my new coiffured hair and I didn't care that we all looked similar. We were all so proud to have been accepted by Pan Am and we were prepared to toe the line and do whatever it took to get a job with them. Nobody wanted to mess this chance up.

It was so different from the little hairdresser's in Walthamstow High Street where I had been getting my hair cut since I was a child. I remember going there when I was about six, and I was talking so much the hairdresser had got quite annoyed. 'If you don't be quiet, I'll cut your ear off!' she had told me. Needless to say, petrified with fear, I'd sat as still and quiet as a statue for the rest of my appointment. There was certainly nothing pampering about that experience, and it was a world away from Coiffures Americana, with its blue chandeliers and glossy magazines.

Another part of the course that I enjoyed was the deportment and etiquette classes, which were run by Lee Trujillo.

One of the main reasons the hiring team came to the UK was that they believed that British girls were more polished and had better manners and etiquette than many other nationalities. But they still wanted to make sure we stood and walked properly and held ourselves in a way befitting a Pan Am stewardess.

At our first class, we all stood in line as Lee walked amongst us like a glamorous sergeant major in heels, inspecting the troops.

'Shoulders back, head up, Miss Eden,' she said, lifting my chin with a perfectly manicured finger. 'Imagine a wire running from the top of your head, holding you up, and a zip running up your front, holding you in.'

We were taught to cross our ankles rather than our legs, as that looked 'too masculine', and not to wiggle or strut in any way when we walked. As Lee told us: 'There's no jiggling at Pan Am.'

There were also certain ways to hold yourself when you were serving food or drinks to passengers. Lee got a couple of the girls to sit next to each other on chairs, as if they were on a plane, and she walked towards them holding a silver coffee pot. As she was pouring them out a pretend drink, she bobbed down and did what looked a bit like a curtsey.

'I think she's just met the Queen,' Angie laughed.

'That ladies,' said Lee with a flourish, 'is the clipper dip.'

The 'clipper dip' was a signature Pan Am move, where the stewardess bends her knees to pour a drink, rather than leaning over the passenger, which was considered very uncouth.

I loved every minute of these lessons and I felt like I was a student at some elite Swiss finishing school.

Another important part of our training was learning how to treat the passengers. On our first day, Al had given us each a book.

'This is your bible,' he'd said. 'I expect you to read it from cover to cover and learn the rules.'

It was called *How to Win Friends and Influence People* by Dale Carnegie. It was written in 1936 and was one of the world's first best-selling self-help books. It was full of tips like always smile, be genuinely interested in people and make them feel important. 'Remember that a person's name is, to that person, the sweetest and most important sound in any language,' it advised. Consequently, we were always expected to know every first-class passenger's name and to use it whenever we served them.

Other Pan Am golden rules were never to argue with a passenger and not to discuss anything controversial like politics or religion. Flirting was definitely not encouraged, but you were expected to chat to customers once the meal service was over, perhaps over a game of cribbage or gin rummy. Even though it was written more than seventy years ago now, I think some of the advice in that book is invaluable, and I still use it today when I'm meeting new people.

Another important part of the job was keeping your eye open for people who were drinking too much. With free Dom Perignon on board, often from take-off, there was a tendency for some passengers to overindulge.

'Deal with it as discreetly and politely as you can,' Al advised us. 'Just try to put them off, rather than refusing to serve them.'

If someone asked for another drink, instead of saying, 'No, you've had enough,' we were taught to tell them, 'We'll talk about it after the meal service' or 'I'm afraid I'm a bit tied up at the moment, but maybe in a little while,' in the hope that they would get the message or would have passed out or sobered up before they could ask again. It wasn't only the men we were warned to watch out for. We were told that some of the older wealthy women on board were often big drinkers and would easily sink Scotch after Scotch if allowed to. Also, we were never supposed to refer to anyone as 'drunk' just 'intoxicated', as it sounded a little less common.

There was so much to learn, and by the end of the day, my head would be spinning. Our only break was at lunchtime, when we would head to the Pan Am cafeteria, and that wasn't exactly relaxing. From our very first day, as soon as we walked in, the men surrounded us like flies. None of us was prepared for that kind of attention, but I think we all secretly enjoyed it. It was mainly the Pan Am ground crew who couldn't wait to check out the latest class of new stewardesses, but they were nice guys and we quite enjoyed the banter. They always made a beeline for Angie first. As an ex-model, she was devastatingly beautiful, and she was soon dating a mechanic called Barry. We were all constantly being asked out for dinner, but because we were so busy with the training, most of us were too tired to even contemplate going on a date.

At first I'd also declined any invitations because of Ernie. I'd been in America for weeks, but I still hadn't heard a peep from him.

'I can't believe he's not even written to me yet,' I said to Angie.

'That's men for you,' she sighed. 'He's probably still hurt that you've taken the job and come to America instead of marrying him.'

I suspected she was right, especially when I received a letter from my cousin Len's wife Jean. 'Ernest's really missing you and he's desperate to know when you're coming back,' she wrote.

I felt so guilty. I really did care for Ernie, but I was enjoying every minute of being in New York. I wasn't ready to give up this wonderful new life and all the unbelievable experiences I was about to have to go home and settle down like he wanted to.

In his heart, I think Ernest knew that too, and a few weeks later I got another letter from Jean. 'I hope it won't upset you too much, but I thought I'd better let you know that Ernest has started going out with a girl called Margaret.'

'I knew it!' I said to Paula.

All of the time we had been going out, Ernie's mother had constantly talked about someone called Margaret who lived in a big house in a neighbouring street to them in Essex. I'd never said anything to Ernie, but I'd secretly suspected she was trying to fix them up.

'I bet his mother's delighted I'm out of the picture,' I said. 'She always did think her son could do better than marry a girl like me from Walthamstow.'

I would be lying if I said that I wasn't upset by the news, but it was my own fault. I knew that losing Ernie was the risk I had taken when I had come over to America. I felt I was too young to get married and I wanted to have a career first, but I had secretly hoped that perhaps Ernie would wait for me. But on the other hand, I was also a little bit relieved to hear that Ernie had moved on, as it meant I could stop feeling guilty about leaving him behind.

It wasn't as if male attention was in short supply in New York.

One lunchtime, I got talking to one of the operations crew, Danny. He was a friend of Barry, whom Angie had been dating, and he invited me to spend the Easter long weekend with his family in Philadelphia. I wasn't sure about it at first, but Danny assured me it was all above board and that I would have my own bedroom.

'You should go,' said Paula. 'It will be fun.'

We had the whole weekend off and I had never been to Philadelphia before, so I accepted his invitation. He was from a big Italian family and on the first night there, we all sat down to a huge dinner. During the evening, Danny, along with his father and five brothers, kept going off into another room and having whispered conversations, leaving me with the ladies. I was really puzzled about why he was being so secretive and I thought it was very rude to keep leaving the table without any excuse or explanation. But none of the other women said a word about it and I thought it was all very odd.

When I got back to the dorm, I mentioned it to Angie.

'That doesn't surprise me,' she said. 'They were probably talking about mob business.'

'Mob business?' I said. 'What on earth is that?'

'Barry told me that Danny's family have got links to the Mafia,' whispered Angie. 'But you must not say anything or we could be in danger.'

It sounded like something that happened in a film, not in real life, and I was completely horrified. Needless to say, I didn't go on any more dates with Danny!

I was so focused on my training, I didn't need a man in my life. Way above everything else, my favourite part of the course was learning about the food service.

In the 1960s the airlines were all trying to outdo each other with the cuisine they served, and Pan Am's was world class. It was from Maxim's of Paris, a famous French restaurant where all the celebrities and stars used to go when they were in Europe.

There was a huge amount to learn, but I devoured every minute of it. Al and a team of supervisors took us through the perfect service in a mock-up of the interior of a 707 which had been set up in one of the classrooms. It was identical to the aircrafts, down to having exactly the same ovens.

Some of the girls hadn't even cooked for themselves before and suddenly we were expected to prepare haute cuisine for hundreds of people. The first-class meal consisted of seven courses and was out of this world. There was a separate first-class kitchen at the front of the plane, and passengers would be offered a choice of six main dishes: lobster thermidor, fillet of sole Albert, roast chicken, a rack of lamb or veal, tenderloin of beef and perhaps sweetbreads.

I had never heard of sweetbreads before, so I had to ask what they were. When I found out they were the glands from the animal's neck, I was absolutely horrified. I could never bring myself to try them, but the passengers loved them. They were so rare in those days and they were always thrilled when they saw them on the menu.

The roasts were completely raw when they were brought on board and we would have to use a thermometer to make sure the meat was at the right temperature and cooked properly. It was quite tricky and a real skill. One side of the oven in first class had been taken out, so you could get a whole two-foot-long fillet of beef in there, and you had to keep turning it so it wouldn't burn.

First-class passengers would start off with Dom Perignon or Bloody Marys, followed by peanuts and crackers, served at their seat or in the cocktail lounge. Most 707s had around twenty first-class passengers and the majority of them would wander through to the lounge, where they would mingle and get to know each other.

As part of our training, we also had to learn how to mix the popular cocktails of the time, like a Manhattan, a Tom Collins, a Gin Fizz and a Martini. There was a bar on board with full-sized bottles, never miniatures, and we would use a silver cocktail shaker and proper Martini glasses. Each drink would be beautifully presented, with a napkin folded into a fancy shape, a cherry or an olive on the side and an orchid floating on the top.

'This will be good practice for you gals when you're married,' Al joked as we got to work with the silver cocktail shaker.

While the passengers were enjoying their cocktails and a chat, we would be taking orders from the menu, while the other stewardesses would lay the tables. There would be a white linen tablecloth on each one, silver salt and pepper pots and a fresh flower in a vase. The heavy silver cutlery would be wrapped up in a linen napkin and placed on the table too. All meals were served on fine china plates and the drinks were in proper glasses, none of the plastic you get today. It really was like dining in a top-class restaurant at 37,000 ft.

The next job was helping the purser to set up the hors d'oeuvres cart. This really was a production, with a huge silver tureen filled with ice and topped with prawns and large tubs of Beluga caviar. To go with it, you would pour each passenger a shot of neat, chilled vodka.

'Pan Am only serves the best,' Al told us, and we were taught to give very generous servings and let passengers have as much as they wanted. 'If they want three portions of caviar, let them have it.' We all had to learn silver service, which as we found out was very tricky to get right.

During the hors d'oeuvres, we would serve lobster salad with pink mayonnaise. This was always one of the stewardesses' favourites and we all secretly hoped it wouldn't be gone by the time it was our turn to sit down and eat at the end of service. The next course would be soup, often served with a glass of sherry, followed by a Caesar salad, which was always tossed individually at each passenger's seat. Then the main courses would be brought out on a silver tray. If they had chosen a roast like the beef, you would wheel the whole thing on a cart down to the passenger's seat and carve it in front of them.

The mains were served with potato croquettes or pilaf rice and some nicely presented vegetables and were washed down with the finest French wines or more Champagne. Afterwards, there would be a cheese course – whole cheeses on a trolley – then a fruit course, then finally dessert, which always reflected the country you were travelling to. On the Hawaiian routes, we would have coconut cream pies, which we were taught to cut like the hands of a clock, and the European flights would have pastries from Paris. Then we would serve coffee and liqueurs and hand out Camel and Marlboro cigarettes. So much work went into the onboard meals that no one could accuse us of being the 'trolley dollies' that flight attendants are often classed as today.

'Working the first-class galley is the most stressful job, but those girls that can get it right will be in really high demand,' Al told us.

Even in economy class, which on Pan Am planes was called coach class, meals were always served on a tray and passengers would also have Champagne.

Preparing the food was always a huge amount of work, but we also had to learn to do it really quickly. We were warned that on some of the shorter flights, you would only have just over an hour to do the whole meal service.

'You must never appear flustered or rushed,' Al said. 'The passenger wants to get what he has paid for and you should encourage people to relax, take their time and enjoy their meal.'

In order to help us practise, Pan Am staff would come into the mock-up cabin and we would serve them lunch. It was always hugely popular and there were often big queues. Sometimes the trainers would get staff to pretend to be a difficult customer and complain that their beef was overdone or they didn't like the vegetable selection. It was really stressful, but we knew we couldn't get flustered.

One day we had to run through a breakfast service. Pan Am only flew internationally, so most of the flights were long haul. Even in coach class, you had to make scrambled eggs from scratch and there were always two eggs allocated for each passenger. Scrambling eggs on a plane is quite a tricky business which involves breaking them into a large silver soup tureen, adding a splash of cream and then putting them in the oven. Every few minutes you had to get them out and stir them thoroughly to avoid overcooking them. But I was so busy, I forgot about them, and when I opened the oven door I could see they were so overdone they had gone green. It was a quirk of the plane ovens that if you left scrambled eggs in there for too long and didn't stir them regularly, they turned an unappetising bright-green colour.

Lee Trujillo, who was pretending to be the purser on our 'flight', really gave me a dressing-down.

'What a waste,' she said. 'We'll have to throw them away because Pan Am can't serve green eggs to customers.'

'I'm sorry,' I said.

It really was tricky, and it made me feel better that we all made mistakes sometimes, whether it was the flying prawn that Nancy had struggled to control when she was practising silver service, or Janet burning a fillet of beef until it was the texture of leather. It took a lot of practice before we got up to scratch to meet Pan Am's high standards.

But there was one perk on the days when we practised the meal service. After the staff had gone, we were allowed to eat any of the leftovers. The food was so special and it was always a real treat. I always tucked into the lobster, but I loved the Beluga caviar the best. Sometimes it was served with chopped egg whites, onion and Melba toast, other times I would just eat it straight from the tin, but I thought it was the most delicious thing I had ever tasted.

I often felt like pinching myself. It didn't seem real. Here I was, gulping down big spoonfuls of caviar like it was mince and potatoes. It seemed such a long way from the days of rationing during the war and the scrimping and saving that had always been the way at home.

Home was still the one thing that was never far from my mind. Everything I did during training, every wonderful new experience I had or skill I learnt, I longed to share it with Mum and Dad. On the harder days, when I really struggled, I just wished that I could see them for a chat and hear them say, 'It will be better tomorrow, Tink.'

On an evening, we would all troop back to the dorm, completely exhausted. There was just enough time to grab a quick snack and revise for whatever we were being tested on the next day before it was time to fall into bed. But no matter how tired I was, I always got out a blue airmail envelope and filled Mum and Dad in on the latest news. I knew they missed me and I loved getting their letters. 'We're so proud of you, Betty,' Mum would write. 'We've been telling everyone what you've been up to. It all sounds wonderful.'

Even though I had lived away from home for a while before

I had left England, they felt so far away, and I missed them terribly. But I knew I had to give my all to the training. The six weeks were going so fast, and I didn't just want to pass, I wanted to be one of the best. Because I was the only girl out of the group who'd had experience working for another airline, I felt I should be coming out top.

There was what I would describe as a healthy rivalry between us girls. I think Hazel, in particular, saw me as her main competition and was always asking what scores I had got in the tests. Soon it would be time for the final exam, which was my final hurdle to becoming a Pan Am stewardess and the amazing life that went with it. I *had* to pass. The other option just didn't bear thinking about, and there was no way on earth I could go home now.

Chapter Six

Taking Flight

I adjusted my pale-blue wool jacket and skirt and smoothed down the crisp white blouse. Running my hands over the fabric, it felt so luxurious and expensive. Then I pulled on my white gloves and the boat-shaped hat with a plume at the front and looked in the mirror. As I checked my reflection for what was probably the hundredth time, I couldn't help but smile. I had never felt so sophisticated and grown-up in all my life.

'You have done it, Betty,' I told myself. 'You've made it.'

As of today, 14 March 1961, I was a fully fledged Pam Am stewardess. At the age of twenty-two, I was part of an elite group of young women chosen to represent the world's largest and most respected airline, and I still could not believe my luck. After six weeks of intensive training, today was our graduation and all twenty of us girls were heading to Idlewild Airport for a presentation.

Ever since I had been accepted by Pan Am, I'd been desperate to put on that iconic blue uniform. Now that moment was finally here and it felt fantastic.

It had all been made to measure and I loved everything about it, from the beautiful lining to the fact that it fitted me like a glove. It had cost $300, a heck of a lot in those days, and the money would be taken out of our wages for the next two years, but I didn't care. I had never owned anything like it and it felt exhilarating finally being able to wear it. I didn't even mind the uncomfortable regulation girdle that went right down over my thighs, as it gave the pencil skirt a smooth line and helped it cling in all the right places.

I had been so excited travelling into Manhattan for the fittings with a Hollywood designer called Don Loper, who had created outfits for stars like Ella Fitzgerald and Judy Garland. His luxurious studio was based in a huge New York brownstone. An assistant had come out to greet us, we were led down a few steps from street level and were suddenly inside a plush design studio in the basement. I had just stared, absolutely stunned, as I took in the antique furniture, the thick carpets and crystal chandeliers.

There were mannequins everywhere, with beautiful, half-finished creations pinned to them and I'd felt a thrill of excitement as I'd wondered which Hollywood star they were for. Was that Marilyn Monroe's evening gown or Jean Harlow's dress? All of the other girls looked as awestruck as I did. Being fitted for the uniform had really brought it home to us that this was really happening. It had all felt a million miles away from my life back in Walthamstow, that's for sure.

But as well as being thrilled to be able to wear my uniform, I was also very relieved that I had passed the Pan Am training course. Dottie Bohanna had constantly warned us that some trainees in previous years had failed and were immediately sent home, but thankfully none of the girls in my intake had. A few days ago we'd had our final exam and afterwards Alan West had told us that all twenty of us had passed with flying colours to become Pan Am's fifth international class of stewardesses.

'Well done, gals,' he said. 'And congratulations to Hazel for being the star pupil.'

Hazel was ecstatic that she had come first. I was pleased for her, although I was secretly a little bit put out that I hadn't got the highest score, but I was just so glad we had all made it. We never found out our individual scores, but during the daily tests I had always come in the top three and I was really hoping that I would get the top mark.

I was desperate to tell Mum and Dad the good news that I'd passed, but telephoning was very expensive in those days, so as usual I wrote them an airmail letter. A week later I got their reply, saying how thrilled they were for me, which was lovely of them, as I knew they hated me being so far away. It meant a lot to me, knowing how proud they were, and I found out many years later how they would bore our poor relatives for hours with stories of all my comings and goings.

I knew they would have loved to have been at my graduation ceremony, where I was presented with a certificate and, most importantly, the fourteen-carat gold wings badge that said 'Stewardess' on it, which I pinned proudly on my jacket.

Afterwards, all of us girls linked arms and posed on the sweeping staircase inside the Pan American building, as each group of trainees did at the end of their course. The airline's official photographer took a picture with his Kodak Box Brownie camera balanced on a tripod. I've still got that black and white shot and, with our matching hairstyles and uniforms, it's hard to tell us apart. But we all looked so glamorous and there was a real sense of excitement and promise in the air. Unlike most young women in the early sixties, we were all about to embark on this amazing career, and we couldn't wait to start work and put everything we had learnt into practice on our first flights.

There was no time for celebrations. A couple of days later we had to leave the dormitory where we had lived during our training. It didn't take me long to pack the two suitcases I'd been permitted to bring with me from the UK and move my things into a rented furnished apartment in Jackson Heights, a bustling neighbourhood of Queens. It was very basic but homely and we had chosen it because it was on the way out to the airport. It was $60 a month each and there were six of us sharing three bedrooms – myself, Paula and Angela, and the three Japanese girls, Jo, Florence and Mimi. There was no need for any big goodbyes with the other girls because everyone had found a place in the same area, so it would be convenient for work.

However, one harrowing event threatened to put an end to my Pan Am career before it had even started. The girls and I were tidying up one afternoon and we put our rubbish outside in the bins as usual and thought nothing of it. However, a few days later, I was horrified to receive a summons to appear in court for a crime described as 'loose garbage'. The letter informed me that an envelope with my name and address on it had blown out of the bin and some mean so-and-so had picked it up and reported me to the authorities for not tying up the bag properly.

It sounds ridiculous now, but this really was a crime at the time, and I was fearful about the implications it would have on my Pan Am career if I was found guilty. I was pretty sure that being a convicted criminal was a definite no-no when it came to being employed by the world's most prestigious airline.

I was so scared, I hardly slept a wink the night before I was due in court. On the day of the case, all five of my roommates came with me, as a show of solidarity, and we trooped arm-in-arm down to the local magistrates court in Jackson Heights. We sat there for hours amongst what I can only describe as a motley bunch of criminals who were up for various unsavoury offences like drunk and disorderly and breach of the peace. I had never seen such a grungy group of misfits in all my life, and we were all terrified. Meanwhile, my mind was churning with worry about what was going to happen to me.

Finally the judge called my name and it was my turn to address the court.

'I'm so very sorry and embarrassed, your honour,' I said in a pitiful voice, my legs trembling. 'I didn't know anything about the rubbish not being secured properly until I got the letter.'

The judge looked at me sternly, banged his gavel and bellowed: 'Three dollars and three days!'

I immediately burst into tears. Three days in jail! All I could think was, how on earth was I going to tell my poor parents? My second thought was: 'I can't go to prison, I've got a flight to catch.'

Then the judge looked at me over his glasses, smiled and said, 'Only joking, Miss Eden. Just three dollars will do.'

The cheeky beggar had been having me on, but I was too relieved not to be going to jail to be angry. Although $3 was quite a lot of money in those days, I would have paid £300 if that was what it took to get out of that horrible court and put an end to my nightmares about being locked up.

With the threat of incarceration lifted, in April 1961, I was assigned my first proper flight – a seven-hour overnighter over the Atlantic from New York to Lisbon, Portugal. It took me at least two hours to get ready, partly because my hands were shaking so much I could hardly do up the buttons on my uniform! I was flying with Sheila Harris, another graduate from my course. Sheila was a very tall girl and she was friendly enough, although she and I were never particularly close. But it was reassuring to be with someone else who was as nervous as I was, and we got the bus to the airport together. Flying was a big deal in those days; it was something exciting and out of the ordinary, and people went to the airport just to watch the planes take off and land. There was nothing like the security there is today and you could just wander freely onto the tarmac and even hop onto the planes to have a look inside.

The bus was packed and when Sheila and I got on in our distinctive blue uniforms, everyone turned to stare at us, which felt very strange. Half an hour later, we pulled up outside the Pan American terminal at Idlewild, which was known as the Worldport. It had only been opened in 1960 and it was very futuristic and modern. It looked like a white flying saucer on legs that had just landed from outer space! Pan Am had one round-the-world flight in each direction every day and also flew to eighty-two countries, so the terminal was always very busy and exciting. There were all sorts of exotic sights, including people who seemed to be carrying their worldly possessions with them, like furniture and opulent jewellery, and men with real gold in their teeth.

As Sheila and I walked into the airport in our high-heeled black court shoes, our heads held high and shoulders back, like we had been taught in our deportment classes, I felt so proud. The crowds literally parted as we walked through and everyone turned to look, as if we were film stars. Men grinned at us and women gave us envious glances or asked where we were flying to.

A little girl came running up to us and said, 'When I grow up I want to be just like you.'

I felt so special, but it was also a bit odd to have all this attention focused on us. I knew that we were very lucky, as it was the dream job for a young woman, but for the first time it also felt like a huge responsibility. A little voice inside me was questioning, could I really do this? When the chips were down, was I really up to the job?

I'm sure the uniform definitely helped. From that very first day, I learned that when one puts on a uniform, it's like you become a different person. It gives you courage and a sense of accomplishment. Even now, all these years later, when I'm in a difficult situation, I imagine I'm wearing my Pan Am uniform and it gives me the confidence to believe I can tackle anything.

Our first port of call was the captain's briefing, to meet the crew we would be working with. There were four in the flight deck – the captain, first officer, second officer and an engineer. Then there were eight stewardesses and myself and Sheila, who were classed as 'supernumerary' stewardesses, which meant we had just come out of training.

'As you know, you're on probation for six months and today there will be a check purser on board who will observe you working during the flight and then write a report up afterwards,' a supervisor told us.

'I feel sick just thinking about it,' whispered Sheila.

I was determined not to mess it up and let my nerves get the better of me. But we had a few more hurdles to get through before we could even get on the plane.

At a pre-flight briefing like this there was always a grooming check, to make sure that our appearance and uniform were in order and that we were wearing our regulation girdles. I knew this was done with a pinch or slap on the bottom, but it was still a shock when the supervisor breezed past and gave our industrial-strength girdle elastic a quick ping. In fact, Sheila visibly jumped and I gave a little cry of surprise as I felt the sting on my thigh.

'Well done, ladies, it looks like everything is in order,' she said.

Thankfully, on this flight, it was a female supervisor, but sometimes it could be a male. We just got used to it and accepted it as part of the job.

You were always expected to remember every single part of your uniform, down to the white silk scarf you tied around your head to keep your hat on if it was windy and the smock you changed into when you were serving food. We had been warned during training that if anything was missing, you were really in trouble and would get a good dressing-down from the supervisor. Even now, if I'm feeling a bit stressed about something, I will often have a nightmare that I've turned up for a flight and have forgotten something.

'Phew, I'm glad that's over,' I sighed, as the briefing came to a close.

'That's nothing,' said another stewardess. 'Just you wait until weigh-in time.'

If there were three words designed to put the fear of God into a stewardess, it was 'weigh-in time'. Every month, at a pre-flight briefing, the supervisor would get the scales out and everyone would step on them to check that we hadn't gone over our maximum weight. My hiring weight was 8 st 6 lb and the most I was allowed to weigh was 8 st 12 lbs.

'Anyone who goes above their maximum weight will be immediately suspended from flying duties and pay until they regain their correct weight,' Lee Trujillo had warned us during training.

Poor Janet had looked like she was going to burst into tears when she'd heard that. Thankfully, throughout my career, I never went above my maximum weight, but that pressure was always there, and it was a real worry. Our livelihood depended on us being a certain weight and no one wanted to experience the shame of being grounded.

'I can't believe I'm surrounded by all these lovely things to eat, yet I can't touch any of them,' Janet always said. 'It's like torture.'

She got into a real flap around weigh-in time and made sure she starved herself for a couple of days beforehand.

When I look back, I can't believe how times have changed. There is no way you could be forced to get on the scales at work now, but in the 1960s we just accepted that looking your best and being 'well proportioned', with a nice figure, was part of the job.

Another part of the job that we dreaded was being pulled in by the supervisor. Thankfully it only happened to me once, a year into my career.

'Betty, please can I have a quick word in my office?' she had asked at the end of a briefing.

I was absolutely horrified. I knew you were only taken into the office if there was a problem, like you'd put on weight and needed a warning before weigh-in, or your eye shadow wasn't the right shade.

'Miss Eden, I'm afraid your hair has got a bit too long and is well over collar length,' the supervisor had told me. 'I'm afraid I'm going to have to write it up in the book and I would appreciate it if you could get to the hair salon as soon as you can.'

'I'm dreadfully sorry,' I'd said.

It might sound silly, but I was genuinely upset at the time, because if something was written up in the book, it would remain on your file permanently.

Thankfully Sheila and I had passed all the necessary grooming checks for our first flight and with the briefing over, it was time to go on board and prepare the 707 for the 150 passengers. Like all of the Pan Am aircraft, which were always referred to as clippers, it had distinctive blue seats and matching blue carpet down the aisle. I had been assigned to work in the first-class cabin, assisting the other stewardesses with serving and clearing food and pouring wine. It was extra nerve-wracking, as I had to do all of this while being observed by the check supervisor, who was sat in the last row of first class and would write a report on me after the flight.

As I waited to greet the passengers, I ran through everything we had been taught in my mind. Don't discuss politics, religion or other airlines and always call passengers by their names. It was easier said than done. There was a seating plan taped to the side of the bar, but there were a lot of names to remember.

And I couldn't forget the golden rule: smile, Betty, smile.

'Welcome to Pan Am,' I grinned as the first few first-class passengers started to board from the Clipper Club in the airport, where they had been relaxing.

It was mainly wealthy businessmen in suits, some of whom had brought their wives along. If you were a housewife in the 1960s, it was often the done thing to accompany your husband on a far-flung business trip. You could see the sights, but mainly it was a way of checking he didn't get up to mischief in a foreign country!

I took the passengers' coats and hung them in the onboard cloakroom. Then, when they had settled in their seats, I handed them their little leather kit bags, which contained all sorts of luxury goodies, like hand and face cream, razors, slipper socks, eye shades and face freshener. There was Chanel perfume for the ladies and aftershave for the gentlemen.

I loved watching everyone get on in their 'best' clothes. Flying

Me during the Second World War, aged three, with my beloved Teddy. Mum took me to a photographer's studio so she could get a picture to send to Dad.

My handsome dad, Sidney, in 1940 just after he was drafted into the Royal Fusiliers.

Being crowned the runner-up in the 1955 Walthamstow Carnival Queen contest. I was a bit disappointed that I hadn't won but I got to meet the famous American comedian, Alan King.

I might not have been the queen but I still felt like royalty at the Walthamstow Carnival as we were driven through the streets on the back of a huge American convertible car.

Soaking up the sun on the beach in Benidorm with the girls in 1957. I was desperate to go abroad and I saved up for years to be able to afford a package holiday.

I was so pleased to get a summer job at Silver City in 1958. I flew across the Channel to France and back up to six times a day in one of these B170 Bristol Freighters which carried 14 passengers and three cars in the nose of the plane.

Once I'd overcome my terrible airsickness, I loved working as a stewardess especially the stylish navy uniform we got to wear.

I was delighted when they kept me on after the summer and I started working on charter flights to Europe.

Winging Her Way Around The World

No one was more stunned than me when I was one of 17 British girls chosen out of the thousand who applied to be a trainee stewardess for Pan American Airlines in New York. I even made the headlines of the local paper, the *Thanet Times*.

The *Daily Mail* came to interview me and some of the other girls during our six-week training course at Idlewild Airport in February 1961.

IN a land of get-up-and-go, American airline executives lost no time in going to Britain to recruit one of the most potent weapons in their sales armoury. . . .

Which is how I happened to meet five British air-hostesses-in-training at Idlewild.

ANGELA VAUGHAN (extreme left), 22, is a former model from Wolverhampton; BETTY EDEN, 21, was a secretary in Waltham-stow; ANNE LOWES, 22, is from Cheshire, and graduated in chemistry; JENIFER MILLWARD, 22, taught in Stratford-on-Avon; LEONIE HOLLINGSWORTH, 23, from Bookham, Surrey, was a receptionist.

The lavish living British girls like so much here means they sometimes have to give up things they took for granted at home. Things like having their hair done. In New York the cheapest shampoo and set costs almost £2—a perm more than £8.

Still, I suppose you can't expect everything. Even here.

You could hardly tell us apart as we posed on the sweeping staircase of the Pan American building after our graduation ceremony. I felt so special in my new uniform that had been made-to-measure by a top designer.

Straight after graduation, my dream finally came true. I transferred to San Francisco and started to fly around the world.

I made lifelong friends with the other stewardesses and anyone who wore the same blue uniform was considered a 'Pan Am sister'.

Waiting to welcome the First Class passengers on board at Los Angeles Airport. You were always expected to know their first name and greet them with a smile.

Flying was always fun but it was hard work too, especially preparing a seven-course gourmet meal in such a confined space.

After the passengers had been fed, it was our turn to grab a quick bite to eat in the first class lounge.

I had so much fun travelling to exotic, remote and far-flung places. Flights were so infrequent in those days we'd often have layovers up to a week long.

On a day out with other Pan Am crew members to Pagsanjan Falls in the Philippines.

I'll never forget taking my parents on the trip of a lifetime to Hawaii. They couldn't believe it when we landed and garlands of flowers were placed around our necks.

Kent and I on our wedding day in San Francisco on 16 March 1968. I was the last of the Pan Am girls from my training course to get married.

in the sixties was a real event; people were excited to be going on a plane and you dressed up and made an effort. When I see people slouching through airports these days, in their tracksuits and trainers, I shudder. Flying was an occasion and ladies wore shift dresses or suits, with hats and gloves, high heels and even fur coats. Gents would wear sports coats or smart business suits and ties.

These were the halcyon days, when there were no problems about travelling with liquids or aerosols. In fact, passengers would bring their own cigarette lighters and penknives on board. Airport security was at a minimum and there was no such thing as scanning machines. People and their luggage were sometimes subjected to a search, but it was mainly to prevent food items from being brought into the country.

My stomach was in knots as we took off, which I put down to first-day nerves. But as we reached altitude, I felt a familiar griping feeling in my belly.

'Not now. Come on, Betty,' I told myself, trying to ignore it.

But when the griping turned to churning and I tasted a horrid salty liquid in my throat, I knew I couldn't stop what was about to happen next. I was going to be sick!

Even though I'd been flying for a year over the Channel to France from the UK, up to six times a day, I occasionally suffered from air sickness. I was hoping the larger planes and the higher altitude of the Pam Am flights would mean it didn't happen with my new job, so I hadn't mentioned it during training, or told any of the other girls. But now I knew there was no avoiding it.

I ran to the loo and shut the door, just in time to be violently sick. I was so mortified, I didn't tell any of my new colleagues what had happened. I just smartened myself up and went back to work, determined to get on with my assigned duties. At least my sanctuary had been the first-class toilets, where there were individually wrapped scented soaps and soft, fluffy towels to freshen myself up with.

I took off my court shoes and changed into the smock and flat ballet shoes we were permitted to wear during the meal service. My first job was to help the other stewardesses serve cocktails at the lounge bar in first class. There was a J-shaped padded-leather seat where passengers could enjoy a drink, and in the middle was a cocktail bar. The air was thick with cigarette smoke as I took the orders for Martinis, Manhattans and Old Fashioneds. But as I opened a bottle of brandy and the pungent alcoholic fumes hit my nose, I felt my stomach heave. I grabbed a linen napkin, pressed it to my mouth and dashed to the near-est toilet, where I was sick again.

'Please, God, make this stop,' I moaned, with my head halfway down the bowl.

Ten minutes later, I was still feeling a bit fragile, but had man-aged to compose myself. So I headed back to the galley, just in time to help serve the hors d'oeuvres. There was an older male purser in charge of the cabin that day and he liked to do things with a bit of flair and flourish. Just as he was about to start serv-ice, he dropped some dry ice into the silver trolley. All the passengers gasped and broke into a round of applause as he wheeled it into first class, the dry ice erupting out of the top of the trolley like a spectacular volcano.

Unfortunately, I was still feeling a bit green around the gills, so I was horrified when I was handed a huge silver tureen piled high with the finest seafood, including lobster and giant prawns, topped off with a mountain of caviar. Not what you want to see when you are feeling a bit queasy, but I was determined that this wasn't going to beat me. I tried my best to focus on the job, but as I scooped up a large pile of the black, slippery fish eggs and deposited them on a passenger's china plate, I felt an acidic fizz bubbling in my throat.

'I'm so sorry, Mr Smythe,' I said, gagging. 'I'm just going to have to check something in the galley.'

'At least I remembered his name,' I told myself, as I bolted down the aisle and practically threw myself through the toilet door, where I collapsed in a heap on the floor.

I was so embarrassed. Here I was, on my first flight, desperately trying to prove myself, and I'd spent most of it with my head down the toilet.

After six hours of going backwards and forwards to the bathroom, I was in a real state, exactly like I used to be in the early days at Silver City. So much for being a glamorous, sophisticated Pan Am girl! But I felt even sicker when the check purser beckoned me over to him, saying he wanted a word. Oh, imagine the shame if I was sacked on my first flight!

'It's not unusual to be air sick at first, dear,' he said kindly. 'I'm sure it will pass.'

Then he showed me the report he had written. 'Miss Eden strikes me as someone who works very hard and will become a very valuable employee. However, on this particular flight, she seemed to spend most of her time in the powder room.'

I was mortified and completely shattered, but there was no time to rest. My next job was to take dinner to the crew in the cockpit. The pilot and the first officer were never allowed to eat the same food, in case they both got ill, but I wasn't sure what was in the covered bowls. I politely knocked on the cockpit door and introduced myself.

'Hello, captain,' I said, putting down the bowls. 'I'm Betty Eden and it's my first flight today.'

'Well, hi there, Betty, and welcome to Pan Am,' the pilot replied, giving me a friendly smile.

Around fifteen minutes later, I heard the cockpit bell ringing, which meant a stewardess was needed, so I rushed back in to find the captain and the first and second officers sat there with grim faces.

'I'm so sorry, Betty,' the captain said gravely, 'but I'm afraid the food you brought us didn't agree with the first officer. In fact, the poor man has been quite ill.'

He handed me a paper cup which, to my horror, was filled with a watery yellow liquid with lumps of what looked like carrots and peas in it. I apologised profusely and rushed back to the galley with the cup of vomit.

I was horrified. Not only had *I* been sick, now I had successfully managed to poison the cockpit as well. I went and told one of the other stewardesses what had happened and handed her the offending cup. She took one look at its contents and burst out laughing.

'No one's been sick, dear,' she smiled. 'That's just the vegetable soup we served them for dinner. I think you have been the victim of a first-flight prank.'

I felt very silly as she explained that if the cockpit heard it was a stewardess's first flight, they would often play a prank on them. It was almost like an initiation.

I'm sure the crew in the cockpit were splitting their sides, but it was all too much for me. By the time we landed in Lisbon in the early hours of the morning, I was completely exhausted and extremely happy to be back on the safety of the ground. Thankfully I had managed to nip to the bathroom to re-do my rouge and lipstick and tease my hair, so I didn't look too wrung out as I said goodbye to the passengers.

There was a limousine waiting for the crew and we were whisked off to the Hotel Aviz, an elegant place on Praca do Rossio, where I was sharing a room with Sheila. We were both so tired, we didn't have any energy to chat, and I felt much better after a couple of hours' sleep. Later that day, we met up with the other girls to go shoe-shopping and explore the local cork factory.

'This is the life,' I told myself.

It was so exciting to have three days in a city I'd never been to before and it softened the blow of my first disastrous flight somewhat. I had been desperate to make an impression, and I had certainly done that, but for all the wrong reasons!

I was still embarrassed I'd been so sick, but I was determined I would conquer it. After all, I had to. I was a Pan Am stewardess now. This was the job of my dreams and there was no way I was giving it up.

Chapter Seven

Going West

As soon as the cabin door opened and I saw the little green Morris Minor parked on the tarmac outside, my heart leapt. It could only mean one thing: I was home at last.

It was an incredible feeling, walking down the steps of the 707 in my Pan Am uniform to see Mum and Dad waiting there, and I will never forget the look of pride on their faces when they saw me.

'I told you I'd be back,' I said, throwing my arms around Mum and giving her a big hug.

'You look lovely, dear,' she said.

I could tell Dad was pleased as punch to see me too, by the big smile on his face as he helped me with my bags.

It was April 1961 and, despite my poor parents thinking they would never see me again, the second flight I was assigned was to London. So it meant I would be able to sneak in a night at home with Mum and Dad before I flew on to Paris.

As I've said, there was hardly any airport security in those days, so they were able to drive right up to the tarmac outside Pan Am Operations at London Airport to meet me.

I was so excited to see them and to be able to tell them in person all that had been going on. I talked non-stop in the back of the car, hardly pausing for breath, as we drove around the North Circular. Mum wanted to know everything, so I told her all about the training course, the girls and my first flight to Portugal.

'It sounds wonderful,' she said.

'I'm so eager for you and Dad to come over and see it all,' I told her.

One of the many perks of working for Pam Am was that we were given a month's holiday every year and we only had to pay the tax on any flights we took during that time. We also got an additional two free tickets a year, which meant I could treat my parents or Geoffrey to flights over to America, or take them somewhere nice on holiday.

I had only been gone for ten weeks, but everything at home had changed. Mum and Dad had given up their council house in Walthamstow and were now living with Dad's mother a couple of miles away in Epping Forest. Nana Eden was in her eighties and had been getting increasingly frail, so they had moved in to help take care of her. It was a big decision for them, as they had lived in a council-owned property for many years, since before the war, and they had been one of the first couples in the area to be offered one after they'd got married. But once they had left the system, they were unlikely to qualify for one again, as the rules had all changed.

It was strange going back to Nana's three-bedroom semi instead of our old house, especially as it meant I didn't have a bedroom any more. It didn't feel like my home and for the first time it really hit me that I had left for good.

With Dad out at work all day, it was Mum I felt for the most. It was a much bigger house than our old one, but it must have been so hard for her, having to live with her mother-in-law, especially as Nana Eden was a feisty old bird.

Nana still wanted to be in charge of everything and at midday every day she insisted on taking over the kitchen and making a full hot meal for her youngest son, Bert, who owned a tool business down the road. Mum would take herself off shopping and walk for miles and miles, just to get out of the house and keep out of Nana's way.

Although she complained about everything, Nana liked being the centre of attention. I think she secretly enjoyed being fussed over and, as soon as I arrived, she had a face like thunder. While Mum, Dad and I chatted, she just sat in her chair, mumbling under her breath to herself.

'Oh don't mind her,' said Dad. 'She's just having a hissy fit because she's not the queen bee for once.'

Geoffrey was fifteen now and was busy revising for his O-levels up in his bedroom. Like most teenagers, he was a man of few words.

'Oh, hello, Betty,' he said when he saw me, quickly burying his head back in his book.

'You would think I'd just walked in from the shops,' I joked to Mum.

But we had so much to catch up on. I couldn't believe it when my parents got out some newspaper cuttings that had been written about me. I felt like a celebrity as I read the story in the *Thanet Times*, with the headline: 'Air-minded girl's dream comes true'. There was even an article in the *Daily Mail* about the British stewardesses who had been selected by Pan Am, and I was one of the five girls in the black and white photo.

I was so pleased to see my parents, but after one of Mum's

delicious steak and kidney pies and a restless night's sleep on a camp bed, it was soon time to leave again. After I had packed up my things, I walked into the living room to find Mum looking wistfully out of the window.

'Sometimes I stand here watching all the other mums and daughters walking past arm in arm, going off to do their shopping, and I'm sad that's not you and me,' she sighed. 'I'm so proud of what you're doing, Betty, but I really miss you.'

'I know, Mum,' I said, squeezing her hand.

In those days, young women generally didn't leave home until they got married. It wasn't Mum's intention, but I felt guilty that I wasn't there, helping her out with the housework and the shopping, like all the other girls my age did with their mothers. It was so hard being apart, as Mum and I were so close. I knew it was much harder for her, as while I was off doing all these new and exciting things, she was living the same life, just without me in it.

But there was no time to dwell on it. Dad put my bags in the car and took me to a hotel in central London, where I was going to spend the last night with the rest of the crew, so I could leave for my flight early the next morning.

I could tell Dad was sad to see me go, but as usual he kept his emotions hidden.

'See you soon, Tink,' he said, giving me a kiss goodbye.

I felt a lump in my throat as I watched him drive off. Would leaving always be this hard?

But I knew I had to get back to New York, as there were important decisions to be made. Now we were qualified, everyone on our course had to choose a permanent base, depending on which routes we wanted to specialise in. There was a lot of debate amongst us girls about who wanted to go where. Some people knew immediately where they wanted to be, like Paula, who got her transfer to Seattle so she could be near her boyfriend. I believe they eventually got married, although sadly she didn't keep in touch. Others were adamant they wanted to stay in New York, but I wasn't sure. All through the course, our head trainer, Alan West, had been telling us how great California was.

'You gals don't want to stay in the east; you want to come out west to the sunshine,' he had said.

I had never been to San Francisco before, but Al had told us about the wonderful scenery, the amazing weather and how you could be in three different environments in the same day, from the ocean, to the desert, to the mountains.

Although I loved New York, San Francisco had a large Pan Am base and out of there you could fly to places I had only dreamt of visiting, like Australia, the South Pacific, Hawaii, India, Thailand and Japan.

In the end, ten of us decided to transfer to San Francisco – me, Hazel, Sandra, Angie, Angela, Nancy, Janet, Mimi, Florence and Jo. I still wasn't 100 per cent sure, especially as I was worried about what Mum and Dad would think, as being on the west coast would mean that I was even further away from the UK. So I wrote them a letter explaining my dilemma and Dad sent a telegram back: 'Since you prefer the west, you should go for it. All thrilled for you.'

You paid by the word in those days, which is why it was so short and sweet, but at least it made me feel like I was making the right decision. The funny thing was, because Pan Am didn't fly domestically within the United States, to get to our new base in San Francisco, we would have to fly from New York to London, then out again to California. So, once again, it meant I got a couple of days at home, and this time I took the three Japanese girls with me to meet Mum and Dad.

In all honesty, I was a little bit worried about bringing Mimi, Florence and Jo back, as Mum and Dad had never met a Japanese person before and the only experience they'd had of the country was the brutal reputation of the Japanese military during the war. It had been fifteen years since the war had ended, but there was still a strong anti-Japanese feeling in the UK. Even in the early sixties, the Japanese were considered a barbaric, cruel race, and Dad's generation still talked about the 'atrocities of the Japs'.

But I didn't say anything to the girls, and I need not have worried. They were such kind, sweet, gentle people, and Mum and Dad took an instant liking to them and were so pleased to meet some of my new friends. Even Nana Eden managed to be polite and not make any disparaging comments as we all tucked into Mum's roast beef, Yorkshire pudding and trifle.

The girls had never been to London before and they loved it. We wandered down Carnaby Street, which was *the* place to hang out in the sixties, a great place for people-watching. There were lots of fashionable independent boutiques selling clothes designed by people like Celia Birtwell, Ozzie Clark and Mary Quant. One of the most famous items to emerge from this area was the miniskirt, which was invented by Mary Quant in the sixties and named after her favourite car – the Mini.

The so-called Swinging Sixties started in Carnaby Street and the Kings Road, where bands like Small Faces, the Who and the Rolling Stones played and Mods hung out. The Mods drove Vespa or Lambretta scooters and wore Parkas, tailor-made Italian suits with button-down-collar shirts and winklepicker shoes or Chelsea boots. Female Mods had short hair and wore men's trousers and shirts and pale-pink or white lipstick. I used to see the odd Mod around Walthamstow Market, but it wasn't a style for me and I think my parents would have been horrified if I had started to dress like that, as Mods were seen as quite rebellious.

The girls loved window shopping on Carnaby Street and they also got their hair cut by a fashionable new hairdresser called Vidal Sassoon, who had a salon on Bond Street. They had poker-straight hair, so the asymmetric, choppy styles he gave them looked fantastic.

A few days later the four of us left London and flew into San Francisco for the first time. Al had told us about certain areas that were convenient for the airport and were popular with flight crew, so Mimi, Jo, Florence and I got a Greyhound bus down to a sleepy little town called San Mateo, twelve miles south of the city.

'What a pretty little place,' said Mimi.

It was boiling hot as we walked up the main road of the town, which was called El Camino Real. It was lined with eucalyptus trees and beautiful Spanish-style houses that were painted white with red tiled roofs. They all had large, lush gardens filled with orange and grapefruit trees and exotic, brightly coloured flowers, like oleander and birds of paradise, whose beautiful scent you could smell as you walked past.

'Everywhere is so clean and pristine,' I said.

It was completely different from the grey and grimy streets of Walthamstow, where one had to constantly loop around the pavement to avoid piles of dog mess and no one thought twice about winding down their car window and tossing an empty cigarette packet into the road.

After a few hours of trudging around in the heat with our suitcases looking for 'to let' signs, we were exhausted and rapidly giving up hope. But in a last-ditch attempt to find a roof over our heads, I stopped a respectable-looking elderly lady in the street to ask if she knew anyone who might have a room available to rent.

'We would be so grateful,' I said. 'We're really desperate.'

'Well, I have a friend, Mrs Allen, who has space in her loft,' she told us. 'You might want to talk to her.'

She led us to a detached, Spanish-style house and rang the bell. A very elegant older lady answered. She was tall, with dyed blonde hair, and was wearing smart trousers and a blouse. The woman explained our predicament to her friend.

'Well, you girls had better come in,' she said, looking us up and down. 'I'm Mrs Belle Allen and my husband is Mr Chauncey D. Allen, but he's not home at the moment.'

The house was full of old-fashioned chintzy furniture, there were huge dried flower displays everywhere and all of the settees, which were covered in a flowery material, had plastic covers on them to keep them pristine. She showed us around the loft, which was one large room with two double beds in it and a little kitchenette with an electric hob. It would be a bit of a squash, but I was sure the four of us would hardly ever be home at the same time and, as the saying goes, beggars can't be choosers.

'It's perfect,' I said.

'Well, I don't know,' Mrs Allen sighed, pursing her lips. 'I've never had lodgers before and I'm not sure I can have four of you up here.'

'Please,' I begged. 'We'll be away on trips most of the time, so you will hardly ever see us and we're very tidy.'

I think she felt sorry for us, as she eventually agreed to take us in.

'You can call me Auntie Belle,' she said. 'And you can address Mr Allen as Uncle C. D., after his initials.'

We had thought Dottie Bohanna was strict at the time, but

Auntie Belle was in a whole different league. We had only been there for five minutes before she was laying down the law.

'You must keep the place spotless, turn the wireless down after 9 p.m. and definitely no gentlemen callers,' she said.

'Dottie Bohanna, eat your heart out,' I whispered to Mimi. 'It's like having another house mother,'

We soon realised that Auntie Belle was one of a kind. Even though she was in her eighties, she was very fit and every day, without fail, she went for a swim in San Francisco Bay. Everyone in town knew her and she was always interfering in other people's business and telling them what to do. That applied to us girls too. She would have strong opinions about what we should and shouldn't do and which boys were suitable for us.

Mimi had been asked out on a date by a local man one evening. But when he arrived at the front door to collect her, Auntie Belle looked him up and down and then took Mimi to one side.

'He's not for you, dear,' she told her. 'I don't think he's husband material.'

'I know he's not,' said Mimi. 'We're just going for dinner.'

But Auntie Belle had a heart of gold and would do anything for anybody. One night I came home to find a couple of sailors sat around the dining table.

'The poor things looked like they needed a good feed, so I brought them home for tea,' she told me.

'And before you get any ideas, I don't think they're suitable companions for you girls,' she added.

As always, poor old Uncle C. D. sat quietly in the corner, minding his own business, not daring to ask why two strangers were now tucking into his dinner.

'Get these young men a drink, Chauncey,' she told him.

'Yes, dear,' he said wearily.

Auntie Belle definitely wore the trousers in the house. Uncle C. D. was a kind, gentle man, who, at the age of eighty, still ran his own engineering company and went into work every day. Auntie Belle bossed him around, but I think he secretly enjoyed it and he relied on her completely.

Auntie Belle was always complaining about us, but I think she was actually very proud of the fact that she had four Pan Am stewardesses living with her, and she told everyone about us. She was always popping up to the loft under the pretence of needing to discuss something important, and we could never get rid of her. Like Dottie Bohanna, we realised that she came up and checked how tidy the place was whenever we were gone.

She seemed to take a special liking to me and she would insist on taking me shopping to Gump's Department Store – always telling me what to buy of course. Every week, if I wasn't away on a trip, she would put on a hat and cocktail gloves and take me to Blum's, which was a nice restaurant full of elegant ladies that lunched. I knew how keen she was on good manners, so the first time we went, I ordered a hamburger and, trying to be ladylike and polite, I started to eat it with a knife and fork. But when Auntie Belle saw me, she almost choked on her salad.

'You do not eat a hamburger with cutlery. For goodness' sake, just pick it up and bite it!' she hissed.

We had been living there for a few months when, one night, Auntie Belle invited me into the living room and sat me down.

'Uncle C. D. and I have been thinking,' she said. 'Since your parents are so far away back in England and we don't have any offspring of our own, we would be very interested in adopting you.'

I was so surprised, I didn't know what to say. At first I thought she was joking. Did 22-year-old women really get adopted? But I could tell by the look on her face that she was deadly serious.

'Would you mind mentioning it to your parents, dear, and ask them if that would be all right?' she said.

'Er ... well, I'll mention it to them, but I very much doubt that they would go for it,' I stuttered.

I was completely taken aback. Perhaps I should have been flattered that she viewed me as the daughter she and Uncle C. D. had never had, but I didn't want to upset my parents, who I suspected would be horrified by the idea.

When I next wrote to Mum and Dad, I casually mentioned in passing what Auntie Belle had said and, before I knew it, they had written directly to her. Auntie Belle told me she'd had a letter from Dad, thanking her for her kind offer, but saying that on this occasion they would decline! Understandably, I could tell they were a bit put out that someone wanted to adopt their only daughter.

But for all her interfering, I secretly liked having someone like Auntie Belle in my life. I missed Mum and Dad so much and it was nice to have a surrogate family in America. Thanks to Auntie Belle, I also had a surrogate sister. Shirley Mstowska was a 15-year-old girl who lived a few doors down the road. Her mother, Vlada, was a widow and worked long hours, so Auntie Belle took Shirley under her wing and looked after her every day after school. She really enjoyed teaching her all the niceties she felt a young girl needed to know, like good manners and – most importantly, according to Belle – how to treat older people with the utmost respect!

Shirley was a very sweet girl and she was so impressed by the fact that I was a Pan Am stewardess. She was fascinated by my job and looked at me with these big eyes when I told her all about my trips, hanging on to my every word.

'I wish I could be like you,' she would tell me.

She was a very clever young lady, and she ended up being a school teacher and then training as a lawyer. We still keep in touch all these years later.

So, I had my American family and a place to live, and I really started to settle into life in California. Everyone in San Mateo was friendly and when you would pass people in the street they would smile and nod at you.

When I first got there, I'd smile back and politely say, 'It's lovely weather, isn't it?'

But Auntie Belle soon set me straight.

'People will look at you strangely if you say that,' she said. 'It's always sunny here.'

I also had a ready-made social life. Angie, Janet, Hazel and Sandra had all rented an apartment in a block about ten minutes' walk from us. They had a swimming pool, so we would often go round for a dip and a barbecue. Needless to say, a group of young Pan Am stewardesses soon attracted the boys, and whenever we were by the pool, we were never short of male attention.

We would all sit around chatting and the boys would play 'Kumbaya' on their guitars. It probably sounds strange now, but as well as rock and roll becoming fashionable in the early 1960s, there was also a revival of folk music, with bands like Peter, Paul and Mary becoming popular.

There was a bunch of handsome but impoverished law students living in the apartment below the girls. They never had any money and the girls took pity on them and would often make them dinner or take them out.

One afternoon we were having a barbecue and one of them came to join us.

'Here comes F-F-Fred,' whispered Hazel.

'Why do you call him that?' I asked.

'You'll see,' smirked Janet.

Fred was very ordinary-looking, not the kind of man you would notice at a party.

'H-h-hello, ladies, I wondered if I could come and j-j-join you,' he stuttered.

'Oh, Hazel,' I whispered. 'You are wicked.'

Poor Fred may have had a terrible stutter and been Mr Average, but he was funny and kind, and he and Hazel ended up dating.

Everyone knew each other in the apartments, and they were a hotbed of gossip.

We were lying around the pool one morning when I saw a man in a suit let himself out of one of the apartments and scurry off down the stairs.

'Who's he?' I said. 'Has he just moved in?'

Sandra and Janet gave each other a knowing look.

'I think he's one of Miss D'Angelo's overnight guests,' said Sandra.

'Honestly, that woman will spend the night with any man who has two legs and a pulse,' said Janet.

Beverley D'Angelo was one of the stewardesses who lived in the building. I always thought she looked a bit common to work for Pan Am, with her stringy blonde hair and thin lips. She always wore the wrong colour lipstick to work and I was surprised that no one had ever pulled her up on it.

Beverley had a bit of a reputation and was always the talk of the apartments for bringing men back to stay the night. In 1961 sex was not something my friends and I ever discussed and no young woman wanted to be seen as having loose morals. Even if people were in a serious relationship and were intimate, they certainly didn't talk about it in those days.

'Mark my words, she'll have trouble finding a husband,' said Janet.

It was a real case of double standards between men and women then. If a woman was considered 'easy', it would be known but not talked about and her reputation would definitely affect her attractiveness in the eyes of men – other than for one-night-stands of course. Young men, however, were actively encouraged to sow their wild oats before settling down, and that didn't affect their desirability as potential husbands.

As a Pan Am stewardess, I was starting to realise that male attention was something that came with the job. There were some men who seemed to take great pride in the fact that they would only go out with air hostesses.

The girls had found their apartment through an estate agent in San Mateo called Bing. He obviously couldn't believe his luck that a group of Pan Am girls were living in the area and he tried to date all of us, one by one. He started off with Angie first, because she was the prettiest, and then he went down the line. Some of the girls went out to lunch with him initially, but when we realised what he was doing, the rest of us turned him down. He would often drop by the apartments under the pretence of needing some information, and I happened to be there one afternoon with Sandra when he called round. As soon as Sandra went to the toilet and was out of earshot, he swooped in like a vulture.

'You're a beautiful young lady, Betty,' he said. 'In fact I've always thought you were the prettiest out of all you Pan American girls. Could I take you for dinner one evening?'

I couldn't believe his brazen cheek and I decided to teach him a lesson.

'Sandra,' I shouted, 'didn't you say Bing had asked you out to lunch last week?'

'I think you know my friend Angie too,' I told him.

Bing's face was as red as a berry and, realising he'd been rumbled, he made his excuses and left.

'What a creep,' said Sandra, when I told her what had happened. 'Janet said he'd asked her out too.'

'He's not even in the least bit appealing,' I said.

He was tall and blond, but I didn't find him attractive in the slightest, and it was obvious he just wanted the prestige of having a Pan Am stewardess on his arm.

But as well as meeting new men, an old face from my past suddenly popped up.

I received a letter from Danny, the man who worked as Pan Am ground crew at Idlewild, whom I had dated briefly during training. 'Hello, Betty, I hear you're in San Fran these days. You're a great girl and I'd love for us to hook up again. Perhaps I could come and visit you?'

I wasn't really keen on the idea, particularly because of my suspicions that he was involved in the Mafia, but I was a bit of a coward when it came to saying no to people and there was no way I wanted to get on the wrong side of him or his family!

'Lovely to hear from you,' I wrote back. 'If you want to come and stay, I'll book you into the local motel for the night.'

But when I mentioned Danny's visit to Auntie Belle, she wasn't at all happy about the idea.

'I have spoken to Uncle C. D. and we have agreed that this young man is only allowed to come up to the loft in the daytime,' she said. 'What would your parents say if they knew I was allowing you to bring gentlemen up to your living quarters?'

'He's just an old friend,' I said. 'There will be no funny business.'

I tried to reassure her that Danny had no ulterior motive, but unfortunately that wasn't the case. As soon as he arrived, Danny made it perfectly clear that he wasn't happy about the sleeping arrangements.

'I can't believe you've booked me into a motel when I could just stay here with you,' he said. 'Go on, Betty, please let me stay.'

'There's no way on this earth that's going to happen,' I told him.

But he was so annoyed. I obviously hadn't lived up to his expectations, and he left that evening in a huff and I never heard from him again.

'What a jerk,' said Sandra, when I told her what had happened.

A few years later, I was working on a flight to Japan, and when I pulled open the aircraft door at Haneda Airport, who should be standing on the other side, two feet away from me, but Danny. We were both as embarrassed as each other and I mumbled, 'Fancy seeing you here.' Thankfully we never bumped into each other again.

Although my personal life left a lot to be desired, things were improving at work. After the disaster that was my first flight, I was still desperately trying to prove that I was up to the job. Another of my earliest flights was a trip across the Pacific to Japan. During the pre-flight briefing, the chief purser and the captain would assign everyone roles.

'Any volunteers for the first-class galley?' the chief purser asked.

'I'll do it,' said Mimi.

While most of the stewardesses avoided volunteering for the first-class galley, Mimi, Florence and Jo seemed to love it. It was hugely stressful cooking all those meals to order and presenting seven courses to such high standards, but the Japanese girls seemed to thrive on the pressure and quickly developed a

system to make sure everything was perfectly cooked and beautifully served. I always assumed it was because they were a little
bit shyer than the rest of us girls and they preferred that to dealing with the passengers in the cabin.

'Miss Eden, I'd like you to work the coach-class galley,' the
purser told me.

As a new stewardess, I knew this was a baptism of fire. For
a start, the coach- or economy-class galley was right next to
the toilets in the tail of the plane, which meant it would swing
around and was a lot bumpier than the rest of the aircraft. It
wasn't great for my air sickness, but there was one window in
there, so I could focus on the horizon , which I'd learnt helped
if I was feeling a bit queasy.

It was cramped in there too. It was only a 6ft by 6ft area, with
chilled cabinets on one side and ovens on the other, so it got
quite hot and claustrophobic during the meal service. It was
such a confined space that there could only be one stewardess
working in there, so it was going to be my sole responsibility to
prepare meals for 160 passengers.

'Right. Focus, Betty, focus,' I told myself, as the crew all
boarded the plane. I remembered the 'six Ps' Al West had taught
us during our training – Prior Planning Prevents Piss Poor
Performance! It wasn't a very sophisticated acronym, consider-
ing the high calibre of Pan Am, but it certainly stuck in our
minds, and it was something I always remembered throughout
my career.

I took a crumpled piece of paper out of my bag, which was a
list of all the duties I had been assigned to do and the order in
which to do them. There was also an official guide we could
refer to on board, which showed pictures of how everything
should look, from where exactly the wine glasses should sit on
the passenger's tray, to the fact that the meat or fish should

always be placed at the five o'clock position on the plate, which was a technique Pan Am had copied from some of the world's finest restaurants.

While the other girls working in the cabin were welcoming passengers and showing them to their seats, I took off my blouse, jacket and heels and changed into my short-sleeved smock and flat pumps, ready to begin the hard work. I turned on the ovens and put in the huge foil pans of chicken Veronique with grapes and white wine which was going to be the main course, as well as the bread rolls to warm up. Then, immediately after take-off, I pulled down the large shelf which spanned the whole width of the galley and started to pile up the plates, a dozen at a time.

As I worked, I was amazed at how I instinctively knew exactly what to do next, without having to refer to my list. Weeks of training and all those practice meal services had really drummed into us what needed to be done. On each tray, I methodically placed a shrimp salad, a strawberry tart and a selection of cheese and biscuits.

'Are you OK in there, Betty?' checked the purser.

Beads of sweat were dripping down my forehead by now as I worked at breakneck speed.

'Yes, ma'am,' I said. 'It won't be long now.'

There wasn't a second to think, or even feel sick, as I placed four meals on each tray and handed them to a stewardess to serve. When I got the nod from the cabin that everyone had finished their starter, it was time to serve the main course. I dished out portion after portion of chicken (making sure it was in the correct position of course), along with some potato croquettes and broccoli.

Two exhausting hours later, my hair and clothes smelt of food and I was knee-deep in rubbish and surrounded by piles of dirty trays, but the meal service was almost over. It had been hectic and tiring, but the main thing was that I had done it. And I think I'd done it well.

'Very well done, Betty,' said the purser. 'You did a great job in there.'

We lowered the lights so the passengers could sleep, but the hard work wasn't over for us. There always had to be one stewardess in the cabin on duty, so we took it in turns to walk up and down the aisle, checking everyone was OK and bringing people drinks.

Before I knew it, it was time to get back into the galley and start preparing breakfast. Each passenger was served a warm breakfast of sausages and scrambled eggs. Two eggs were allocated for each person in economy class, so that meant scrambling 320 eggs.

'I don't think I want to see another egg as long as I live,' I sighed as I cracked shell after shell into a huge silver tureen. It was quite a bumpy flight too, so every time the plane jolted, I ended up with gloopy egg yolk all over my clothes, and by the time I'd finished, it was splattered all over the galley too. I stirred and stirred them until my arms ached and then tipped the whisked eggs into huge foil pans and put them into the oven along with the sausages, which were warming up.

'Don't forget about them, Betty,' I told myself.

There was no way I wanted to repeat the green eggs incident from training. But it's true that you learn from your mistakes, and every five minutes, I opened the oven and gave them a good stir. With an hour to go before we landed in Tokyo, breakfast was served bang on schedule and not a green egg in sight.

By the time we landed in Japan, I'd been on my feet for thirteen hours and was completely exhausted. But for the first time since joining Pan Am, I felt like a real stewardess.

'I think I've proved to myself that I can really do it,' I told Mimi.

'Of course you can,' she said. 'And you're a natural with the passengers.'

It was hard work, but I was enjoying it.

It was just a short trip and we had to fly back to the States the next day.

Thankfully for me, on the return leg of a journey, you were always assigned a different position from the one that you had worked on during the outward-bound flight. This time, I was delighted to get the first-class cabin.

'Remember, preparation is the key,' the chief purser told me.

So as soon as I got on board, I started folding the white linen napkins into pretty fan shapes and doing fiddly little jobs like putting olives and cherries into glasses for the Manhattans and Martinis, so I wouldn't have to waste valuable time doing it later. Soon it was time to greet the passengers and take their coats and hats.

'Remember to use their names as early as you can,' another stewardess advised me.

Trying to be organised, I took their drinks orders before take-off, although because of customs rules and regulations, we weren't allowed to serve them until we were airborne. There was only ever a maximum of twenty-four people in first class, but it was still tricky carrying twenty-four champagne flutes on a tray while walking down the aisle of an airplane.

'Go carefully,' the purser advised me. 'It can take a while to get the hang of it.'

But, to my amazement, I quickly learnt the knack of balancing the silver tray in my left hand while holding onto the seats for support with my right and still managing to look graceful and elegant at the same time.

Then I went round the cabin to take the passengers' orders.

'Try the beef, Mr Reynolds,' I told one man. 'It's always delicious and it's cooked exactly the way you like it.'

I tried to be efficient but not hurried, polite and friendly but not overbearing. I took great pride in my job, whether it was mixing the perfect Manhattan or laying all the tables beautifully. It might sound silly, but I got so much satisfaction from seeing how lovely the tray tables looked, with the crisp white linen tablecloths draped over them, the pretty orchids in vases and the heavy silver cutlery wrapped in linen napkins.

I remembered that when serving wine, the foil on the bottle should always be neatly trimmed and not torn, and that the lids of any condiments given to the passengers should already be loose, so they didn't have to struggle with them.

These were all little things, but were considered hugely important by Pan Am, who wanted to provide the ultimate five-star service on board its jets.

I quickly realised that working in the first-class cabin was my favoured position. I was always upbeat and smiley and, most of all, when the meal service was over, I loved chatting to the passengers.

We had been taught not to ask people personal questions unless they volunteered the information, so I would play chess or cards with them, or they would ask about the country we were travelling to.

'What can you tell me about Berlin, dear?' asked one of the passengers who was due to catch a connecting flight to Europe when we landed.

I wasn't going to tell him that I'd never been there either.

'I'll get you the Pan Am world guide that we have on board, Mr Briggs,' I told him. 'Then you will be able to read all about it yourself.'

If I had thought scrambling 320 eggs in coach class had been a challenge, then the first-class breakfast was equally demanding in a different way. There were a lot fewer people to cater for in first, but they could order their eggs exactly how they wanted them, poached, scrambled or fried. Poached and boiled were fairly straightforward, as we would just put them in boiling water, but trying to fry an egg in an oven was always tricky. Thankfully, because I was working in the cabin on this journey and not the galley, I didn't have to worry about it.

The other good news was that although I still felt air sick, I started to learn ways to control it, so I didn't spend the flight throwing up. Whenever I felt queasy, I would try to look out of the window and focus on the horizon , or chew on a dry bread roll. I also knew not to eat anything acidic before a flight.

Things were also looking up personally as well as professionally. I went to see the girls at the apartments one day and, as we were lying by the pool, I felt someone watching me.

'Do you know that man?' I asked Sandra.

'No,' she smiled, looking at him over her sunglasses. 'But I'd like to.'

He was certainly very handsome; in fact, he could have passed for a film star. He had lovely thick, short, dark hair, dark eyes and luscious lips. Not to mention his tanned, athletic body.

'He's coming over,' whispered Sandra.

Sure enough, the good-looking stranger was sauntering casually over to our sun beds.

'Hello, ladies,' he said. 'I'm Chuck Welch. Do you gals live in these apartments?'

'My friend Sandra does,' I said. 'I live in town.'

We started chatting and I was secretly delighted when Chuck perched on the end of my sun bed. As well as being handsome, he was also very funny and polite. I told him that we all worked for Pan Am.

'What do you do?' I asked.

'I'm in computers,' he said.

'Oh, lovely,' I said, completely mystified as to what that meant. I'd never heard of computers before. Chuck must have noticed the puzzled look on my face as he started to tell me about this machine that sounded a bit like a typewriter but could do lots of other amazing things as well.

'That sounds very exciting,' I said.

'Believe me, they're the future,' he said. 'We'll all have them one day.'

We chatted for ages. Chuck told me he was originally from New York State and, despite his good looks, he seemed very down to earth and friendly.

'Would you like to go out for dinner with me, Betty?' he asked.

I could see Sandra winking at me out of the corner of my eye and suddenly I felt myself blushing.

'Yes,' I said. 'That would be lovely.'

That night Chuck came and picked me up. Auntie Belle couldn't resist hovering by the window as he pulled up outside in his Ford Falcon.

'Ooh, this fellow's a snappy dresser,' she purred approvingly when she saw Chuck walk up the path in a smart black suit, crisp white shirt and fashionably thin black tie. I knew he must be special to get the seal of approval from Auntie Belle, who was notoriously hard to please.

I was utterly hooked by this handsome, confident man, and we started dating. He was very easygoing, a little bit too laid back sometimes for my liking.

Chuck shared his apartment with one of his work colleagues,

Pete. He took me round there one day and I was absolutely horrified. There were heaps of clothes everywhere and dirty dishes
piled up in the sink.

'This place is like a pig sty,' I said.

'Is it?' he said. 'Neither Pete nor I are very good at playing
house.'

I couldn't believe they lived in such squalor and I tried to
avoid going round there from then on.

Despite his untidiness, I'd really fallen for Chuck. The only
problem was, we weren't able to see each other that regularly,
as I was always away with work. But he didn't seem daunted by
that fact and, unexpectedly, I soon had a bit more time on my
hands.

One thing none of us girls expected when we moved to San
Francisco was to find ourselves on the picket line a few months
into our new jobs. But that's exactly what happened in May
1961. When we first became stewardesses with Pan Am, we
were told we had to join a union, so we all became members of
the Transport Workers Union, or the TWU, as that was the one
all of the other girls belonged to. It was the same union the
cockpit crew joined, and when Pan Am announced plans to
reduce the number of engineers they employed, they decided to
go on strike. If the flight engineers went on strike, it meant
everyone in the union had to go on strike too.

So, much to my dismay and despite the fact that I was very
happy with my new job, we were taken off the payroll by Pan
Am, and every day for a week, we had to go down to Union
Square in the centre of San Francisco and walk around with
placards.

'This is ridiculous,' said Angie as we all trooped down there.

'It's so demeaning,' grumbled Janet, never one to mince her
words.

To be honest, I found it really embarrassing too. There I was, in my nice new uniform and my pristine white gloves and hat, having to walk around carrying a huge sign saying, 'I'm on strike'. Understandably, the general public didn't have much sympathy for us. Some women came over to me as I was walking up and down and gave me a disgusted look.

'Why are you complaining, lady?' one of them said. 'You've got one of the best jobs in the world.'

'I'd kill to do what you do,' said the other.

They were right: I had nothing to moan about. In fact, I just wanted to get on and do my job

Thankfully, a couple of weeks later, the dispute was settled and we could all resume our duties. Now I finally felt confident that I could do this job and do it well, and I could get on with what I had been longing to do for so long. It was time to see the world.

Chapter Eight

Living the High Life

There are some moments in your life that you will always remember like they happened yesterday, no matter how much time passes. For me, one of those defining moments was the first time I arrived in Hawaii.

It was July 1961 and it was my first 'exotic' trip working for Pan Am, and everything about it was truly magical. It was there that it really hit me that this was my job now, this was really happening, and it was almost too good to be true. My ambition had always been to travel the world and now, at the tender age of twenty-two, I had achieved that, and it felt wonderful. Not only that, but I was being paid to live my dream.

Angela Kirby was working on the same flight to Honolulu and neither of us could wait to get there. It was a nice, easy five-hour daytime trip, and there was a happy, relaxed atmosphere on board. Most of the passengers were heading off on holiday, so they eagerly tucked into the Dom Perignon and I think every-one was a bit merry by the time we landed!

As we stepped off the plane, what struck me first was the

warm, perfumed air. Local music was playing and beautiful Hawaiian girls wearing grass skirts or muumuus, which were long, loose, brightly coloured cotton dresses, came to greet us. I had never seen anything like it, and it took my breath away. They put leis, which are garlands of tropical flowers, around our necks and handed us cups of fresh pineapple juice. After five hours of free Champagne, the passengers gulped it down, as they needed a bit of sobering up!

There was no airport building in those days, just a ram-shackle old hut where the luggage was taken, but even that seemed charming and exotic to me. Then, when we had collected our cases, we climbed into the stretch limousine that was waiting for us. Wherever you went in the world, there was always a car there to take you and the rest of the crew to your hotel.

In the limo, we were handed an envelope with our 'per diem' in it. This was our allowance for the time we were away. We got at least the equivalent of $20 a day in local currency, which was quite generous and always a lot more than we needed. We never saw a hotel bill and our dry-cleaning was always paid for, so we just used our per diem to buy food outside of the hotel. When I was away on trips, I never even had to touch my salary, which was wonderful. Our starting wage was $300 a month, the equivalent of £125 in those days, so we were very well paid compared to most women in the sixties, and it was certainly a vast improvement on the £28 a month I was paid at Silver City.

The limo took us straight to the five-star Royal Hawaiian, which was the crème de la crème of the hotels on Waikiki Beach. It was the first hotel in Waikiki, and its nickname was 'the Pink Palace of the Pacific' because the building was a striking candy-pink colour. I loved everything about it, from the beautiful mahogany-wood-panelled reception area, to the lush gardens filled with exotic flowers and tropical fruits that I'd never seen before, like papayas and mangoes.

Because flights were so infrequent in those days, you could have anything up to a week at a destination, and on this trip we had two days to explore Waikiki.

Angela and I were like two excited school girls and, much to my embarrassment now, the first thing we did was go out and buy ourselves grass skirts. We must have looked like such unsophisticated tourists as we strolled down the beach in them, arm in arm, but we didn't care. As we wandered across the golden sand and paddled in water that was so clear it looked like gin, I almost had to pinch myself.

'It's just so beautiful,' said Angela. 'I can't believe we're really here.'

'Me neither,' I sighed. 'It seems a long way from Walthamstow.'

The next morning, we put our worries about our weight restrictions to one side and tucked into a wonderful breakfast of eggs, Portuguese sausage and orange bread. Then, after we had eaten, we literally hopped over the wall onto the beach. I sat on the sand and listened to the sound of the waves crashing on the shore, while palm trees swayed in the gentle breeze. In the distance, I could see lush green mountains and to the left of me was a dormant volcano called Diamond Head.

'I think this is the most beautiful place I've ever been to,' I sighed to Angela.

It was certainly a million miles away from the grey sand and murky water of Benidorm that I had saved up for years to visit. As I sat there, I made myself take a mental note of that beautiful beach and how happy I felt. Even now, I can still conjure up a picture of Waikiki in my mind, and it instantly calms me.

Then, as eager as always to get a tan, I lay out on the sand in my white bikini with orange flowers.

'Wow, you're daring,' said one of the American stewardesses when she saw me.

'What do you mean?' I asked.

It was only when I looked around that I realised Angela and I were the only women on the beach wearing bikinis. They had just become fashionable in England in the early 1960s, and there had even been a song about them, Brian Hyland's 1960 hit 'Itsy Bitsy Teenie Weenie Yellow Polka Dot Bikini', which tells the story of a shy young girl who won't come out of the sea because she is wearing a revealing bikini. But it was suddenly apparent that the rest of the world hadn't followed suit. In the 1950s some Catholic countries, like Spain, Portugal and Italy, had banned women from wearing bikinis and they were considered so risqué, they were prohibited in some American states and you could be fined for wearing one.

The American Pan Am stewardesses were all wearing swimming costumes or modest, boyish-looking two-pieces that covered their stomachs and waist, and I could tell they thought we were a bit racy. But I was secretly quite proud of the fact that Angela and I were fashion trailblazers. By the time Ursula Andress emerged from the sea in a white bikini in that iconic scene from the first James Bond film, *Dr No*, in 1962, every young woman was wearing one.

That night Angela and I went to explore the local restaurants. As darkness fell, the beach looked even more magical, lit by a line of flaming torches called tikis. We tucked into teriyaki salmon and mahi mahi fish, as well as a local delicacy, a savoury purple porridge called poi. There were three different consistencies – one-finger poi, two-finger poi and three-finger, which was the thickest. We got the giggles as we tried to eat it the way the locals did, by scooping it up with our hands and sucking it off our fingers.

After a second day of sunbathing on the beach, it was time to go back to our rooms and rinse out our white gloves in the sink, so they would be dry in time for our flight back to San Francisco the next morning.

Thankfully that visit to Hawaii wasn't my last, as most of the Pan Am flights to the South Pacific would fly out via Honolulu, so I was there frequently – up to two or three times a month. Sometimes I'd drop my dry-cleaning off on one trip and pick it up the next time I was there. It's still one of my favourite places in the world, probably because it holds such happy memories.

After that incredible experience, I couldn't wait to find out what my next trip would be. Even though the four of us girls shared Auntie Belle's loft, we were always away and it was very rare to find all of us at home at once. Pan Am had over 300 routes, which were referred to as lines, and on average there were three flights on each line. We each had to do at least one line a month and you could bid for the ones you wanted depending on your seniority. We needed to fly seventy hours a month and anything above that was classed as overtime.

It was always very exciting to see which line you had been given and where in the world you would be going, especially in the beginning, when everything was so new. It would depend on which routes you had been assigned, but we were away on average for just over half the month. Our time off could be broken up into a few days or one large chunk – it varied from month to month.

There would be just enough time to go home, get my hair done, catch up with Chuck and whichever of the girls were around, then it was time to be off again.

'You're hardly ever home,' said Chuck. 'Don't you hate being away so much?'

'Not at all,' I said. 'I love it.'

In all honesty, I was having the time of my life. It was hard work on the plane, and the long flights were gruelling, but it wasn't as if I was on the aircraft for fourteen days straight. There was plenty of time for lying on a tropical beach, shopping and sightseeing in an exotic new country.

When we were away on trips, we always stayed in the best five-star hotels. An important part of being a Pan Am stewardess was being able to chat to the passengers and advise them on where to go, so we needed to know about the top-class restaurants, the most luxurious hotels and fashionable shops. The staff at these places knew that, so wherever we stayed, we were treated like VIPs in the hope that we would recommend their establishments to our passengers.

When we first started flying, the senior stewardesses took us under their wing and gave us tips about where to go when we were in a certain city. Before long, I knew the best place in Sydney to get your hair done, where to go for a manicure in Tokyo and where to get a suit made in Hong Kong.

Can you imagine staying at the best hotels in the world, the same places frequented by film stars and presidents, and never seeing a bill? Not only that, I was being paid to do it. It really was the job of my dreams, and I just felt so, so lucky. I remember checking into Raffles Hotel in Singapore and being totally awestruck by the size of my suite. It was bigger than the entire terraced house I grew up in and was the height of luxury, with its dark-wood furniture, amazing views and huge bed.

Certain parts of the world that we flew to were still quite remote and Pan Am was so worried about the crew getting food poisoning at some hotels in these far-flung places that we would even have our own catering facilities. When we stayed at the Royal Princess Hotel, which was a lovely olde-worlde place in Bangkok, we had our own crew kitchen and dining room. There was a chef who would make you whatever you fancied to order, and I loved tucking into banana pancakes with coconut syrup. It really is a good job I didn't put on weight easily in those days!

Because flying was still so rare in the 1960s and was something only wealthy people did, we often went to places where there were hardly any tourists.

One of my earliest trips, in 1961, was to Pago Pago, which is pronounced Pango Pango. I'd never even heard of the place and it was only on the flight over that another stewardess told me it was a little island in the South Pacific and the capital of American Samoa. Its real name is supposed to be Pango Pango, but legend has it that the missionaries didn't have the letter N on their typewriters, so from them on it was called Pago Pago instead.

We landed at 3 a.m. local time and I couldn't believe it when I opened the plane doors to find that a huge crowd had gathered to greet us. The whole town had turned out to welcome the locals that were returning home and there were people singing, dancing and playing instruments.

'I've never seen anything like this,' I gasped.

A big jet was such a rare sight for them that everyone had got up in the middle of the night to witness the spectacle.

Pan Am only flew there twice a week, so it meant I had four days to explore this beautiful, unspoilt place. There was only one hotel, the Intercontinental, which was right in the foothills of the Rainmaker Mountain, but there were no pavements and the main street was just a dirt track lined with rickety market stalls.

It was fascinating finding out about a different culture and I loved hearing about all the local customs. The strangest one was, if a family had lots of sons and no daughters, they would raise one of the boys as a girl. They would give him a girl's name and dress him in girls' clothes, and as he got older he would learn how to cook and clean and help his mother, like a daughter would have done. Sometimes, when these boys were older, they would go back to living as a man and they were quickly snapped up by the local women, as they were considered a real catch because they were so handy around the house!

Travelling really opened my eyes to all these different cultures and even though places like Pago Pago felt really remote, I always felt very safe there.

But my flights were not always to exotic, tropical destinations. On my first trip to Tokyo, we stopped off in Alaska for the night. Before we landed in Anchorage, the captain radioed ahead and ordered two cooked giant king crabs. I couldn't believe it when I saw the size of these beasts. They were 3 ft wide, with legs as long as my arms, and they were so heavy it took two of the cockpit crew to carry each of them.

The first thing that struck me about Alaska was how cold it was. By the time I'd walked from the aircraft to the crew car, the hairs inside my nose had frozen. But that was the least of my worries.

'Betty, as you're the most junior person on the flight, the party's in your hotel room,' laughed the purser.

The whole crew piled into my room, put newspaper down on the floor and then proceeded to tuck into the giant crabs, along with some leftover white wine from the flight. Everyone left later on, but the overpowering fishy whiff did not and I spent the entire night trying to sleep in a room that smelt of crab. I'm sure I did too by the morning.

I thought Alaska was such a strange place. If we went in

winter, we hardly saw daylight at all, and if I was staying there in summer, I had a hard time going to sleep because it was light practically all the time. Later on in my career, I was on the first Pan Am flight that flew into Anchorage after the Good Friday earthquake in March 1964. It was one of the worst recorded quakes in North American history and hundreds of people were killed. It was strange and a little bit eerie, walking down the main street, which had been completely destroyed, and seeing the cinema which had slipped down a crack in the ground and all the buildings that had fallen into the sea. At the airport, there were huge cracks in the tarmac and the control tower had collapsed, so they'd had to build a temporary one.

The first time I flew to Manila was also memorable. It was a bustling Asian city and the most popular form of transport were jeepneys, which were brightly coloured trucks that were made from US military jeeps left over from the Second World War. We were guests at the iconic Manila Hotel, which was *the* place to stay in the city, where presidents and stars like Charlton Heston and Marlon Brando stayed when they were in town.

One night the manager insisted we came to the top-class hotel restaurant for dinner.

'You must try this,' he told me, handing me a Champagne flute with what looked like a pink oyster at the bottom. 'It's a local delicacy called a balut.'

'Oh, how lovely,' I said. 'What is it?'

I was horrified when he explained that it was a raw, fertilised duck egg that allegedly had aphrodisiac properties. The idea turned my stomach, but I didn't want to offend him, as he had been so kind. There was only one thing for it: I took a deep breath, closed my eyes and swallowed it down in one go. I managed it, but even now the thought of that jelly-like blob slipping down the back of my throat makes me feel dreadfully sick.

It was while I was in Manila that I was invited by some local Pan Am crew that I was flying with to go and shoot some rabbits.

'What a terrible group of people,' I thought, assuming it was some barbaric local custom that I no way intended to be part of. But they kept asking me if I was sure I didn't want to go grab my swimming costume and come with them.

'Definitely not,' I said, slightly puzzled. 'But what has a swimsuit got to do with shooting bunnies?'

It turns out I hadn't understood their accents and the crew had meant 'shoot some rapids' not 'rabbits'. I felt so embarrassed, but luckily they thought it was funny. Eventually I did get my swimsuit and we had a lovely afternoon 'shooting the rapids' and swimming at Pagsanjan Falls.

I soon learnt that travelling was a good way to indulge my love of fashion. I'd always liked nice clothes, although I had never had the money to buy them before. But in some of the Asian countries I visited, you could get a whole outfit made for a few dollars. On long-haul flights, after the meal service was over and the passengers were asleep, I would sit on the jump seat and flick through *Vogue* magazine, ripping out pictures of some of the beautiful designer dresses that caught my eye.

Like a lot of young women at the time, Audrey Hepburn was my style icon. *Breakfast at Tiffany's* had just come out in 1961, and I loved all of the clothes Holly Golightly wore in the film.

Whenever we had a layover in Bangkok, I'd buy some Thai silk and then when we landed in Hong Kong, I would arrange for a man called Mr Wong to come and meet us. Some of the older stewardesses had told us about him and he was a funny, smiley little fellow who hardly spoke any English. We handed him our pictures from *Vogue* and a bundle of Thai silk and he took our measurements and copied them for us. The next time

we were in the country, he met us at Kai Tak Airport and we
sneaked into a little office behind the Pan American check-in
desk to have a final fitting. It was always great fun to try on
our glamorous new creations as quickly as possible before we
had to rush onto the aircraft to welcome the passengers on
board.

I had some lovely shift dresses made in yellow and pale pink,
with matching collarless, knee-length coats, exactly like Holly
Golightly's in *Breakfast at Tiffany's*. Up until the early 1960s,
women never wore trousers, but thanks to the actress Katharine
Hepburn, they had just become very fashionable and Mr Wong
rustled me up several pairs of Capri pants. But my favourite of
all was a knee-length, asymmetrical dress in emerald-green Thai
silk. One shoulder was embroidered with tiny, tubular-shaped
beads, and I felt so stylish in it.

Another of my favourite places to visit was Papeete, which is
the capital of French Polynesia. It was exactly how you would
imagine a desert island to be. In fact, the film *Mutiny on the
Bounty* starring Marlon Brando was filmed there in 1962, a few
months after I went there for the first time.

The flights were so infrequent that we always had a week
there before we had to fly home, so we would get out of our
uniforms as soon as we landed and jump on a two-hour ferry to
one of the islands, Moorea. I say 'ferry', but it was more like a
long, flat boat with a little motor and fifty people packed onto
the back. It was mainly full of locals who had been to the markets in town and sometimes there would even be a crate of
chickens or a sheep on board. Someone would be strumming a
ukulele and the locals would join in and sing Tahitian songs. I
was always exhausted from working on the flight all night, so I
would lie there and watch the flying fish jump out of the trans-
parent, turquoise water.

If there was one place on earth that summed up the definition of paradise for me, then I would say Moorea was it. I wasn't the only one who thought so. In early 1961 three bachelors from California – Hugh Kelley, Jay Carlisle and Don 'Muk' McCallum – decided to ditch their jobs as a lawyer, stockbroker and salesman, get on a yacht and go in search of paradise. They ended up in Moorea and sold everything they owned to buy a vanilla farm. But after a while the bottom dropped out of the vanilla market, so they decided to build a hotel on the island, which they called the Club Bali Hai.

They were tanned, buff, funny, clever guys and it became a popular place for us Pan Am girls to hang out. The Bali Hai boys, as they were known, loved being surrounded by young, beautiful air stewardesses, and they were terrible flirts. They became quite famous. There was a story about them in *Life*, the most popular weekly magazine in America, and Jay even featured in a TV advert for Camel cigarettes.

The first time I went to Moorea with some other stewardesses, the hotel had just opened and Jay was waiting on the little pier as the boat docked. He looked up at the brilliant-blue, cloudless sky and sighed: 'Another terrible day in paradise.'

And what a paradise it was! The hotel consisted of a series of basic little thatched bungalows built over the crystal-clear water. At dinner, everyone would just sit around one big table and eat whatever was served up. We would always be tired from the long flight and if we got there too early and our rooms weren't ready, they would take us to a long house with a big thatched roof and we would all crash out on the floor. It must have looked quite funny, all of us Pan Am crew asleep in a row, like we were having a grown-ups' pyjama party.

We spent the days sunbathing and swimming, and this was where I snorkelled for the first time. The boys had built a wooden bamboo raft with a bar on board, which they called the Liki Tiki, and they would take us out into the middle of the ocean and we would jump off the side. Muk would strum away on his guitar and serve us cocktails while we soaked up the sun. The water was amazingly clear and I couldn't believe it when I put my head under and saw all these schools of brightly coloured tropical fish.

Sometimes the Air New Zealand crews would join us on the island and they were a wild bunch. Their flight attendants were predominantly male and they certainly liked to drink and party. We Pan Am girls would watch their antics with wide-eyed horror and we would avoid them like the plague.

The crew hotel we all stayed at in Papatee before our flights home had a freshwater pool in the reception area, and one day the Air New Zealand boys caught one of the eels that swam around in it and proceeded to barbecue it, much to the hotel manager's horror.

In between all these amazing trips around the world, it was always nice to have a few days at home to catch up with the other girls.

One day I went round to see Sandra, who was all excited. One of the supervisors at Pan Am knew she was single and had suggested she get in touch with a friend of his, Mike Marini.

'I called him and he sounded lovely,' she told me. 'He's invited me round to his place and said to bring some of you girls with me, as his friends will be there.'

Unfortunately most of us were working, but Angie was off and she had agreed to go.

'How did your big date go?' I asked Sandra a few days later, when I was back in the country.

Sandra rolled her eyes. 'Mike was a lovely guy,' she said. 'But he took one look at Angie and that was the end of me.'

It was a running joke amongst us that no red-blooded male could ever resist Angie, the blonde bombshell with the fabulous figure.

'Don't worry,' Sandra said, smiling. 'There are no hard feelings. Mike introduced me to one of his friends, Jim, who seems like a nice guy.'

A few days later, I got to meet Mike Marini for myself when he invited us all to go waterskiing.

'He hasn't got much hair, Betty, but he's a lovely guy,' Angie told me.

He was the only boy in a huge Italian family and even though he was in his mid-thirties, he still lived at home with his parents. They owned a successful linen company that supplied all the top restaurants in the area and they had a huge house with a pool bigger than the one at the apartments. They also had their own boat, and Mike took us out on it to the nearby Stockton Sloughs.

It was obvious by her puppy-dog eyes that Angie was head-over-heels with Mike. He was a little on the short side and thin on top, but he had a magnetic personality, was full of fun and had a big group of friends whom he went bodybuilding with. He completely swept Angie off her feet by showering her with gifts and taking her to elegant restaurants.

I'd never been waterskiing in my life, but Mike was really patient when explaining the technique to me. But every time he revved up the boat and we started to move, I fell flat on my face in the water.

'You can do it, Betty,' he said. 'Let's try again.'

'I can't,' I wailed.

Thanks to Mike having the patience of a saint, after several failed attempts, I finally managed to stand up on the water-skis. But we were going so fast, I was terrified, and proceeded to scream my way around the lake, while everyone else in the boat laughed hysterically.

'Betty, you'll have to meet my friend Brad,' Mike told me afterwards, when we were safely back on shore.

'Oh, Mike,' groaned Angie. 'Don't you dare try to fix her up with Brad. No one ever fancies him.'

Brad was a fireman, but the poor bloke couldn't seem to find himself a girlfriend because of his front teeth, which stuck out over his bottom lip like a chipmunk's.

'I don't think Chuck would appreciate me seeing someone else,' I told them.

So, one by one, all of us girls started to go steady. Sandra seemed smitten with Mike's friend Jim, a tall, handsome electrician, and Hazel had ditched F-F-Fred and started dating Gary Carter, a salesman who lived in the apartment block.

But while we were all settling into life in San Fran, I knew the Japanese girls were still very homesick. In the autumn of 1961 Florence and Jo requested a transfer back home to Hawaii, so they could be closer to their families. Although I had grown very fond of Auntie Belle, I thought it would be nice to have a place of my own, without rules and regulations and someone breathing down our necks the whole time. So Mimi, Sandra, Angie and I decided to rent a house together.

We found a lovely white clapboard cottage with a white picket fence and a garden full of orange and lemon trees a bit further down the coast in Hillsdale. I was dreading telling Auntie Belle we were moving out, and it took days for me to pluck up the courage.

'Well, to be honest, I'm very disappointed, dear,' she said after I'd broken the news to her. 'It's like losing one of the family.'

I felt terribly guilty.

'You can come and see us in Hillsdale whenever you want, and you've still got Shirley,' I told her.

I was going to miss her and her funny, interfering ways, not to mention Uncle C. D., but I knew we would keep in touch. In fact, Auntie Belle insisted on coming down with us on moving day, to help us settle in.

Even though there were four of us in the new house, we were all away so often that we were like ships that passed in the night. We were hardly ever there at the same time, so we adopted a stray dog, a black mutt we called Harry, to keep whoever was at home company. But the poor old thing didn't know if he was coming or going. When I was there, I would let him sleep on the bed; when Sandra was there, she'd make him sleep on the floor; when Angie was there, she'd make him sleep in the kitchen; and when Mimi was there, she kept him outside.

We moved in at the end of October 1961. On one of the first nights we were there, Mimi and I were at home together when there was a knock at the door.

When we opened it and saw a group of children dressed as witches, goblins and ghosts, we were completely puzzled.

We were even more confused when they yelled, 'Trick or treat!'

'I'm sorry, but I don't know what you mean,' I said and they looked at me strangely.

'It's Halloween,' a little witch told us. 'You give us a treat or we play a trick on you.'

'Oh, that doesn't sound very nice,' I said.

Halloween wasn't something that we celebrated in England in the 1960s, and neither Mimi nor I had ever heard of trick or treating. Because we were hardly ever at home, we didn't have much food in the cupboards, just a bowl of oranges and lemons from the trees in the garden, so we gave the children some of those. But, much to our horror, the trick or treaters kept coming and before long we had run out of fruit. So Mimi rummaged through the cupboards in a panic, to see what else she could find. Those poor children's faces were a picture when, instead of the sweets and chocolates they were expecting, we presented them with a couple of cans of tuna and a rusty old tin of tomato soup.

'You must be kidding,' sighed one little boy, who was dressed as a ghost.

Mimi and I just closed the door and collapsed into a fit of giggles.

America was slowly starting to feel like home, but although I loved my job, I still missed my family terribly. Now I just needed to convince them to come over and visit me, to see this wonderful country for themselves. But as I was about to find out, that was going to be easier said than done.

Chapter Nine

Family Ties

We had been in our new home in Hillsdale for nine months when it was time for my first annual month off. And I had a plan up my sleeve.

'How do you fancy a free trip around the world?' I wrote to my brother Geoffrey back in England.

He was sixteen and at high school, and I knew Mum was worrying about how to entertain him over the six-week summer break. Dad was busy working and Mum had just got a job at Sainsbury's, in the butter department, chopping it into pats, so I knew they wouldn't be able to take that much time off. So, as I was entitled to some free flights, I thought it would be nice to give my little brother a treat.

Geoff, who was only used to holidays in Margate, was beside himself with excitement. I picked him up in London and we flew to Frankfurt, where I had booked us two rooms in a nice hotel. But the poor boy was left red-faced a few hours after we'd got there. Geoff was having a bath when he saw this long cord hanging down from the ceiling and, out of curiosity, he pulled it. He was nothing less than mortified when a maid came rushing in, thinking he was in distress and needed help.

'I can't believe she saw me stood there in the altogether,' he said.

From Frankfurt, we went to Istanbul, then we flew to Bangkok, where we stayed at the crew hotel, and then on to Hong Kong. A man called Fred Collars, the manager of the Pan Am base there, kindly invited us to dinner with his wife and ten children. They served us a huge plate of chicken feet, which I knew was a local delicacy, but Geoff had never seen anything like it before and his horrified face was a picture.

'Excuse me, what have you done with the rest of the chicken?' he politely asked them.

From there, we went to Tokyo, and then on to Honolulu and back to California. Geoff had an amazing time, but even more enjoyable was his new-found fame when he went back to school.

'That's the boy that went round the world,' other pupils in his year would whisper to each other, and he lapped up his celebrity status. No one we knew went abroad in those days, never mind to several countries.

Life with Pan Am was certainly never boring. I had only been back from my round-the-world trip for a month when, in September 1962, Sandra and I were called in to see our supervisor.

'How do you girls fancy going on a little adventure?' he said.

He explained that the British Tourist Association was bringing over a London Routemaster bus and driving it across the United States, to promote the UK. They wanted two British Pan Am girls to go along and invite the public to come on board and talk to them about Britain. He had suggested that Sandra and I would make good ambassadors, and it meant we would get a month off flying duties to travel around the country.

'It sounds like fun,' I said, and Sandra agreed that it would be a good way to see more of America.

So, a few weeks later, we set off on our mission. I had to wear my Pan Am uniform, but Sandra was horrified when she was handed a Beefeater's costume that consisted of a top hat, staff, fishnet stockings and the tiniest pair of shorts that I had ever seen.

'Well, it will be a chance to show off your lovely long legs,' I teased, but she was not amused.

The Routemaster was being driven by a man called Mervin Pulford, who held the title of Britain's champion bus driver. He was a roly-poly, chirpy chap who could talk the hind legs off a donkey. He was very jolly and was always cracking jokes

'Awight, gurls?' he said in his cockney accent. 'I fink I'm the luckiest geezer in the land, getting to drive you two crackers around.'

Merve drove us around the country in a plush tour bus that had bunk beds on board, and we would meet up with the Routemaster in various cities around America. We drove thousands of miles across the length and breadth of the country. It was mostly fun, but at times it could be very boring, especially when we were travelling through places like Kansas, where it would just be field after field of corn and nothing else to see for hours.

It was quite dangerous too. At one point we had to get from Salt Lake City to Denver, but there was treacherous, deep snow. Mervin lived up to his champion bus driver title and bravely drove the bus through the Rockies to get there in time for the next day, while we took a tiny plane through a raging storm.

Wherever we were in the country, local TV crews would come out to film us and although it was a bit nerve-wracking at first, I got used to being interviewed for television.

During one part of the tour, Sandra and I had to go to Las Vegas and bus the delegates arriving for the American Society of Travel Agents from the airport to their hotel. All these middle-aged businessmen were delighted to have two Pan Am stewardesses to greet them, especially as one was dressed in a skimpy Beefeater's outfit.

'Welcome aboard,' I told them over the mic. 'Our pilot today, Captain Pulford, advises me that we will be cruising at an altitude of three and a half feet and a speed of forty-five miles per hour. We will land at the hotel in fifteen minutes, so please fasten your money belts.'

A few weeks after we got home, we both received letters of commendation from the Pan Am Division Service Manager, thanking us 'grand little ladies' for our efforts.

Working for Pan Am, I never knew what adventure would be waiting round the corner, and I was enjoying every minute of it. But even though I loved my new life, I still got homesick from time to time. Thankfully, because I could choose my routes, I would pick trips that went through London and would often make it home once a month. I was also determined to keep in touch with my old friends back home, but much to my dismay, after only a few months of working for Pan Am, contact with them had already started to peter out.

'If you're over here for two years, then we've got you,' Al West had told us during our training.

He had also warned us that we would probably lose touch with old friends back home, but that we would make new ones. In my mind, I still intended to go back to England one day and, no matter how inevitable, I felt quite sad about losing touch with some of my closest childhood friends, people like Betty Potter, who had lived in the same street as me growing up.

We had been so close all through high school and after we'd

left, she had gone to work in a bank, where she had met her husband, Richard. He was a nice chap and they had got married very quickly. But I had to face the fact that our lives were going in completely different directions and we hardly had anything in common anymore. I would try to see her on my brief visits home, but there are only so many times you can say, 'Remember when we did this?' It was too expensive to phone and I was conscious that if I wrote and told her what I was doing, it would look like I was bragging. I didn't want it to seem like I was boasting about all these wonderful places I was visiting, while she was hanging out a line of washing. My life just seemed so far removed from hers.

By now, all of the girls I knew from home were getting married and having children, including my closest cousins, Jill and Peggy. Peggy had married a Welsh pig farmer, so her life could not have been any more different from mine. I felt like I couldn't really talk to them about all the things that were going on in my job, as we had been taught when we were growing up that bragging about your achievements was vulgar.

I think that's why the other stewardesses and I formed such tight friendships with each other. They were like-minded people who shared the same lifestyle, and you could have conversations with them about what you had been doing and no one would think you were full of yourself. While our peers at home were settling down, getting married and having children, we were enjoying having careers and exploring the world without having to have husbands by our sides, which was rare for a young woman in the early 1960s. I was sure I wanted all that one day, but there was still so much I wanted to see and do first.

But Al West was right. It seemed that for every friend I lost touch with back in England, I made a new one in America. There was Brenda Lee from Leigh-on-Sea, who I would fly with quite often out of San Francisco. She was from a class four years before me and had been flying with Pan Am since 1957, so she showed me the ropes. Once we were on a round-the-world flight together and had a few days in Hong Kong, where she took me to buy my first string of real pearls – a rite of passage for any new stewardess. We got the boat out to an island, where I chose a lovely strand of pearls with a solid-gold clasp. Both the necklace and my friendship with Brenda have endured the years.

There was also a familiar face from my past. Dawn Hester, who I had lived with when I worked at Silver City and who unfortunately wasn't chosen for Pan Am, sent me a letter to say she'd got a job with Trans World Airlines (TWA) and was going to be based in St Louis.

'I'm so pleased for you,' I wrote, 'but why don't you try to get a transfer to San Francisco? You would love it here.'

I was so happy when, in November 1962, she did. It was perfect timing, as Mimi had just decided to transfer back to Hawaii, so Hazel, Dawn and I decided to rent an apartment in central San Francisco. It was great being roommates with Dawn again, and our ground-floor flat was right at the top of one of the city's steepest hills, so we had to get used to the loud ringing of the cable car bell every time it passed.

Two other Pan Am girls also decided to move in with us. Pauline Smith was in the intake a year after ours and she was an ex-ballerina from London. She was very elegant and skinny, with big hands and feet, and she had long, glossy dark hair that she used to iron to keep poker-straight. She was a nice girl and fun to be around, although I could tell that she fancied herself a bit. Her friend, Jan Tucker, also came to live with us. She was an American girl from California and was a very quiet, gentle person.

I loved being in the centre of the city, close to all the shops and cafés, rather than in a sleepy suburb. In fact, it was there that I met a gay man for the first time in my life. Bruno was one of the stylists at my hairdresser's, and he was dating another hairdresser called June. I knew they were a couple, but when I went in one day to get my hair set, they weren't speaking to each other.

'Have you two had an argument?' I asked her.

'Only about the fact that he prefers men,' she said.

'What do you mean?' I asked.

June explained that Bruno was gay, but because it was so frowned on, they had a long-running agreement that she would pretend to be his girlfriend.

'Oh,' I said. 'That's a bit different.'

The word 'gay' meant happy or carefree to me. I didn't know there was such a thing and, I must admit, I was quite shocked. I suppose I had led a fairly sheltered life. No one I knew in England was openly gay and even in San Francisco, a place that over the years has become a gay Mecca, it was still considered shocking in the early 1960s.

Unlike today, there weren't any openly gay stewards or stewardesses when I was working for Pan Am. But when I look back now, I realise that a lot of the older male pursers were probably homosexual. I remember one in particular, Bob, who I flew with quite a bit. We were talking about relationships one day and both bemoaning the fact that we had not met anyone we were really taken with.

'Don't worry,' I'd told him. 'You'll meet someone one of these days.'

'Oh no, I'm nothing but a little old lady,' he'd said.

It was only now I'd found out about Bruno that I understood what Bob had been telling me. Despite all my travels, I wasn't very worldly wise, and meeting a gay man really opened my eyes. It's amazing how times have changed and how modern society has had to become so much more accepting than in the sixties.

I loved living in the centre of San Francisco, and there was one thing I desperately wanted more than anything in the world – for Mum and Dad to come out and visit me and see it for themselves. I was always asking when they were coming over, but Dad was busy working, so I didn't want to put pressure on them.

But, in March 1963, Mum finally agreed to fly over to San Francisco for a holiday. She had never been abroad or on a plane before, and I knew she was nervous about the twelve-hour flight. I could tell Dad was worried about Mum coming all that way on her own too, but he was very proud of her.

As an unmarried stewardess, your parents were allowed one free return coach-class ticket to anywhere in the world once a year, and they only paid 10 per cent tax for any flight after that. Once you were married, your spouse took that benefit.

It felt lovely to be able to treat Mum to her air fare over to San Francisco, and we arranged it so that I was working on the same flight, so I could check she was OK. She wore her best dress and coat and Dad took us to the airport and helped her check in while I had my pre-flight briefing. My supervisor allowed me to board the plane along with the passengers, so I could take Mum to her seat and get her settled.

'This is your seatbelt, which goes across your lap,' I said, showing her how to click the buckle in and release it. 'Now, don't be frightened when we take off. The engines sound quite loud and it might feel a bit bumpy, but remember, that's normal.'

'I'll be fine, Betty,' she reassured me. 'I'm too excited to be nervous.'

But I could tell from the look in her eyes that she was a little bit anxious. I wasn't surprised. I knew this was a big deal for her, flying thousands of miles away from home for the first time, especially without Dad by her side.

'Well, I'll come over again when we're at altitude, to see how you're doing,' I said, squeezing her hand.

When I went back to see her after take-off, Mum had a huge grin on her face.

'That was amazing,' she smiled. 'I can't believe how tiny everything looked down on the ground.'

She thought it was incredible, and I loved watching her reaction as she tucked into the gourmet food and enjoyed her first taste of Champagne.

'It's so lovely to see you in action, dear,' she told me.

'You should try to get some sleep, Mum,' I said. 'It's a long flight. You'll be exhausted by the time we get there.'

'Sleep?' she said. 'There's no way I'm going to sleep, love. I might miss something.

I was so proud of the way she was savouring every minute of this new experience, and I knew it was reassuring for her to have me with her on the journey.

We got a taxi from the airport to the new apartment, where Mum was staying with me. She met the other girls and the next day I invited Chuck round for lunch. He turned up with a big bunch of flowers.

'It's lovely to meet you, Mrs Eden,' he said, shaking her hand, and I could tell Mum was impressed.

'Isn't he handsome?' she whispered to me.

Unfortunately, a couple of days later, I had to do an overnight trip to Hawaii and leave Mum behind. I explained the American currency to her and left her plenty of food and a list of instructions about how everything in the kitchen worked.

'The girls will look after you and I'll take you over the road and introduce you to the people in the grocery shop,' I said. 'Then if the girls are out and you need anything, you can just ask them.'

'Don't you worry,' Mum told me. 'It's not as if we don't speak the same language. I'll be fine.'

But when I got back from my flight the following day, I came home to find her in a terrible state.

'Oh, Betty,' she said. 'There's been an earthquake.'

Mum explained that she had been on her own in the flat when she'd felt the ground shaking. Tremors were a normal occurrence in San Francisco and we knew the drill was to crouch down in a doorway, as they were the strongest part of the building, but poor Mum had never experienced anything like it in her life. Convinced that the ground was about to open up and swallow her whole, she had run out onto the street in a blind panic.

'I thought I was a goner, Betty,' she said. 'I ran screaming into the shop across the road and all the cans and bottles on the shelves had fallen onto the floor and smashed.'

The tremors had only lasted a few minutes, but I could tell she had been really frightened. But before the drama of the earthquake, Mum had been having a great time. She told me how she had walked into town and gone to Woolworths in Union Square, where she'd spent hours looking at the animals in the pet department.

'I couldn't get used to the money, love, so I just paid for everything using dollar bills,' she said, handing me a huge pile of coins. 'Sorry about the change.'

To get over her fright and give her a bit of a change of scene, I arranged for us to go up to the Lake Tahoe ski resort with Jan and Pauline. Neither of us had ever been skiing before, but I thought it would be fun to show Mum some other areas. Jan had a car, so we were going to drive the four hours up there, but on the way, we hit some bad snow and Jan's little car was really struggling.

'I've got some snow chains in the boot,' she said.

It was illegal to drive in snow without chains, but none of us had a clue how to fit them to the tyres. We all stood there, shivering in the snow, trying to figure it out.

'We'll have to ask someone,' said Pauline.

'But there's hardly anyone around,' said Jan. 'And how can we make sure they will stop?'

I could see Mum was looking worried too, so I came up with a plan.

'Mum, lie down in the middle of the road,' I told her.

'What?' she said. 'What on earth would I want to do that for?'

'It will look like you've fallen in the snow, and no one's going to drive past a damsel in distress.'

Poor Mum looked a bit bemused as she lay down in the road, but she was as cold as the rest of us, so she was willing to give it a go. The girls and I lurked in some nearby bushes, just to make sure she didn't get run over. Thankfully she had only been there for five minutes when a car full of young men pulled up. They didn't seem to mind that they had been tricked into stopping. I think they were just relieved Mum was OK.

'We thought the old lady was dead,' one of them said.

'Hey, less of the old!' Mum told him. 'I'm only in my fifties!'

Soon we had the snow chains on and finally we made it to our destination. We all crammed into one motel room and had a fun few days exploring Lake Tahoe. Mum was used to my harebrained schemes, but she couldn't wait to tell Dad all about it when she got home.

'Oh, Sidney,' I could imagine her saying. 'I'd only just survived an earthquake and then you'll never guess what they made me do.'

I was so desperate for Dad to come over and see America too, as I knew he would love it. I was seeing so many amazing places and I really wanted to share it with him. When he retired, in 1963, I knew there was no excuse anymore.

'I want to take you and Mum on holiday to Hawaii,' I told him. 'It's my treat; it won't cost you a penny.'

For months I kept asking, but his response was always the same: 'I don't think so, Tink.'

Mum wanted to come back to San Francisco, and she was getting as frustrated with Dad as I was.

'I know there's something bothering him,' she said. 'But he refuses to tell me what it is.'

On one trip, I was in London overnight and Dad came up to the crew hotel in Piccadilly to see me. As usual, the subject soon turned to the holiday in Hawaii. After months of tearful conversations and countless letters, I was starting to get really annoyed by the fact that he was being so stubborn.

'I don't understand it, Dad,' I said. 'Why won't you come on holiday with me and Mum?'

'I just don't fancy it,' he told me.

'Please, Dad, I'm begging you,' I said. 'It would mean so much to Mum and me. If it's the flight you're scared of, I'll be there on the plane to look after you.'

'No, it's not that,' he said, shaking his head.

'Well, what is it then?' I asked.

'I just don't want to do it,' he said.

By now I was so frustrated and annoyed with him, I burst into tears.

'When you die, you won't have been anywhere else in the

world,' I sobbed. 'Think about all those places you showed me on the maps when I was a little girl and how wonderful it would be for you to see some of them for yourself.'

Dad had a very expressive face, and he sat there looking so worried. Then, to my utter astonishment, he said, 'All right, Betty, I will. I'll come.'

I couldn't believe it, I was so happy.

'Thank you,' I said, flinging my arms around him. 'You'll love every minute of it, Dad, I know you will.'

It was only then that he confided in me the real reason that he'd never wanted to go abroad. You had to have various jabs in the 1960s when you travelled outside Europe, and one of them was the smallpox inoculation, which Dad had had to have when he joined the army during the war.

'I know it sounds silly, love, and that's why I never even told your mum. But I had such a bad reaction to it during the war. I had a dangerously high temperature and I was seriously ill for months,' he told me. 'I couldn't bear the thought of the same thing happening again, so I thought, why risk it?'

'Oh, Dad,' I sighed. 'You silly thing. You should have said. Mum and I would have understood.'

'I just felt a bit foolish,' he said. 'A grown man scared of a few injections.'

Mum couldn't believe he had kept his fears to himself either.

'You're a funny old fish, Sid,' she scolded. 'I knew there was something bothering you.'

Mum was delighted that Dad had finally agreed to come.

'I can show you all those places in San Francisco that I've been boring you about for months,' she said.

Dad kept to his word and bravely put his worries to one side and had the injections. Thankfully he hardly had any reaction this time, which was a huge relief to all of us.

So, in July1963, I had a month off and I took Mum and Dad over to Honolulu for two weeks. Dad put on his smartest suit and Mum got all dolled up to get on the plane, and I had made sure I was working on their flight from London, so I could look after them. I loved watching their faces when we landed in Hawaii and the hula girls came to meet us and put the leis of tropical flowers around their necks. They were as amazed as I had been on my first visit. Jo and Mimi were there to collect us and take us to the little apartment that I had rented on Waikiki Beach.

That night we went out for dinner to a Japanese restaurant which had low tables and we all sat on cushions on the floor. I was a bit worried that it would all be a bit too much for Dad, as he was a picky eater at the best of times.

'These look like maggots,' he said, examining a plate of fried rice.

Then the waitress put down another bowl in front of him.

'What on earth is this?' he asked.

'Octopus, sir,' she said.

Poor Dad's face dropped but, good on him, he tried it. He threw himself into everything on that holiday, and it was lovely to see. Mum and I were in hysterics when he put on a sarong-type garment the local men wore, called a pareo, and posed for a photo. He was such a good sport and really got into the spirit of things.

I made sure we saw all the sights. I took them to Kapiolani Park and the zoo, and we watched a hula show and ate fresh pineapple from a hut in the pineapple fields, but Dad loved the warm, clear sea of Waikiki Beach the best. He even taught Mum to swim while we were there. One afternoon I was sunbathing while Dad took Mum in the water, when suddenly I heard her shouting.

'Look, Betty, my legs are off the ground,' she shrieked. 'I'm swimming! I'm swimming!'

She was so proud of herself. It was so nice for me to watch my parents enjoying this wonderful experience, and I felt really happy that I could do this for them. I suppose in a way it eased my conscience and made me feel better about leaving them and going to America. At least now I could see they were getting some benefits from my job too, and I was giving them the chance to have experiences that they would never have been able to afford themselves.

It was the first time Dad had been abroad and as long as he lived, he never forgot that holiday. It really was the trip of a life-time for him. When I dropped them off at San Francisco Airport to catch their flight home, Dad's eyes filled with tears.

'Thank you, Betty,' he told me. 'I've had such a wonderful time. I'm so glad I came.'

That first holiday to Hawaii completely changed Dad's life. There was no stopping him after that, and he wasn't going to miss out on anything anymore.

But, unfortunately, life wasn't always full of such happy times. Something happened in November 1963 that is indelibly etched in my mind and changed America for ever. It was Friday 22 November and Sandra and I weren't working, so we decided to go into town to do some shopping. We'd just stepped out of the door when Sandra realised she'd forgotten her bag, so she dashed back into the apartment to get it. Five minutes later, she ran back out, tears streaming down her face.

'Oh, Betty,' she sobbed. 'It's awful.'

She looked devastated.

'What is it?' I asked. 'What on earth has happened?'

'The president has been shot,' she wept. 'He's dead, Betty. I heard it on the radio.'

Immediately we ran inside, put the radio back on and listened in stunned silence to the terrible news. I couldn't believe what I was hearing, and I started to cry too. President John F. Kennedy had been on a state visit to Dallas, Texas, when he had been assassinated. They had already caught the culprit – a man called Lee Harvey Oswald. Two days later, while Oswald was being transferred from police headquarters to prison, he was shot and killed by a nightclub owner called Jack Ruby live on television.

I had never been particularly interested in politics, but everyone knew JFK. We had arrived in America just as he had been elected and, as far as I could see, the country had never known a leader like him before. He was young, handsome and charismatic, with two cute children and a beautiful wife, and everyone had seemed full of hope and optimism about what he was going to do for the country. Now he was dead, and it just didn't seem real.

Even for two non-Americans like Sandra and me, the news was shocking and overwhelming. We weren't sure what to do, so we decided to walk into town. Wherever we went that was all people were talking about, and it felt like the whole country had stopped. Traffic had come to a standstill in the streets as people gathered around the cars that had radios to listen to the news. In the city centre, crowds had packed into department stores to watch the television sets. I'll never forget that haunting image of Jackie Kennedy, still wearing the Chanel jacket that was soaked in her dead husband's blood.

Men and women wept openly in the street, while some people prayed. It was as if the whole nation had gone into shock. Everywhere was eerily quiet, apart from the sound of TVs and radios and people whispering to each other, trying desperately to make sense of what had happened. Schools closed early and children were sent home, businesses shut down. The whole country, if not the whole world, was grieving. It was one of those defining moments in history. Everyone can tell you where they were and what they were doing when they heard that the president was dead. I can remember every detail of that day, even down to the chocolate-brown A-line coat with the faux-fur collar and very high heels I was wearing.

A state funeral was held on the following Monday and was broadcast live on television. It was declared a public day of mourning and there were five minutes of silence across the country to mark it. Even though I wasn't American, I found it all so upsetting. Who could fail to be moved by the sight of the president's three-year-old son John Kennedy Junior, whom everyone affectionately called John John, as he stood bravely saluting the coffin of his dead daddy?

Not only had a family lost a husband and a father, and a young, energetic man been murdered in the prime of his life, but the hopes and dreams of a lot of American people had died that day with the president, and it was all so terribly sad.

Chapter Ten

Dangers in the Sky

It had been nine long, gloomy months since the assassination of President Kennedy and the country needed something to boost morale and lift its spirits. That something came in the form of four young men from Liverpool.

When I arrived at San Francisco Airport that day for work, there was total and utter pandemonium. Thousands of young people, mainly screaming girls waving placards and banners, crammed into the arrivals hall along with hundreds of journalists. And the reason for this sheer and utter madness? The Beatles were coming to America.

It was August1964, and the whole place was buzzing. Their Pan Am flight had left London Airport and the Fab Four were due to touch down in California that afternoon. I couldn't believe the crowds as I tried to fight my way through the airport to get to my pre-flight briefing.

I had first heard of the Beatles when I'd gone home on a visit and my cousin Len's wife, Jean, had played me their record, which I'd thought was terrific. Their very first visit to the US had been six months earlier, when they had taken the country by storm. In just a few days, the band had cracked America and 'I Want to Hold Your Hand' had stormed to the top of the charts.

They had also started a new craze for long, shaggy hair amongst the previously clean-cut American men. The press had never seen anything like it before and they loved making fun of their hairstyles, calling them 'shaggy Peter Pans' and describing their 'sheepdog bangs'.

Now the Beatles were back to do their first American tour, kicking it off with a sell-out gig at the Cow Palace in San Francisco.

Unfortunately I was working, so I couldn't go and see them perform, but just witnessing the spectacle at the airport was exciting enough. The atmosphere was electric as I tried to fight my way through the mobs of hysterical teenage girls to check in for the crew briefing for my flight. I heard later that the cleaners sent on board after their 707 had landed had gone through the ashtrays, picked up the Beatles' cigarette butts and sold them for hundreds of dollars.

I loved their music, but the Beatles also struck a deeper chord with me. They were from very ordinary, working-class backgrounds, just like I was, and it reinforced the idea that you didn't have to have attended the best schools, gone to university or speak with a cut-glass British accent to achieve success or do something with your life.

A bit like the Beatles, I really felt I was living the dream in America. I was still enjoying my work – well, all except one part of it. Safety training had continued to be the bane of my life, even though it was probably the most necessary part of being a stewardess. Every six months we had to do a refresher course and if you failed, you would be taken off the payroll and grounded until you passed. Our supervisor always told us, in no uncertain terms, 'If you want to keep working for Pan Am, you have to pass this course.'

So there was a lot of pressure, knowing that your whole career was riding on it. Much to my horror, it was even more harrowing in San Francisco than in New York, as we had to do it in the sea rather than a swimming pool. They put an old aircraft on floats in the Bay, and we would all sit on board, like we were on a normal flight, until the captain shouted, 'Abandon!' They would even pump smoke into the plane to make it more realistic. Even though I knew it was only a practice, it was terrifying, and my heart was always thumping as I scrambled onto one of the life rafts.

Even by the mid-1960s, flying was still relatively new, and a lot of people falsely believed that it was very dangerous. So much so, you could even buy life insurance at the airport. There were special dispensers where you filled out a form, inserted some coins into a slot and out came a policy, which you could then put in the nearest post box to send to your family before you boarded your flight. I always found it amusing when passengers gave a round of applause when the plane landed, as if it was such a surprise and a relief to them that we had all survived and touched down safely.

But even though I was aware of any problems that could occur, I knew that statistically they were very rare. In fact, in the 1980s, long after I had hung up my wings, I helped out at a 'fearful flying' course that a retired Pan Am captain used to run. His opening line of the seminar was always: 'I was going to drive up here today, but then I realised it's twenty-five times safer to fly on a commercial jet than drive my own car from Florida.'

I have heard that during the 1950s and 1960s, fatal accidents occurred around once every 200,000 flights, but today airline safety is so much better, mainly because there have been so many advances in the technology used in the cockpit and there is high-tech equipment like satellite navigation systems. I believe that fatal accidents now occur less than once in every two million flights. That sort of statistic really puts it into perspective, but it still doesn't stop some people being absolutely petrified of flying.

During my career, when I questioned passengers, they often said they were afraid because they were not in control, unlike when they were driving a car. My advice to people is to always pay attention to the safety demonstration, even if you're a frequent flyer, as each aircraft is different. I always do and I also make sure that I count how many rows there are to my nearest exit, so even in thick smoke, I would know exactly where to get out.

Thankfully, in the whole of my career, I never once experienced an emergency landing or had to pull the slides out. Sometimes the oxygen masks had come down, not because of a lack of oxygen, but accidentally, because of turbulence.

Even though I was properly trained, it didn't stop me feeling frightened every so often, and I never quite got used to the severe turbulence we would experience on some flights. There were some scary times during the monsoon season, when we would be coming out of the Far East. It was always at night, so it was dark, and there were thick, heavy clouds all around us and the plane would be lurching all over the sky. Sometimes we would be rocking and rolling all the way across the Pacific.

It was only natural that the passengers would get worried. A lot of them were Catholic and they would get out their rosary beads and start praying out loud in the cabin, or occasionally people would start to cry. I would try to go round and reassure them, but if it was very bad, we would have to be strapped into our seats too. I was often on the back jump seat in the tail of the plane, facing the opposite way to everyone else, and I couldn't see a thing out of the tiny window next to me. Even as an experienced flyer, it was still very scary. I would be all alone back there and the tail of the plane would be swinging around the sky. It was noisy too. Sometimes I could swear that there was someone banging on the door trying to get in, it was that loud.

Things would fly out of the overhead compartments and sometimes the plane would drop so sharply, it would make your stomach lurch. You could always guarantee that at the worst point, there would be some silly passenger ringing his bell, expecting you to get him a whisky. I had heard about flights where the turbulence had been so bad, stewardesses were bounced off the ceiling and had been seriously injured. So if I did have to get up to see to a passenger, I always made sure I clung on to the top of the seats for dear life.

Even on the very turbulent flights, we would still have to do a meal service, which was always a challenge. On many occasions, I wouldn't be able to take the drinks trolley out, because there was too much of a risk that the glasses and bottles would smash, and scrambling eggs for breakfast was always tricky if it was bumpy. I found turbulence particularly hard, as it often made me feel sick, especially if I was working in the back galley, as that moved around the most. So in between scrambling eggs, I would be in and out of the toilet or chewing on a dry bread roll, as that always helped. Thankfully, over time, my airsickness did subside, but it took a good year.

Mimi and I were once on a terribly rough flight from Tokyo to Honolulu. We were both working in coach class at the back of the plane and were trying to serve the passengers a type of cold soup called vichyssoise. Mimi was walking down the aisle with a tray of bowls when the plane lurched violently. I watched in horror as the tray flew into the air, hit Mimi on the head, almost knocking her out, and then all three bowls of cold soup came down over some unsuspecting passenger's head.

'Oh my goodness,' Mimi gasped. 'I'm so sorry, sir.'

The poor fellow was covered from top to toe in vichyssoise, but his ordeal was just beginning. The next thing I knew, Mimi had whipped off his shirt, washed it in one of the basins in the toilets and then hung it out near the ovens to dry. Then, much to my amusement, she proceeded to make him a shirt out of a pile of linen napkins from first class, using safety pins to attach them all together. The poor man was just sat there with a puzzled look on his face, while Mimi fashioned him this bizarre-looking homemade shirt, not knowing whether to laugh or cry.

'There you go,' she told him. 'You would never know what had happened.'

But most of the time turbulence wasn't in the least bit funny and I learnt techniques to keep myself calm. If it was a really bumpy flight and I was feeling anxious, I would sit on the back jump seat, let my arms hang down by my sides, take deep breaths and try to make my body go completely limp.

I will always remember the flight from Los Angeles to London when I got talking to an elegant older lady. We were chatting about the job and the stresses and the strains, and I told her that I still hadn't got used to bumpy flights. I could tell she was a wealthy lady and a frequent flyer, and she said, 'Whenever I fly and it gets a bit rough, I picture myself as a seagull floating on the air currents at Pacific Palisades Beach in LA. I just close my eyes and imagine I'm relaxing my wings and I let myself be carried gently along by the current.'

I thought it was such a lovely, calming image and it stayed with me throughout my career. Whenever I had a bad flight, I would close my eyes and imagine I was that seagull, being pulled along by the breeze, and it really helped to reassure me.

I certainly needed something to relax me after a flight in September 1964, during the monsoon season. It was night time when we took off from Manila and there was already a ferocious storm brewing. I was strapped in the jump seat at the back of the plane when suddenly I saw a flash of bright light and something zigzag down the blue carpet in the middle of the plane. Oh my goodness, we'd been hit by lightning!

But by the time I had registered what it was, it had already gone.

'What was that?' I heard some of the passengers whisper. 'Did you see it?'

But I didn't tell them and, thankfully, it hadn't done any damage. I was really shocked, as most airplanes have small prongs coming off the wings and tail, known as static discharge wicks, which are there to deflect lightning, so it was really unusual that it had come inside the aircraft.

But perhaps the most dangerous and frightening incident in my career happened later the same year. I was flying from Tokyo to Honolulu and we were four hours into the seven-hour flight when the captain called the purser into the cockpit. When she came out, I knew immediately by the serious look on her face that something had happened. I felt sick to my stomach as she gathered all of the stewardesses together at the back of the plane. Then, in hushed tones, she told us there was a potential emergency situation unfolding on board.

'The captain has just informed me that two of our four engines have failed and he is worried the same fault could affect the last two,' she said.

Worryingly, neither the pilot nor the engineers knew at this stage what the problem was that was causing the malfunction. No one said anything, but I could tell we all felt as uneasy as each other. The possible scenarios ran through my mind. This is where the 'point of no return' comes in. What's now become a common phrase in the English language actually originates from a technical term in air navigation. It refers to the point on a flight which, due to fuel consumption, means that a plane can't return to the airport it took off from. On this particular flight, we were past the point of no return. Once you get beyond that point, you have got to keep going. But we were still three hours from our destination, and the problem with the Pacific is that it's so vast, once you get past the point of no return, there is nowhere to go.

Except for one place. In the northern part of the Pacific was Wake Island. Even though it's called an island, it is actually made up of three little stretches of land in a boomerang shape with a lagoon in the centre. Pan Am flights would occasionally have to stop there to refuel or drop off a passenger, as it was a military base for the American navy. This also meant there were mechanics there, in case any flight experienced a problem.

Thankfully we were almost at Wake Island, otherwise we would have had to make an emergency landing in the sea. Even though we had lost half of our engines, amazingly, the plane didn't feel that different, apart from a little bit more vibration than normal.

We didn't want to alarm any of the passengers by talking about engine failure, so we deliberately kept it vague. The purser made an announcement that due to a 'slight technical problem' we would have to land on Wake Island. It took us forty-five minutes to get there and, believe you me, it felt like the longest three-quarters of an hour of my life. As the plane touched down safely on the ground, I breathed a huge sigh of relief.

Wake Island is a very desolate place and there's hardly anything there except sand and scrubland. In the 1940s the USA built an air and naval base there, as well as barracks, and there was also a little chapel. So while the mechanics attended to our plane, I walked across the tarmac to the chapel, where I said a silent prayer of thanks that we had survived an engine failure and avoided having to make an emergency ditching into the sea. The island is still used today as a place to land by the US military and some commercial planes, as well as for emergency landings like ours.

After a frightening experience like that, I must admit that I did think to myself: 'Why am I doing this?' I vowed that when I finally got off that plane in Honolulu , I was never getting on another one again.

But I went and powdered my nose, put on my gloves and hat and said goodbye to the passengers. Then I walked off the aircraft into the beautiful Hawaiian sunshine and I thought, 'Why was I worried? It's fine. I survived.' Amazingly, I forgot about it in an instant.

In the winter of 1964 there was sad news from England. One morning I received a letter from Mum telling me that Nana Eden had passed away after being admitted to hospital with a broken hip. They had suspected that I wouldn't be able to have any time off to come home for the funeral, so by the time I got the letter, poor Nana had already been laid to rest. Even though Nana had been hard to cope with in her old age, I felt very sad for Dad and his brothers Jim and Bert and his sister Cathy.

In her will, Nana had split all of her possessions between Dad and his surviving siblings – their brother Ed had died years before I was born. I knew Mum and Dad were worried because that included Nana's house, where they were still living and which had been valued at £1600. My parents had given up their council house years ago and there was no way they could afford to pay Dad's sister and brothers £400 each for their share of Nana's house, so they faced the prospect of having to sell it and look for somewhere else to live. Dad was in his early sixties by now and had stopped working, so I knew they were worried about how they were going to survive and where they were going to spend their retirement.

Ever since I'd started working for Pan Am, I'd been paid a pretty good salary that I hardly had to touch most of the time because I was away on trips. Now I had just over $3000 sat there in the bank. It was the most money that I'd ever had in my life and I had been puzzling over what to do with it for months. Now suddenly I had the answer.

On my next visit home, I handed Dad an envelope with a cheque inside for £1200.

'What's this, Tink?' he said, with a shocked look on his face.

'It's for you, Dad,' I told him. 'It's so you can pay off your brothers and sister and keep Nana's house.'

But Dad had always been a proud man and I knew it would take a lot of persuasion to get him to accept the money. True to form, he handed it straight back to me.

'Absolutely no way,' he said. 'She can't do that, can she, Ruby?'

Mum just looked completely stunned.

'Yes, I can,' I told him. 'Otherwise it will just be sat in the bank and I'll still be worrying about what to do with it.'

'I can't take it,' Dad said.

'Please, I'm begging you,' I replied, pressing the cheque back into his hand. 'More than anything in the world, I want you and

Mum to have this money, to say thank you for all you have done for me.'

Dad was so choked up, he was speechless. Mum had tears running down her face as she threw her arms around me.

'Oh, Betty,' she said. 'Thank you.'

My parents had never owned their own home before, and I knew it meant the world to them. Dad had never earned huge amounts of money and they'd always lived in council houses or rented properties, and having that security meant so much to them. It felt wonderful for me to be able to do this.

Each little thing I could do – like taking them on holiday and coming up with this bit of money, helped to justify the fact that I had left them to come over to America.

The money really did make a huge difference to their lives and eased them of any financial worries in their retirement. They stayed in Nana's house for another decade and then moved to a nice bungalow in Woodford Green that they were able to buy outright because of the profit they had made from selling Nana's house. My parents were always grateful for that helping hand, although we didn't talk about it after that. It's not something I went round telling people – in fact, I don't think even my brother Geoffrey knew – but it's one of the things that I'm most proud of in my life. It was a chance for me to show my parents just how much they meant to me and how grateful I was to them.

Now Mum and Dad were nicely settled, and the same could be said for many of my fellow Pan Am stewardesses. One by one, the girls were getting married and leaving the company in order to become wives and mothers. Angie was the first when she walked down the aisle with Mike Marini, and she left almost immediately to become a housewife. Then Sandra and Jim tied the knot and she resigned from Pan Am too. Angela finally married

Charlie Blue Eyes, the pilot she had been dating since she left the UK, and they moved to Arizona, where he had been transferred. It wasn't long before Hazel married her boyfriend Gary, and then Janet Brown walked up the aisle with Derek, a British engineer.

I was pleased for the girls, but I knew marriage was a long way off for me. None of my friends or my parents ever expressed concern about the fact that I wasn't engaged or married yet. I think Mum always secretly hoped that I would meet a nice British chap and come home to live.

'Would you like to get married?' Sandra asked me one day.

'I would,' I said. 'Just not right now. I'm happy for you girls, I really am, but I love working and having a career. There's plenty of time for me to settle down.'

'What does Chuck think about it?' she asked, but I just shrugged.

Chuck and I had been dating for over a year now. I suppose I was a bit of a coward when it came to discussing the future, and I didn't want to hurt his feelings. Whenever he tried to talk about our relationship and where it was going, I would successfully change the subject.

'I love you, Chuck,' I would tell him. 'And I enjoy spending time with you.'

I'd only been a stewardess a few years, and I felt like there was still so much more for me to see and do. I didn't want to have to give all that up to get married and run a home.

At first Chuck had been quite accepting of my job and the fact that I was away a lot, but over time, he had got more and more fed up with it.

'You're hardly ever here, Betty, and we don't have much time together,' he complained.

'I'm sorry,' I said. 'But you know that's the nature of my job. I have a few days at home, then I'm off again.'

I just wasn't sure if he was the man I wanted to spend the rest of my life with.

Then fate stepped in to make a decision for me.

One night Chuck took me out for dinner. 'I've got some news,' he said. 'My company is transferring me to New York.'

'Oh,' I said, surprised. 'When?'

'I have to leave as soon as I can,' he said.

It was a shock and I was sad to see Chuck go, but I knew this would be a good test of our relationship.

'I'll miss you, Betty,' he told me.

'I'll fly over and see you whenever I can,' I said. 'And we can talk on the phone.'

As the weeks passed, Chuck and I called each other as much as we could. But with him working long hours in the week and me spending most of my time in the air, it was difficult for us both to be at home at the same time to chat. It was nigh on impossible for either of us to find the time to fly out to see each other and, as the months went by, the phone calls started to fizzle out.

At first we would speak once a week, then it was once a month. There was no emotional goodbye or difficult conversation, but soon I realised it had been weeks since we had spoken, and eventually we lost touch altogether. Six months after he had moved to New York, I heard on the grapevine that Chuck had got engaged to an American Airlines stewardess. To tell you the truth, I was a little bit miffed that he had moved on so quickly, but I knew in my heart that it meant that he wasn't the right man for me

'I suppose if she works on domestic flights, she would be around a little bit more than I was,' I sighed to Hazel.

'It just proves that you weren't right for each other,' she said.

I was friends with a couple of English Pan Am stewardess,

twins called Jill and Jo Holland. Jo was dating a doctor from the local naval hospital, Brad, and when she heard about Chuck, she insisted on matchmaking me with one of Brad's friends.

'There's a doctor who would love to meet you,' she said.

He was called Bob Searcy and he was originally from Kansas but was doing an internship at the hospital. I had nothing to lose, so I agreed to go on a double date with her, Brad and Bob. My first impressions weren't great. He seemed a very studious, serious character, and was short and wore horn-rimmed spectacles.

'He's a bit geeky,' I whispered to Jo.

'Give him a chance,' she said. 'He's a lovely man.'

I wasn't sure if we had much in common, but Bob seemed kind and chatty, and when he asked me out, I accepted.

A couple of nights later he picked me up and took me to a pokey little club in the centre of San Francisco called the Library. Suddenly loud rock and roll music started blaring out and Bob whipped off his tweed jacket.

'Come on, Betty,' he yelled over the music. 'Let's show them how it's done.'

Much to my surprise, he pulled me onto the dance floor and started to go wild to the music. He was the most fantastic dancer.

'You certainly know how to move,' I said.

'I like to strut my stuff,' he said, beads of sweat dripping down his face.

I loved dancing too, and Bob would take me to hidden little clubs around San Francisco. Rock and Roll had inspired all sorts of dance crazes, like the Mashed Potato, the Fly, the Hully Gully and the most popular one of all, the Twist.

My relationship with Bob was fun more than anything serious and when he was transferred back to Kansas, I ended up dating another medical student, Graham Kretchman.

Even though most of my peers had now left Pan Am to get married and have children, I enjoyed my job and was keen to progress. Ambition was still seen as a rare quality for a woman in the 1960s to have, but it had always been my plan to become a purser and, in late 1964, I was delighted to get promoted. Although I'm not one to brag about my own achievements, I was very pleased with myself, as San Francisco was such a large base and I was the first one from my course to make purser.

It was an important role, as the purser was the manager in charge of the cabin. It was their job to make all the announcements over the tannoy, assign where the crew worked, oversee the meal service and the bar, and fill and clear the aircraft with customs at foreign ports.

You were invited to apply for the position, then you did a day-long course and took an exam at the end of it. If you were successful, you would be on probation until you passed a check flight, where you were assessed by a supervisor. As part of your application, your superiors would also look through your file. This was the record of your work with Pan Am and contained reports from staff members and details of any incidents, such as failing a grooming check or going over your required weight, as well as letters of commendation from passengers.

In the 1960s people were often so impressed by the service and the level of care and attention we would give them that they would put pen to paper to thank us personally. At the front of the plane there was always Pan Am letter-headed paper, envelopes and pens, and some people would write to their friends or family members and we would post it for them at our next port. Often they would write to us too and say thanks for a great flight. Our superiors would send us copies of letters that came in from grateful passengers and I've still got many of them today.

I took great pride in my work and it always meant so much when someone took the time to write and thank me. Can you imagine that happening now? Not very often, that's for sure. But even in this day and age, if I have been on a flight and seen great customer service, I will always make sure I find out the person's name and I make a point of writing to the airline.

I was so looking forward to starting my new role. Little did I know that something was going to happen on one of the first flights that I was in charge of that would haunt me for the rest of my career.

Chapter Eleven

Problem Passengers

I was extremely excited about becoming a purser, but also very nervous. One of the first trips I was in charge of was a round-the-world flight that I was picking up in Bangkok and taking on to Hong Kong and then Tokyo. As I walked out of the airport onto the tarmac, I could see the incoming crew coming towards us, and before they cleared customs, we had a brief moment to chat.

'Are you the purser?' one of the cockpit engineers asked.

'Yes, I am,' I said proudly.

'Well, just to let you know, there's a rhinoceros in the hold and he needs bread, milk and sugar every two hours.' he said. 'He's on his way to Seattle Zoo.'

'Oh, yes, of course,' I smiled.

Did he think that I was born yesterday? *A rhino in the hold?* How ridiculous! I knew when someone was taking me for a ride and I suspected it was a trick, like the ones pilots played on new stewardesses. Someone had obviously told him that I was a newly qualified purser and he was having a great laugh at my expense. Well, I wasn't a wide-eyed stewardess anymore and I certainly wasn't going to fall for it this time.

'I'm not stupid. I know when someone's pulling my leg,' I told the engineer.

'It's no joke, miss. Go down there and see for yourself,' he said, before walking off.

Even though I was convinced it was a prank, as we boarded the plane, something niggled at me. I gestured to one of the stewardesses, a girl called Jackie Chung, to come over.

'I know this sounds rather silly,' I said. 'But would you mind checking in the hold, just to see if there is a rhinoceros down there?'

Poor Jackie looked a bit surprised, but off she trotted. I was sure she was going to come back and tell me it was all a joke, but she returned ten minutes later with a stunned look on her face.

'Well?' I asked.

'You were right, Betty,' she said. 'I didn't believe it at first, but there's a huge rare white rhino down there. I've never seen anything like it.'

'Good grief,' I sighed.

Of all the situations I had expected to have to deal with when I became a purser, this was not one of them. Jackie informed me that there was a man tending to the beast, which thankfully was tethered up. I still didn't have a clue what they were doing in the hold, and who had allowed it in the first place, but the passengers were about to board, so I had other things to think about. We were filled to the gills that day and there was a big tour group in first class. In fact the flight was so busy, there wasn't one empty seat, and four of the ladies from the tour group had to sit in the first-class lounge. On busy flights they were classed as assigned seats, as they had seatbelts.

The first leg of the journey, from Bangkok to Hong Kong, was only three hours long, which didn't leave us much time to prepare, serve and clear a seven-course meal service. So as soon as we took off, I got the trolley set up and started preparing the first-class hors d'oeuvres. I headed to the first-class lounge to serve the four elderly ladies first, and I was quite pleased, as I was managing the tricky business of silver service. It was all going swimmingly and I was just serving out the caviar, when suddenly there was a loud noise and the cockpit door burst open to reveal the scruffiest man I had ever seen. He had an unkempt beard, was wearing dirty jeans and was holding a smelly, filthy bucket.

'Need to get rid of rhino slop,' he grunted.

I realised, with horror, that he must have climbed up the ladder from the hold, which came up at the rear of the cockpit. But before I had time to object, he had opened the first-class toilet door and proceeded to tip the contents down the loo. He was making so much noise and swishing around this disgusting bucket of God knows what, that the wealthy, well-dressed women sat in the first-class lounge couldn't fail to notice him. They looked absolutely appalled, their mouths gaping open in disgust, as they watched this spectacle unfold.

But the horror didn't end there. Before I could stop him, he went into the galley, pushed Jackie aside and started tearing the tops off sugar packets with his grubby hands and tipping them into the bucket, obviously meaning to give the rhino a bit of a snack.

At this point, one of the old ladies leaned over and asked me: 'Is that gentleman a crew member?'

'Heavens no,' I said. 'He's just downstairs in the hold looking after the white rhinoceros.'

She didn't believe me, and obviously thought I was being a smart Alec, as she turned to her friend and said, 'How rude!'

I was getting really stressed by this point. I grabbed the grubby man's arm and ushered him towards the cockpit, so he could go back down the ladder to the hold.

'You can't come up here again,' I hissed.

I hadn't got a clue who had given him permission to come on board, but I was pretty sure that transporting a man plus a live rhino in the hold had broken every rule in the Pan Am book.

Thankfully, when we landed at Hong Kong, he didn't emerge again, or on the two-hour journey to Tokyo either. As purser, it was my job to record anything significant that had happened during the flight in the log book for the next crew to see, but what on earth could I say? 'Rhino in the hold. Needs bread, sugar and milk every two hours. The best of luck!' I wrote.

The new crew was already coming on board the aircraft before I left, and one of Pan Am's most senior pursers was in charge that day, a chap called Barney Sewicki. He put on his glasses and was reading the log book when I heard him say, 'Miss Eden, what the devil is this?'

He must have seen my entry about the rhino.

'It's true, Barney, it really is,' I said.

But he obviously didn't believe me, so I shrugged my shoulders and walked off.

I had never been more relieved to get off a flight, and I had no desire to see the rhino or his unsavoury companion ever again. A few days later, I landed in Honolulu on another trip, and I saw that Barney Sewicki was in an outgoing crew. He waved at me in customs.

'You were right about that rhino, Miss Eden,' he shouted.

'I told you,' I smiled.

It certainly wasn't funny at the time, but that story followed me all through my Pan Am career. I'd be at a crew party or on a layover and someone would say, 'Aren't you the purser who had the rhino on board?'

I found out later that each of the two captains who had allowed the man and the rhino to travel in the hold as a favour to someone had been fined $1600 each, which was a great deal of money in those days. Apparently the man had tried to bring one over before, to sell to the zoo, but the poor thing had died because no one was allowed to sit with it in the hold and feed it.

Rhinos were not the only animals that caused problems on board some of my flights. The restrictions were very relaxed in those days and domestic animals were allowed in the hold. Sometimes snakes or birds would get loose and the pilot would send an engineer down from the cockpit with a flashlight to sort it out. Whenever we had dogs in the hold and we stopped for a few hours, I would go and check on them. It was so cold and dark down there and I always felt really sorry for them.

Passengers were even permitted to take animals on the flight with them, which often caused chaos. You were allowed up to a maximum of two animals per cabin and they had to be able to fit into a carrier that was small enough to go under the seat but still had enough room for the pet to turn round in, so mainly it was small dogs, cats and birds who would travel this way.

On one flight from the Far East, a lady had brought her two Siamese cats along. We had just finished the meal service and I'd turned off the lights so the passengers could get some sleep, when I heard a commotion coming from the last row in coach class, where she was sitting.

'My cats,' she sobbed. 'They've gone.'

'What do you mean by "gone"?' I asked.

'I let them out of the cage for some fresh air, but they've run off,' she said.

There was only one thing for it. Another stewardess and I got on our hands and knees and tried to find these blooming cats. The passengers must have wondered what on earth we were doing, crawling around on the floor in the dark.

'Here, kitty, kitty,' I whispered.

There was so sign of them at first, but when we heard a scream coming from the first-class cabin, we knew we had finally found our escape artists. The intrepid pussies had gone all the way to the front of the plane, startling sleeping passengers by brushing up against their legs. Thankfully they were soon safely back in their cage and their mistress was under strict instructions not let them out again.

Another time, an elegant Oriental lady was travelling with her beloved mynah bird, whom she called Mr Timmy. On that particular flight, we were due to stop at Wake Island, so she brought the cage out onto the tarmac and I was puzzled when I saw her open the cage door and let the bird fly off. When it came to getting back on the plane half an hour later, she point-blank refused.

'I'm not going anywhere until Mr Timmy comes back,' she said.

Of course we all knew that the bird had flown off for good and wasn't coming back, but the poor lady was distraught.

'I was just letting him out for some fresh air, like I do at home, and he always comes back then,' she wept.

It took a lot of persuading before she would get back on the plane and she spent the rest of the flight sobbing in her seat, clutching the empty cage.

It wasn't just the passengers who brought animals on board either. One day we were checking into the Royal Manor Hotel in Honolulu when I heard a strange rustling coming from one of the little trees by reception. Much to my surprise, when I pulled back the leaves, there was a little monkey looking back at me.

'What on earth?' I gasped.

'Oh, don't worry, he's mine,' said another Pan Am stewardess, who was checking out on her way to the airport.

She explained that she had bought him in Manila and was taking him back to the US to keep as a pet.

'I've had a word with the captain and he said it's OK for me to bring the little chap on board,' she said. It was certainly the most unusual souvenir I had ever seen!

It wasn't only animals who caused me problems. There were plenty of misbehaving human passengers too. The US Merchant Marines had a clause in their contract that said they could travel first class to get to their vessels when they had a foreign posting, and unfortunately it meant that we got some really shabby fellows on board. You had to be careful with the seamen and the free alcohol, as they could get quite rowdy. I remember one sailor who insisted on taking off his smelly socks and shoes and resting his grotty feet on the seat in front of him. I had to have a quiet word with him and he got quite bolshie.

'I'm entitled to be in first class as much as anyone else,' he shouted.

'Well, that's fine,' I told him. 'But please take your feet off the seats. You don't see anyone else doing that.'

Unfortunately, from time to time, there were some creepy men who wouldn't leave the stewardesses alone. If a passenger was getting a bit over-friendly, I quickly learnt ways to deflect it. I would just smile or turn it into a joke, or if it was getting too much, disappear to the other end of the airplane. The stewardesses would stick together and the girls would warn each other if a passenger was getting a bit frisky.

'Keep your eyes on row 13F,' someone would whisper as we passed in the aisle, or '12B, wandering hands'.

We would always try to knock it on the head before it got serious. If a passenger was very persistent and we really did feel threatened, we would get the cockpit crew involved. I remember one stewardess telling me how a respectable-looking businessman had cornered her in the back galley, but thankfully most of the men I came across were well behaved.

Pan Am girls were generally seen as quite aloof and almost untouchable, unlike some of the other airlines at the time, whose stewardesses promoted a much sexier image. The girls who worked for Pacific Southwest Airlines (PSA) wore brightly coloured mini–dresses, and by the end of the sixties, their uniform consisted of hot pants and go-go boots. One of their adverts featured a photo of the stewardesses posing raunchily in their uniforms, with the cheeky caption: 'PSA gives you a lift.'

In the 1960s Braniff International Airways hired Italian designer Emilio Pucci to design new uniforms and he came up with patterned mini–dresses, as well as a bizarre-looking space-bubble helmet to protect the stewardesses' hair when they got off the plane! We found their get-ups very amusing and it made us very grateful that we worked for Pan Am.

I couldn't believe how suggestive some of these uniforms and adverts were and I thought those stewardesses were really leaving themselves open to all sorts of behaviour from male passengers. By the late 1960s, airlines were really sexing up their image, and National Airlines had a whole advertising campaign which used pictures of the stewardesses saying: 'Hi, I'm Kim, fly me' or 'Hi, I'm Diane, fly me.'

It sounds terribly big-headed now, but us Pan Am stewardesses used to look down our noses at those other airlines. We

used to call them 'Pan Am dropouts', as we knew everyone
applied to work with our airline first.

With free alcohol on board our flights, we always had to be
vigilant and make sure the passengers didn't overindulge too
much, but occasionally one would slip through the net. One day
I was working on a flight from Honolulu to Tokyo and there was
a passenger on board called Mr Johnson. He looked like a typ-
ical respectable businessman, but before long, I realised he had
completely overdone it on the Whisky Sours.

One of the stewardesses came to see me in the first-class
galley. 'I think Mr Johnson's rather intoxicated,' she said. 'He's
taken his trousers off and is refusing to put them back on
again.'

'Good Lord,' I said.

I looked down the aisle to see him staggering out of his seat
in just his shirt, tie and tight white briefs.

'Come here, you pretty little thing, and get me another drink,'
he slurred.

'Mr Johnson, please go and put your trousers back on and sit
down,' I told him politely. 'I don't think the other passengers
want to see you in this state of undress.'

'I'm not putting my trousers on until I get another drink,' he
roared, before stumbling over.

'Pan Am will not tolerate this kind of behaviour,' I told him
firmly. 'Now please go and sit down, sir.'

'Oooh,' he mocked. 'Go home and put your curlers in. Don't
you tell me what I can and can't do. Now get me another
Scotch.'

That was it. As far as I was concerned, he had well and truly
overstepped the mark and it was time to call for extra help. So
I did what we were told to do in these situations and informed
the cockpit. The captain sent the burly first officer to give Mr

Johnson a good talking to, but he wouldn't calm down and was still refusing to put his trousers back on.

'Unfortunately we are going to have to drop you off at Wake Island, where you can stay until you dry out,' the first officer told him.

To say Mr Johnson wasn't happy about that would be an understatement. But the first officer kept to his word and when we landed, he was marched off to the military barracks to sleep it off. And he certainly had plenty of time to sober up.

'When's the next flight to Tokyo?' I asked the first officer.

'In three days,' he grinned.

Mr Johnson was going to wake up with one heck of a hang-over and I was sure that he wasn't going to be happy about being seventy-two hours late for his meeting. A week later I happened to be on the same plane that had picked him up from Wake Island, and there was a note from the purser in the log book. 'Collected a Mr Johnson who was removed from a previous flight for being highly intoxicated. I am pleased to report that we did not hear a peep from him for the duration of the journey.' I bet they didn't!

It wasn't just the men who were sometimes badly behaved either. On one flight from Honolulu to Los Angeles there was a wealthy woman in her fifties in first class. She was travelling with a very good-looking man who was in his thirties and was obviously her toy boy. She spent the whole flight giggling and canoodling with him, and they ordered endless amounts of Dom Perignon.

'More Champagne, please,' she kept asking, and the stewardesses were constantly filling her glass.

'Oh, Blanche,' I heard him say. 'You really know how to spoil me.'

But when we landed in LA, her toy boy called us over. 'I don't think my lady friend is very well,' he said.

The woman had drunk so much, she was literally passed out cold in her seat, and none of us could rouse her.

'I'll go get the smelling salts and we can try that,' I said.

In the onboard first aid kit, we had an ammonia inhalant which was used to bring someone round if they felt dizzy or had fainted. We wafted it under the inebriated woman's nose, but even that wasn't enough to rouse her from her drunken stupor. Much to her toy boy's disgust, we had to call for assistance from the ground crew, and she was eventually carted off in a wheelchair.

Other times, it was a clash of cultures that caused problems with some international passengers. Many Japanese men would get on the plane and immediately take their suit trousers off, fold them up and hand them to us to hang up, as they didn't want them to get creased on the long journey. But I couldn't let them sit there in their tighty whities, as I called them, for all and sundry to see. This was Pan Am and I couldn't let anyone go trouserless, for fear of upsetting the other passengers.

Another time, I got a shock when I opened the door of the toilet at the back of the plane to find a Vietnamese fellow standing on the loo seat with his legs akimbo, having a wee. He wasn't used to Western toilets, because in his country the loo was literally a hole in the ground. It certainly gave us both a shock. I let out a little yelp of surprise and quickly slammed the door.

Sadly, one passenger that I will always remember is the poor man who died during one of my flights from Honolulu to Los Angeles. He was a very elderly gentleman in a wheelchair and when he came on board, I could see he was extremely frail. I felt sad that he was travelling alone, and he had all his documents around his neck on a string.

I was the purser in coach class that day, but halfway into the five-hour flight, the purser in first class called me up to the galley.

'Oh, Betty, the old man in the wheelchair has died,' she said. 'What are we going to do?'

We were both panicked and, I must admit, I was very scared, as I'd never had to deal with a dead body before.

'Are you sure?' I asked.

'I couldn't wake him, so I checked his pulse several times and there was no response,' she told me.

As discreetly as I could, I went to see the man, who was slumped in the window seat in the front row of first class. He was very pale and had dribble coming out of his mouth, and I just knew instinctively that he had passed away. Very gently, I covered him with a blanket, then we went and informed the captain.

There were only four rows in first class and, thankfully, it was relatively empty that day. The other passengers must have known what was going on, but they were all very discreet about it.

'He's in the best place,' the captain told us. 'There's no point trying to move him until we get to LA.'

He radioed ahead for emergency assistance and as soon as we landed, a team of paramedics came on board before any of the passengers were allowed off the plane. The poor man was declared dead and was carried off on a stretcher, while ground staff tried to trace his relatives. It was all very sad and is something I will never forget.

Unfortunately the men on the ground were causing me as many problems as the men in the air. By 1965, I was dating a

marine called Raymond Sellick. I had met him on a layover in
Okinawa, a Japanese island, where he was stationed. A purser
named Lynn was dating another marine and we ended up
there on St Patrick's night. Lynn's boyfriend, Ritchie, asked if
she could bring some stewardesses with her as dates for the
other marines at a dinner which was being held at the Bachelor
Officer Club.

I got all dressed up in a pink silk shift dress and I was paired
up with Ray. He wasn't the most handsome man I had ever
seen, but there was something I really liked about him, and we
got on well. He was quite chunky, a bit like a big teddy bear, but
he was a nice, kind fellow and I thought we really clicked. After
that weekend, we wrote to each other for a few months, and I
was pleased when he was transferred to Camp Pendleton near
San Diego. In November 1965 he invited me to the Marine
Corps Ball.

'Are there a couple of gals you can bring with you?' he asked,
as he had two roommates who didn't have dates, as they were
just back from overseas duty.

So I invited Jan and Brenda, who I was living with at the time.
But Brenda wasn't really keen on the idea.

'Oh, Betty, we're not going to be fixed up with them, are we?'
she said.

'No,' I told her. 'It's just a chance to put on a nice dress and
have some dinner and a dance.'

They agreed to come, and we decided to fly down and got $3
tickets with Pacific Southwest Airlines. They were so cheap
because they were space-available tickets, which meant that
every time the plane stopped, we had to get off and could only
get back on again if there was room. Normally the flight
between San Francisco and San Diego would take just over an
hour, but we stopped six times in various cornfields and military

bases, so it took us six long hours. We had all been to the hairdresser's that morning for a shampoo and set, but because they only turned one propeller off when we stopped, the other one was still whipping up a storm. So by the time we got there, all three of us were exhausted and had hair that looked like toilet brushes.

Thankfully the marines didn't seem to notice that our hair looked like we'd had an electric shock. Ray introduced us to his friends – a quiet, gentle man called Pat McHenry and John Morris, a tall, handsome guy with a warm Southern accent. Well, as soon as Brenda clapped eyes on John, the pair were chatting and laughing away.

'So much for not being fixed up!' I joked to Jan.

It meant that Jan and Pat were pushed together, but unfortunately that wasn't a successful match. They were both such quiet people, there was hardly any conversation between them. But Ray and I got on like a house on fire and by the end of the night, I had a good feeling about him.

'I really think he could be someone special,' I told Brenda excitedly.

Meanwhile, she and John started dating too. Ray and I wrote to each other and Brenda and I devised a plan to make sure we would see them again, so we organised a party at our apartment and invited them to come up. I got all dressed up in one of my tailor-made silk shift dresses, and I couldn't wait to see Ray again. But as the evening went on, I couldn't put my finger on it, but I just had the feeling that he wasn't as interested as I was.

After the party, I wrote to him a few times, but whenever I invited him up, he said he was busy. The communication between us gradually petered out, and as much as I hated to admit it, Ray just obviously wasn't that keen on me. The rejection did sting though, and I was very disappointed.

But Brenda and John were still going strong and when I next saw John, I couldn't resist asking him how Ray was.

'I'm sorry about you and him, Betty,' he told me. 'Ray's parents are strict Roman Catholics, so maybe he thought he should have been dating someone from the same faith?'

I was upset, but I understood. I knew that some families, particularly Catholics, were very old-fashioned and had strict values when it came to their religion, and they would have been horrified if their son had brought home a British Protestant like me. Perhaps John was right and, as far as Ray was concerned, our relationship could never be a serious one, so there was no point continuing to see each other.

In a way it made me feel better that it was about religion. It gave me a reason. It wasn't that Ray didn't like me – he didn't want to let his parents down. It was frustrating but honourable. It was a real blow, and it made me question where I was going, but I'm a very positive person, not the type to mope. I was convinced that one day I would meet someone special, and he would come along when I was least expecting it. I knew I just had to pick myself up and get on with life.

Chapter Twelve

Princes, Pretenders and Pilots

Working for Pan Am, I was used to dealing with celebrities and over the years I had my fair share of stars on board. On the flights coming out of Los Angeles, you would normally spot a famous name on the VIP list that we were given at preflight briefings.

Some had a reputation for being very down to earth and delightful; others were – how shall I say this politely? – a bit trickier. Elizabeth Taylor and Frank Sinatra, for example, were known as very difficult passengers. Warren Beatty, unsurprisingly, was a bit of a ladies' man who liked to flirt with the stewardesses, while Joan Crawford was known to travel with her own cool-box containing a bottle of vodka.

Pan Am's policy was to acknowledge VIPs but not treat them any differently. In fact, I remember one man who was loosely related to the Kennedys, who thought he could use his family connection to sweet-talk his way into getting a free upgrade to first class. Even when I said no, he would not let the matter lie and in the end I had to get the captain involved, to tell him in no uncertain terms that his ticket said coach and that is where he would be sitting.

We were taught to always treat famous people discreetly. Of course everyone knew who they were, but if they didn't want to chat or interact with you, then you respected that and gave them their privacy. Thankfully the other passengers tended to respect that too.

That was definitely the case with the Mamas and Papas, who were on one of my flights from LA to London. It wasn't hard to spot them, as they came on board all dressed in matching chocolate-brown crushed-velvet suits and sunglasses. I must admit, I was a bit worried when I saw the size of Mama Cass. She was a great big mountain of a woman, but thankfully the group was in first class, where the seats were a bit wider. They sat in the last row and didn't say a word to anyone or even each other, so I immediately knew to give them their privacy, and they slept all the way to London.

Other well-known faces were very friendly and loved to chat. On one flight from London to LA, I had the English actor Robert Morley in first class. He'd been in lots of films, like *Oscar Wilde*, *The Young Ones* and *The African Queen*, but he tended to play the pompous Englishman rather than the handsome lead. He was a large, rotund chap in his fifties, with bushy eyebrows, three or four chins and rubbery lips. So he was no oil painting, but he was very friendly and chatted away to the other passengers and stewardesses. After the meal service was over, I sat with him in the first-class lounge.

'Would you like me to show you my party trick, Mr Morley?' I asked.

'Is that sort of behaviour really allowed on Pan Am, dear?' he joked.

'Don't worry, it's just palm reading,' I said.

I grabbed his hand and started to analyse all the lines, just like I had taught myself to do when I had worked for *Prediction* magazine all those years ago.

'The good news is, there's going to be just the one marriage for you,' I teased.

'Well, my wife will be pleased,' he smiled.

He was a lovely man, and one of the nicest stars that I flew with.

Mum, bless her, had the chance to meet her own hero, thanks to Pan Am. One Christmas Day I was working on a flight which was taking Mum back from San Francisco to London, as she had been to visit me. I didn't mind being on duty on Christmas Day. There was always a lovely atmosphere on board and there was roast turkey and crackers and the Champagne flowed freely as usual. As I was the purser and it wasn't a full flight, I managed to upgrade Mum to first class and she was even more delighted to find that her seat was across the aisle from a Hollywood legend.

'It's Cary Grant,' she whispered to me with a big beam on her face.

'I thought you might like that,' I said. 'Merry Christmas.'

Cary was in his sixties by then and was travelling with his wife, the actress Diane Cannon, who was extremely attractive. They were both very friendly and pleasant to all the girls and they even said hello to Mum when I pointed her out to them! It certainly turned out to be a 'merry' Christmas for Cary though. He tucked into the Champagne straight away, and soon he was quite tipsy.

Halfway through the flight, Mum ushered me over. 'Well, he may be a Hollywood star, but he's really annoying me,' she whispered. 'He's so drunk, he keeps dropping his spectacles and I have to keep picking them up.'

Poor Mum was not amused, but she's certainly never forgotten meeting him.

We were also used to politicians and royalty travelling with us, the most memorable being my run-in with a playboy prince on a flight from Honolulu to LA. As we prepared the plane for the passengers, the morning papers came on board and all of the stewardesses crowded around the latest edition of the *Honolulu Star*.

'Have you seen this, Betty?' they said.

The front page of the paper had a story about a Saudi Arabian prince. He was a notorious party animal and playboy, and on this particular trip, it was alleged that he had spent the week holed up in his hotel room with a go-go dancer. It described how the prince was sporting 'a dime-sized diamond on his ring finger' and was going to be leaving Honolulu to go back to the mainland that day.

A few seconds later, one of the ground crew came in. 'Just to let you know, there's an important VIP on board today and he has a large entourage with him,' he said.

As soon as we saw the handsome young man in his long white robes, we all knew straight away it was the prince from the newspaper.

I was working in the first-class galley that day, and I was busy preparing the meal service for the flight when one of his entourage came in. He didn't speak very good English and the only bit I could understand was something about the prince wanting mashed potato.

'I'm dreadfully sorry, sir,' I said. 'But please tell the prince that it's potato croquettes with dinner today.'

The man looked a bit puzzled and shook his head. 'No, no,' he said. 'Prince wants to learn mashed potato.'

Then, much to my amusement, he started to knock his

knees together in a comical fashion. Suddenly the penny dropped.

'Ah,' I smiled. 'You mean the prince wants to learn the Mashed Potato dance?'

'Yes, yes,' the man nodded.

'Well, tell His Royal Highness to come up here and I will see what we can do,' I told him.

He came up to the first-class galley and I gathered all of the stewardesses together.

'The prince would like to know how to do the Mashed Potato,' I told them. 'So come on, girls, let's show him.'

We all stood in a circle and started to do the dance, while the prince watched.

'First, you turn your ankles in and out like this,' I demonstrated. 'Then you slide your feet backwards and forwards and knock your knees together.

'Heaven only knows why it's called the Mashed Potato though,' I laughed breathlessly.

Thanks to my dates with Bob Searcy and the nights we had spent dancing for hours on end in little clubs around San Francisco, I was a dab hand at doing the Mashed Potato and all of the other dances that were fashionable in the 1960s. The prince thought it was hilarious and soon he was joining in with us. God only knows what the other first-class passengers must have thought when they saw us all crowded into the galley, having an impromptu dance with Saudi Arabian royalty.

'His Royal Highness wants to thank you for your help,' said the interpreter afterwards. 'He is now ready to ... how you say? Strut his stuff on the dance floor in LA.'

'It's a pleasure,' I smiled, nodding at the prince.

Soon it was time to land and as the passengers disembarked, I stood by the exit handing them their coats and saying goodbye. As the prince came past, one of his entourage stopped and said, 'His Royal Highness would like to know whether you and the other ladies would like to join him this evening in Los Angeles for some dinner and dancing?'

I was a bit taken aback and wasn't sure what to say. After all, this was a man who was rumoured to have spent the week in a hotel with a go-go dancer and was known as an international playboy. Luckily the captain stepped in.

'I'm afraid these gals have got to get their beauty sleep tonight, as they're leaving for Europe in the morning,' he told him.

The prince looked really ticked off, as I suppose he wasn't used to being turned down. Secretly I was a little bit disappointed too, as part of me thought that dancing the night away with a prince would have been fun.

But soon there was another playboy creating waves amongst the Pan Am staff.

As far as rumours went, it was the most ridiculous one I had ever heard.

'A fake pilot at Pan Am?' I gasped. 'Who on earth would have the gall to do that?'

'Well, somebody has,' said our supervisor. 'And everyone's been told to keep their eyes and ears open to try to catch the rogue.'

It was 1966 and everyone at Pan Am was gossiping about the counterfeit pilot who had been travelling around the world for free on our planes by deadheading on flights. Deadheading was when an off-duty pilot, or any member of the airline crew, could travel for free on any flight. All you needed to do was touch base with the captain and ask if it was OK to hitch a lift on the jump seat (the fold-up spare seat) in the cockpit. It was mainly done when staff lived in one city or state, but needed to start work in another.

None of us could believe the cheek of this imposter, but it was months before he was rumbled. The culprit turned out to be an 18-year-old called Frank Abagnale who, unbelievably, for the past two years, had conned his way onto 250 flights and flown to twenty-six countries after he'd forged a pilot's licence and a fake Pan Am staff pass. Like the rest of us, he had stayed for free in some of the world's top hotels and had all his expenses taken care of. Scarily, he was even invited to take the control of the plane once, while the pilot went to the toilet, but thankfully he'd pressed the autopilot button.

Even though the authorities knew who he was, it was a few more years before the police caught up with him, and that was only after he'd posed as a doctor for a year in Georgia, and then as a lawyer in New Orleans. Abagnale was finally caught in 1969 and was sentenced to twelve years in prison, serving only five after agreeing to help the federal authorities uncover cheque forgers. His exploits were even made into the film *Catch Me if You Can* in 2002, starring Leonardo DiCaprio.

Of course being a pilot is every young boy's dream. Who could forget the scene from that film where Leonardo DiCaprio is strolling through the airport in his Pan Am uniform, with a line of sexy stewardesses hanging on to his arm?

Unfortunately, the reality was a little bit different. Pan Am wanted their pilots to be the best of the best, so most of them were ex-military, which meant they were mostly older men in their forties and fifties. It was more of a paternal relationship between pilots and stewardesses. They looked out for us and generally treated us like you would a niece.

There was no denying they had a fantastic life though, and it was one of the most well-paid jobs in the 1960s. They were on six-figure salaries, which was a massive amount in those days. These fellows lived the life of Riley, as they only worked two weeks out of four, so just about all of them had a second job. I remember one pilot used to trade in pork bellies on the stock exchange; another had an artichoke and avocado farm.

The cockpit was made up of the pilot, who we always addressed as either 'captain' (if we didn't know him that well) or 'skipper' (if we did). He sat on the left-hand side and had four stripes on his uniform. To his right was the first officer, who had three stripes. First officers tended to be a lot younger and were known as captains-in-waiting, and they would take it in turns with the pilot to do landings and take-offs. Then there would be at least one or maybe two engineers in the cockpit. There were never any women in the cockpit. It was well into the 1980s before I came across a female pilot, and I remember being absolutely amazed. Now, thankfully, it's not a rare thing any-more.

Even though the pilots were older and most were married, there were sexual tensions. How could there not be, with crews away on trips together for days and weeks on end? We were all in awe of the captains and even the grey-haired guys looked very handsome and distinguished in their uniforms. They were physically fit too. Every six months, they had to pass a physical examination, so there were definitely no slobs in the cockpit.

Some married pilots had affairs with stewardesses. We were all away such a lot, so they could quite easily lead double lives. But in my experience, it always ended unhappily. I knew several girls who were dating married pilots, so I witnessed for myself the damage that these illicit relationships caused. My friend Jane Fryer dated a married captain for years, and she would always bid to work on the same flights he was on, so they could snatch a bit of time together. They had to keep their relationship hush hush, as it would have been frowned upon.

'He's going to leave his wife and then we can get married,' she always told me, but I was sure he never intended to do that.

I just felt so sorry for Jane. She was such a lovely, kind person and she deserved someone nice in her life. The captain in question was a handsome, respectable-looking man, not the kind you would suspect was doing the dirty on his wife and children. Jane was five years older than me, so I was worried that she was wasting all of her good years on this guy, who I was sure was just stringing her along.

We were all so pleased when she eventually met a passenger on one of her flights who swept her off her feet and she finally ended her relationship with the married captain.

'Oh, Betty, he's such a lovely man,' Jane said of her new beau.

He was a real catch too, by the sounds of it. He was from a family of successful publishers, and he really pursued Jane. Within a few months, he'd met her family back in England and had proposed. He told her to buy an engagement ring that she liked and, as he lived in New York, he would reimburse her on his next visit. So, beside herself with excitement, Jane picked out a beautiful diamond.

But a few weeks later, her dream completely fell apart. It turned out that her new fiancé was a charlatan. He had mental problems, and everything that he'd told her had been a lie. Understandably, poor Jane was completely devastated and sadly I don't think she ever married.

Affairs aside, in reality, a pilot's work was often quite boring. In fact I remember one captain describing his job as 'hours of sheer monotony interspersed with moments of intense panic'. After take-off, a lot of the flight would be quite dull for them. They would sometimes read the paper up there, while the first officer was on duty, mingle with the passengers or walk to the back galley and chat to the stewardesses. Sometimes you would fly with a captain who was known as a sky jockey, a pilot who enjoyed turbulence and bumpy conditions because at least it was a challenge and helped relieve some of the boredom.

On long overnight flights, I would try to keep them company. I would get a big container and put some dry ice into it, tip in some creamers and chopped strawberries, then stir it for ages until it made ice cream. Then I would take some into the cockpit and sit on the jump seat and chat. There was never much room in there, but I loved looking out at the night sky and seeing all the stars. There was something so magical and peaceful about it.

It was in the cockpit one night that one captain told me about his experience of the supernatural.

'I'll never forget that flight,' he told me. 'I had a feeling that something was watching me and when I looked, I saw some bright lights by the left wing. This thing, whatever it was, followed me for a while, then it suddenly did a loop and completely disappeared.'

I listened with wide eyes, completely transfixed. I'd been interested in the supernatural ever since I had worked for *Prediction* magazine all those years ago at Link House Publications.

'There's definitely more life forms out there than we know about,' he said.

After that, I spoke to several captains who were convinced they had witnessed a UFO while they were flying, and I loved hearing their stories. I found it all so fascinating and, to this day, I still believe there is so much out there that we don't know about.

The pilots also found ways to entertain us stewardesses on long trips. One night I had finished the meal service, the lights were dimmed and most of the passengers were asleep as we headed across the Pacific. I was just about to have a sit-down and flick through *Vogue* magazine when I heard the cockpit bell ring.

'Are any of you girls free back there to come and chat to the guys at Ocean Station Victor?' the captain asked over the intercom.

'I'll come and have a chinwag with them,' I offered.

Ocean Stations Victor and November were ex-naval ships that now served as ocean station weather ships in the Pacific. Victor was located midway between Hawaii and Japan and November was halfway between San Francisco and Hawaii. Their main job was to update pilots flying across the Pacific about the weather, as well as providing communication and navigation assistance and helping with search and rescue emergencies. The poor young guys who worked on them had been floating in the sea in the middle of nowhere and hadn't seen a woman for months on end, so it's no wonder they relished the chance of talking to a Pan Am stewardess. We would take it in turns to go and sit in the cockpit and chat to them over the radio.

'What's your name?' the voice asked. 'And what do you look like?'

'Well, I'm Betty Eden and I'm a brunette,' I said.

They would ask us where we had been on trips and what we had done when we were there. They loved chatting us up and I always enjoyed the banter. Of course these ocean stations don't exist anymore because now we have satellite navigation systems.

The other important relationships in a stewardess's working life were those with our passengers, and it wasn't just male passengers. We would often form friendships with all types of people that you would chat to during the flight. On one flight to Hawaii, I got talking to an elderly couple called Jack and Pearl Magowan, who had a holiday home in Honolulu. They were very sweet people and they would always take me out for dinner whenever I was in town.

After the meal service was over, we would spend as much time as possible mingling with the passengers, and even after just one flight with us, people would keep in touch or invite us out. They wanted to socialise with us, and the fact that I was English made me even more appealing. I also made friends with the teenage son and daughter of one of Manila's biggest publishers, who would often fly to California, where they went to college. Whenever Jane and Teddy were at home in Manila, they would send a car to the crew hotel and I would go round to their mansion for a swim and dinner.

But of course a lot of attention that we got was from male passengers.

At that time, Pan Am stewardesses were seen as being on the same level as models and actresses. We were the ultimate trophy girlfriends, and men liked the prestige of having us on their arms and taking us out to dinner. Many of them viewed it as a quick and easy way to find a wife, as they thought that Pan Am had done the hard work for them! The company had already put us through a rigorous screening process and deemed us desirable and attractive enough to work for them. In fact some airlines even advertised the fact that their stewardesses would make the perfect wife. A United Airlines advert in 1967 boasted: 'Everyone gets warmth, friendliness and extra care ... and someone may get a wife.'

It was commonplace to be invited to dinner by a man you had been chatting to when you reached your destination. It was a case of another city, another man. It was normal for us to have

many boyfriends around the world, and there was always someone to take you out for dinner. We got used to being treated to
wonderful meals and being given lovely presents. It was as if
there were different rules for stewardesses. Even if we were
dating someone at home, we would still go out with other men
when we were away with work.

But for most of us girls, it was purely dinner and drinks, no
funny business. There would maybe be a kiss here and there, but
there was definitely no jumping in and out of bed. Promiscuous
behaviour was frowned upon, and we valued our reputation.
Some people are under the impression that Pan Am girls were
like flying Playboy bunnies, but I always put them straight. In
the circles I hung around in, nice girls didn't do that. It was an
unspoken rule, but we all knew that easy girls didn't find husbands.

However, some stewardesses were more forward and didn't
mind who they picked up. There was one stewardess, a voluptuous blonde, who got a bit of a reputation for herself. She
would have dinner with any passenger who asked her, then take
them back to the crew hotel for a night of passion. The rumour
was, if she didn't get lucky with a passenger, she would make
advances towards the stewardess that she was sharing a room
with. Needless to say, none of the girls wanted to be her roommate on trips.

We did have to be careful, particularly in some countries, like
the Philippines. You would check into your hotel and there
would always be sleazy men hanging around in the lobby, looking to take a stewardess out to dinner. They would often pay
staff at the hotel for a crew list and would call all the girls in their
rooms. But we soon got wise to it.

I would be in my room for barely five minutes when the inter-
nal phone would ring.

'Miss Eden, you are the most beautiful woman in the world. Would you like to have dinner with me?' a voice would say.

'No, thank you,' I'd reply politely, before hanging up.

We also had to watch out for married passengers. It was rumoured that some men would remove their wedding rings before they boarded Pan Am flights, so the stewardesses wouldn't know that they were married. They would even use a self-tanning lotion that had just come on the market, Man Tan, to disguise the tell-tale white lines where their rings had been.

But some of the girls didn't mind if they had wives or families. My roommate Pauline was always extremely picky when it came to who she went out with. She was so fussy, she even had a written list of attributes that her perfect partner needed to have, and we often teased her about this. Her requirements meant that her boyfriend had to be wealthy, handsome and a professional who owned his own home. But clearly her list didn't include 'not married' because she dated a couple of married men whom she had met on the plane. She hardly saw them and spent most of her time waiting by the phone for them to call.

One was a top New York financier who wined and dined her and spent lots of money on her. But again, he was never going to leave his wife, so Pauline was left heartbroken. Her next relationship was with a handsome blond lawyer who was also married, but she was devastated when he broke it off.

Pauline did get her happy ending though, many years later, when she married an army officer who was thirty years older than her and ticked off all the points on her list.

Although I never went out with a married passenger, as you will see I certainly had my fair share of dating disasters along the way. Starting off with my relationship with a rock and roll star.

Chapter Thirteen

Lessons in Love

It was so exciting. Although I was used to celebrities flying on my planes, it wasn't every day you got a bona fide rock and roll star on board.

I was working on a flight from Tokyo to Honolulu, and at the pre-flight briefing, I was handed a list of the VIPs travelling with us that day.

'Masaaki Hirao?' I said. 'I've never heard of him.'

'Apparently he's the Elvis Presley of Japan,' one of the engineers told me.

He was obviously a big star in his home country because when we boarded the plane, all of the Japanese passengers, especially the girls, were gathered around his seat asking for autographs.

He seemed like a nice, polite fellow, and he was travelling with a man called Frank Nagai. If Masaaki was the Elvis Presley of Japan, then Frank was the Frank Sinatra, and we were told they were going to Honolulu to perform at a concert.

Much to the stewardesses' delight, after take-off, Masaaki came to the back galley to chat to the girls. He hardly spoke any

English, so Frank had to act as his interpreter. I must admit, Masaaki was very cute. He was small, with an impish face, and was dressed in a rockabilly style, like Elvis, in a tight suit and suede shoes – although his were yellow, not blue. He even had a little quiff like the King's.

'You must give us a song,' I told him. 'I'd love to hear you do one of your numbers.'

'No, no,' he said, shaking his head.

But with all the girls begging and pleading with him, somehow we managed to persuade him to perform. I checked that it was OK with the captain first, then I made an announcement over the PA system.

'Ladies and gentlemen, I'm very pleased to tell you that we just happen to have a very popular Japanese rock and roll star on board with us today who is going to do us the great honour of singing for us.'

All the stewardesses crowded into the back galley, as Masaaki took the mic to sing his hit song 'Crazy Love'.

Well, the passengers thought it was wonderful. They jumped to their feet and started clapping along and dancing in the aisles as Masaaki strutted his stuff. He was fantastic, and all of us stewardesses were bopping away too. We had US Secretary of State Dean Rusk travelling in first class that day and as soon as Masaaki started singing, he came to the back to see what all the fuss was about.

'I didn't want to miss out on all the fun,' he said and he was soon jigging along with the rest of us.

When Masaaki finished, the whole plane erupted with clapping, cheering and whistling.

'Thank you,' I told him. 'You were terrific.'

With Frank interpreting, Masaaki told me he was in Honolulu for three days and was staying at the Royal Hawaiian Hotel.

'He would very much like to see you again while you're there,' Frank told me.

'Oh,' I said, surprised. 'OK.'

I doubted very much that he would get in touch, but the next day, I was lying on Waikiki Beach with Mimi when Masaaki and Frank strolled towards us. Masaaki took his shirt off and joined us on the sand, and Mimi was beside herself with excitement at meeting them both.

Masaaki handed me a piece of paper with his telephone number on it and Frank told me, 'When you next come to Japan, Masaaki would like you to call him so he can take you out.'

'That would be lovely,' I smiled.

I couldn't believe I'd been asked out on a date by a rock and roll star!

A few months later, I was due to have a few days in Tokyo, so I decided to take the bull by the horns and give Masaaki a call. I spoke a tiny bit of Japanese and then he passed me on to his manager, who explained that Masaaki would like me to stay with him while I was in Japan and that he would meet me at the airport. I had to tell the stewardesses that I was visiting Masaaki rather than going on to the crew hotel with everyone else, and they were all very excited for me.

I knew Masaaki was very famous in Japan, but nothing could have prepared me for the scene that greeted me as I walked through customs. There was a grinning Masaaki, surrounded by a huge crowd of hysterical female fans. They were all screaming and trying to grab at his clothes, and it was complete chaos.

'Oh my goodness,' I gasped, as I tried to fight my way through the mob. 'I didn't expect this.'

'This way,' said Masaaki, linking his arm in mine and pulling me through the frenzied crowd towards a red Corvette parked outside.

'Get in,' he said. 'Quick.'

They were even trying to grab at him in the convertible, but he put his foot down and we screeched off to safety. I thought it was all very exciting, and it felt like I was dating one of the Beatles as we sped away from the crowd of fans, the wind blowing through my hair.

Masaaki had an impish charm which I found irresistible and he looked every inch the pop star in a tight grey suit that had flared bottoms with a red lining. Even though I didn't really know Masaaki, I felt safe with him. He lived in a huge house in a gated complex with his parents, which I thought was sweet but not very rock and roll. They were all very welcoming, but his mum and dad didn't speak any English and Masaaki didn't speak much either, so the constant gesturing and sign language got a bit exhausting after a while.

Over the next couple of days Masaaki took me sightseeing and out for dinner, and we shared a few kisses. Even though we didn't speak the same language, he was very romantic and we agreed to keep in touch.

When I told Mum about it when I was next home, she was even more excited about it than I was.

'Guess what, Sidney?' she said to Dad. 'Our Betty's dating a rock and roll star.'

'Ooh, that's a bit different,' he laughed.

A month later, I was passing through Tokyo, so Masaaki invited me to stay again. But on this visit, when we were kissing things got a little heated.

'No, thank you,' I said, pushing him gently away. I wanted him to know I didn't do that, at least not with someone I hardly knew. Thankfully he got the message very quickly, but I'm sure he felt rejected. I don't suppose he was used to being turned down, with all those female fans throwing themselves at him, and I could tell he was a bit put out. But I knew our relationship couldn't progress, not least because we didn't even speak the same language.

We drove back to the crew hotel in Tokyo, where I was due to spend the last night, and we didn't contact each other again.

Men were always asking us stewardesses out. They would leave their business cards or a note on their meal trays, and sometimes we would even get proposals of marriage from over-enthusiastic passengers.

Fred Daniels was a passenger who I met on the plane on the way to Honolulu. We got chatting during the flight and he told me how he was a divorced engineer from Los Angeles.

'How long are you in Waikiki for?' he asked. 'Perhaps you'd like to have dinner with me?'

On this particular trip, I was going to be in Hawaii for three days, and Fred seemed like a nice man. He was a little bit older than me, but good looking, with light-brown hair and kind blue eyes.

'OK,' I said. 'Why not?'

A few days later, he took me out for dinner in Waikiki. We had a nice meal and got on well and, at the end of the night, we shared a quick kiss.

'If you're ever in LA with work, give me a call,' he said.

I thought Fred was a little bit on the serious side for me, but we seemed to have lots to talk about. A month later, I was in LA overnight, so I thought I would look him up. He took me to a lovely restaurant, but he hardly said a word all night and he looked like he was going to burst into tears.

'What is it, Fred?' I asked. 'You don't seem yourself tonight. What's wrong?'

He reached for my hand across the table. 'Oh, Betty,' he sighed. 'I'm completely in love with you. I can't eat, I can't sleep. All I can think of is you. Will you marry me?'

It was the last thing I was expecting and I was so shocked, I didn't know how to respond.

'Um ... I'm ... er ... not sure what to say,' I mumbled.

'Please say yes,' he said. 'Let me buy you a ring. I've never met anyone like you before.'

'But, Fred, I hardly know you,' I told him. 'This is only our second date.'

'Please,' he begged. 'Please say you'll be my wife.'

'Thank you for the kind offer, Fred,' I said, 'but I think I'm going to have to say no.'

That certainly killed the conversation. Fred looked crestfallen and hardly said a word while I ate my meal as fast as was humanly possible. He was a nice man, but too intense, and a little bit obsessive for me. It was a relief when we finally left the restaurant.

'I'm so sorry,' I told him. 'I think you're a lovely man, but I won't be calling you anymore.' I felt terrible, as the poor fellow looked crushed, but I knew it wasn't fair to keep seeing him.

I had been home for a few days when one afternoon the phone rang.

'It's Mrs Daniels here,' said a very angry voice. 'I'd like a word with you, young lady.'

'Mrs Daniels?' I asked. 'I don't think I know a Mrs Daniels.'

'Don't play the innocent with me,' she continued. 'It's Fred's mother. I'm ringing to say how dare you treat my son like that and upset him.'

'I'm very sorry,' I said. 'That wasn't my intention.'

'Well, the poor boy's broken-hearted that you turned down his proposal. How could you be so cruel?'

'I'm sorry, Mrs Daniels, but we hardly know each other,' I told her. 'It was all a bit too much for me.'

'Well, I'm very cross with you for stringing him along,' she huffed before hanging up on me.

I couldn't believe a grown man had got his mum to call me and tell me off! And as for stringing him along, we'd only been out for dinner twice!

Another passenger who proposed very quickly was a gentleman called Mickey Sigler. He was a well-known designer in LA who made shoes for all of the Hollywood stars. We met on a flight to LA, and he was very chatty and pleasant, so I agreed to go out to dinner with him that night.

We were talking away, and I was really enjoying his company, when he dropped a bombshell that quickly killed the conversation.

'Will you marry me, Betty?' he said.

I certainly wasn't expecting that halfway through our first date. We'd only just met and nothing romantic had even happened between us, so I was completely taken aback.

'I ... er ... don't think I'm ready for that,' I told him. 'I'm enjoying having a career.'

I knew I wasn't going to see him again, but a few days later, a beautifully wrapped parcel arrived for me in the post. Inside the fancy box was a pair of glittery high heels. They were exactly the right size and they came with a note:

'Please keep me in mind, love Mickey x.'

Every couple of weeks he sent me another pair, and they were the most stunning shoes I had ever seen. They were always very high heels in bright colours or with fancy patterns cut out of them. As much as I loved them, after three pairs, I knew that I had to put a stop to it, so I wrote to Mickey, thanking him for his kind gifts, but asking him not to contact me again.

You would think that would have been enough to put me off dating passengers, but meeting eligible bachelors was one of the perks of the job. I certainly didn't expect one of them to turn into a stalker. Alan Ball and I met on a flight from LA to Honolulu. He was an author from Chicago, and was very charming, so I agreed to go out for dinner with him. I don't know where he was supposed to be going after that or how long he was in Honolulu for, but I was very surprised when he turned up on the flight I was working on to Sydney two days later.

'Hello there,' he grinned.

'Oh, Alan,' I said. 'Fancy seeing you here.'

'I changed my ticket so I could take you out again,' he said.

'Wow,' I said. 'That's a very grand gesture.'

I suppose I was flattered that a man I hardly knew was flying halfway across the world to go out with me, although it was a bit drastic. But he seemed like a nice man, so we went out for dinner again in Sydney and I didn't think any more of it. However, a couple of weeks later, I was at the crew hotel in London when I got a call from reception.

'Miss Eden, there's a gentleman here to see you,' a voice said.

I thought Dad had come up to London to surprise me, but I was very shocked when I went downstairs to find Alan waiting there.

'Oh my goodness,' I said. 'What are you doing here?'

'I thought I'd fly over and surprise you,' he said. 'I remembered you talking about the crew hotel last time we met.'

That's when alarm bells started ringing. He might have been very charming, but this man was following me around the world, and suddenly I felt very uncomfortable.

'Well, it's very sweet that you've made the effort to come all this way, but I'm very busy today and I fly out again tomorrow,' I told him.

But Alan wouldn't take no for an answer. 'I've flown to England to see you and you won't even have a cup of tea with me?' he said. 'Please, Betty.'

I felt terrible, and he had come such a long way, so reluctantly, I agreed. We were walking down High Street Kensington when Alan suddenly got down on one knee, right there on the pavement.

'Are you OK?' I asked. 'Did you trip?'

He didn't say a word, but reached into his pocket and took out a small velvet box, and I knew instantly what was coming next.

Dear God, no . . .

He lifted up the lid, to reveal a lovely pearl ring.

'Will you marry me?' he said.

'Alan, I'm really flattered, but I'm afraid I'm going to have to turn you down,' I told him.

But he seemed undeterred. 'Take the ring, Betty,' he said. 'Please just take it. You don't have to give me an answer right now.'

'Honestly, I really don't think I'll change my mind,' I said. 'And I don't feel comfortable taking the ring.'

But Alan insisted and, desperate to get him off his bended knee in the middle of the pavement, I took it and put it safely in my bag, so I could give it back to him later.

After half an hour of looking around the shops, I tried to make my excuses and leave.

'I'm sorry, Alan, I have to go round and see my mum and dad now, so I'll have to say goodbye,' I told him.

'That's OK,' he said. 'I'd love to meet your parents.'

This was starting to get a little creepy, but I thought I would just do as he said, then I wouldn't have to see him again. Mum and Dad looked a bit surprised when I turned up with Alan.

'Who is he, dear?' Dad asked, when I followed him into the kitchen.

'Oh, just a friend I met on the plane,' I told him.

But none of us was expecting the announcement Alan made halfway through dinner. We were just tucking into our shépherd's pie when he gave a little cough and put down his knife and fork.

'Mr and Mrs Eden,' he said very seriously, 'I just want you to know that I have very strong feelings for your daughter and I'm hoping that she will reciprocate.'

I just sat there, completely embarrassed, as well as terrified. We had only been out for dinner twice, and I hardly knew this fellow. Mum and Dad were looking at me, equally puzzled. I could see they were thinking, 'Well, she's never mentioned this man before.'

I couldn't wait to get rid of Alan and go back to the crew hotel, but he was very persistent.

'What an enjoyable day I've had,' he said, trying to grab my hand. 'Chicago's not that far away from San Francisco, and I would love to come and visit you.'

That was the final straw.

'I'm terribly sorry, Alan,' I said. 'But I don't think that's a good idea and I'm afraid I'm going to have to turn down your marriage proposal.'

His eyes filled with tears. 'Well, if you would only sleep with me, you would realise you did love me,' he sobbed. 'Please, Betty.'

I couldn't believe what I hearing. 'As tempting as that offer is, on this occasion, I think I will have to say no thank you,' I politely told him. 'Goodbye, Alan.'

Thankfully I never heard from him again, although he forgot to ask for his pearl ring back. I didn't want to be reminded of him, so I gave it to Mum, and she was delighted!

In late 1966 my friend Dawn Hester wrote me a letter. She was still working for TWA, but had transferred from San Francisco to Boston by now. But we still kept in touch and saw each other regularly, and she knew all the trouble I'd been having with men.

'I was on a trip to Uganda last week, Betty, and I met a lovely man on the plane called David, who I think would be ideal for you,' Dawn wrote. 'He's an English police inspector in Entebbe. He's a nice guy, in his late thirties, and I was so convinced that you two would get on well that I've given him your address. I hope you don't mind.'

I was a bit surprised, but he must have been keen, because a few days later, I received a letter from David, saying he would like to take me on a safari and inviting me to come out and see him in Uganda.

Looking back, I can't believe I actually went, but I was always ready for an adventure. Plus I had my month off coming up and I had never been on safari before or seen that part of the world, so it would be another ambition that I could tick off the list. Even though I had never met him, it seemed like a fun thing to do. I don't know what I was thinking, going on what was effectively a week-long blind date. But Dawn had obviously liked David and thought he was a nice chap, so I thought, 'Why not?'

I must admit, by the time I landed at Entebbe Airport, I was starting to have second thoughts, but David was already there, waiting to pick me up. It was such a relief when I saw him. He was tall, handsome and blond, and he seemed like a real gentleman.

I was very excited as we set off in his rickety old jeep to the remote area of the bush where all the game was. We were accompanied by a tracker, a big Ugandan guy dressed in khakis, who I assumed was there to help us find all the wild animals.

It was the beginning of the rainy season, so for the entire three-hour journey, I was thrown backwards and forwards in this rickety jeep, as we ploughed through thick, gloopy red mud. For the first time, I started to worry. I was used to five-star hotels and tropical beaches. What had I let myself in for?

'Don't be a wimp, Betty,' I told myself.

Little did I know what horrors were to come ...

We finally got to the area where we were going to camp, and David and the tracker put up three tents for us. We had been there an hour when suddenly I heard loud voices and I was terrified when a group of tall, skinny Maasai warriors came storming into our camp, clutching scary-looking spears. But the spears weren't what caught my attention.

The warriors were all wearing sarongs and David explained that you could tell how wealthy someone was by the length of their sarong. If they had money, they could afford plenty of material, and their sarongs would go down to their knees. But if they weren't wealthy, like most of these warriors, they could only afford enough cloth to cover their top half, so from the waist down, the majority of them were stark naked. I didn't know what was more frightening – the sight of their undercarriages flapping around in the breeze or their terrifying spears!

'Oh my goodness,' I gasped. 'They're going to kill us.'

'Don't be silly,' said David. 'They're here to help us catch some bait for the leopard.'

'What leopard?' I asked.

I didn't have a clue what he was talking about, and I was horrified when he explained they needed the bait because we were going on a leopard hunt. It was the most barbaric thing I had ever heard, and I was absolutely disgusted. I thought I'd come to Uganda to look at the animals, not kill them! I had never signed up for a leopard hunt, but I didn't dare say anything.

Well, would you want to get on the wrong side of some half-naked Maasai warriors?

David informed me that the first thing we had to do was catch a warthog and kill it for bait. I stayed cowering in the jeep, while David, the tracker and one of the warriors set off into the bush, found a warthog and speared it through the heart. I couldn't bring myself to look as they dragged its bloody body through the soil and attached it to the roof of the jeep. Then they placed it in a tree in the bush close to our camp and took it in turns to see if it attracted a leopard.

Days passed, but nothing happened. In the meantime, we waited at the camp. The tracker was our chef and every night he cooked up a big stew over the fire. I didn't dare ask what sort of meat was in those stews, and even now, I dread to think what it was!

'You must try the doo doos,' David told me one day. 'They're a local delicacy.'

I had thought the fertilised duck egg in Manila was terrible, but that was before I had seen a doo doo. They were bugs that the locals got out of the ground with sticks, left to dry out in the sun until they were nice and crunchy and then poured into big bags. You were supposed to eat them like crisps, but I just couldn't bring myself to try one. I was fed up of creepy crawlies. I had to strain my tea before I drank it because so many bugs landed in it.

The truth was that this safari had turned into a nightmare, and I wasn't really enjoying any of it. I lay there at night, too frightened to sleep because of all the animals making terrifying noises and bumping into the side of my tent. The tracker had a gun, but I was still convinced I was going to be eaten by a lion or a hungry hippo looking for a midnight feast.

Every day I sat in my tent and scribbled in my travel diary.

'What on earth was I thinking?' I wrote. 'I could be lying on the beach in Hawaii.'

To top it all off, because of all the strange food I was eating, I got Delhi belly. It was too dangerous to go into the bush alone at night, so every time I needed to go to the toilet (which unfortunately was quite a lot), I had to call David to come with me with his gun and flashlight, so I could find the hole in the ground.

Needless to say, there was no romance between us. He was a really dear, nice man, but I was so tired, miserable and sick that it was the last thing on my mind.

On the fourth day, I was so bored, I decided to go into the bush with the men and check the bait. David went first, followed by the tracker, then me. Maybe because of a woman's low status in their society, as we trampled through the undergrowth, the tracker let the branches and plants swing back on me as I struggled to keep up with them. They were so prickly, they cut my legs, and I kept yelping. After a few hundred yards of this, David and the tracker held a whispered meeting and it was decided that I was too much of a disturbance to accompany them.

'I'm afraid you're too noisy; you'll frighten the leopard off,' David told me. 'This is no job for a woman. The tracker says you'll have to stay here while we go and check the bait.'

So they left me sitting on a rock, halfway across a ravine. I was absolutely terrified and was convinced that I was going to be eaten alive by some wild animal. They couldn't give me the gun because they needed it to shoot the leopard.

My heart was racing as I listened to all these noises and rustling in the bush. 'I'm going to be eaten by a lion,' I sobbed. 'I'm going to be the bait, never mind the warthog.'

Thankfully they came back quickly, as the bait was still there and there was no sign of the leopard. I made sure I stayed safely back at camp after that experience, and a day later, they returned carrying the body of a dead leopard. As they were hiding in the bush, the tracker had spotted it and shot it. I was so upset, I ran into the tent, as I didn't want to see it, especially as they were about to skin the poor beast and then sell it. If anything, that completely put me off David. I didn't think I could care for someone who could do that to a living creature.

It felt like the longest week of my life, and it was such a relief when it finally came to an end and I could fly back home to civilisation.

I think David felt he had missed out on his chance to show that he really cared for me, because a week after I got back, a postcard arrived: 'The great white hunter doesn't give up all his shots at the first shoot, David x.'

I knew what he meant was: 'Come back and see me again and you will get to know me better this time.' But my heart just wasn't in it. I knew the great white hunter was not the man for me.

I knew I would meet someone one day; I just had a feeling. Unlike most other single girls my age, I wasn't in a rush or a panic, and I never sat at home feeling lonely. If I didn't have anything special to do, I'd call one of the girls, or go and see Auntie Belle. I was away a lot of the time, so it was nice to have some down time when I got home. I liked the fact that domesticity and the kitchen sink weren't looming for me. I was being paid to see the world and was enjoying every single minute of it.

Chapter Fourteen

Turbulent Times

My heart felt like it was about to thump out of my chest as the group of burly men in uniform surrounded me. I felt sick with fear when I saw the machine guns slung over their shoulders. They marched me to a small side room.

'Where are you taking me?' I yelled. 'You can't do this. Please let me go with the others.'

But my words fell on deaf ears. They had seized my passport and now I was being taken off to God knows where.

There had not been many times during my career when I had been genuinely frightened for my own safety, but this was one of them. It had all started as a normal layover in Jakarta. Admittedly, it wasn't my favourite city in the world and usually I tried to avoid going there. It was dirty, the people weren't friendly – in fact they refused to speak to you or even look at you, so you always felt like an alien – and I never felt very safe there.

During the flight, the captain had been told that the British embassy in Jakarta had been fire-bombed and a car that was parked outside it had been set alight.

As the only British member of the flight crew that day, the news had made me feel very nervous. I didn't even know what had happened to provoke this particular attack, but there was always a strong anti-British feeling in Indonesia.

I was obviously right to feel uneasy. Normally, at immigration, we went into a special crew line and after a cursory glance at our passports, we walked straight through. Today, however, the official had taken one look at my British passport and now I had been surrounded and marched off to a small side room. I was terrified. Who knew what they were going to do to me and how long I was going to be held prisoner for?

Thankfully the pilot refused to leave me.

'Don't worry,' he said. 'I'll talk to the officials and we'll soon get you released. They're just using you to make a point.'

'Thank you, skipper,' I said.

But it was hard not to worry. My passport had been confiscated and now I was being held by immigration while the rest of the crew had gone back to the hotel. I hoped and prayed he was right and that eventually they would let me go. But as the minutes ticked by, I started to get more and more worried about what was going to happen to me. I had been there two long hours before one of the officials came in.

'You're free to go,' he said, handing me back my passport.

I didn't ask any questions; I just grabbed my passport and bag and got out of there as quickly as I could. I had never been so relieved to get away from an airport in my life. But even when the captain and I were safely back at the hotel, I still couldn't relax. The whole crew were on edge, and I think we were all relieved to fly out of there the next day.

I can't pretend I knew much about politics back then, but there was one thing that I was certain of in the 1960s: the world was in turmoil.

Generally, the routes that I travelled were OK and I usually felt safe, but I knew that for some of the girls it was a very different story. Stewardesses flying into Saudi Arabia and Kuwait spent the whole trip captive in their hotels, as it was too dangerous for Western women to be seen outside without a headscarf.

Similarly, girls who flew to the Lebanon loved it, but in the mid-1960s Pan Am closed its base there because it had become too dangerous.

Some countries that I travelled to were very corrupt and you had to keep your wits about you. But some of my colleagues learnt the hard way. One stewardess, who I was sharing a room with in Manila, was invited by a local man to dine with him in the hotel restaurant. But she came back a few hours later in tears and shaking like a leaf.

'What on earth happened?' I asked her.

'Oh, Betty,' she said. 'He asked me to bring some guns into the country for him the next time I flew in.'

She had been so terrified of this man that she had pretended that she would try to help him and do as he had asked.

'As soon as we get home, you must tell the managers,' I told her.

Thankfully she did what I'd suggested and requested not to fly into Manila anymore, as she was so scared about what might happen to her.

There was a lot of corruption in the Philippines in those days, which I also experienced for myself. On a flight into Manila, a couple of male passengers invited a group of us stewardesses out for dinner that night. They seemed like respectable busi-nessmen and as there was always safety in numbers, we agreed to go. They took us to an ordinary-looking restaurant, but at the end of the meal, one of the men got up and pulled back a curtain to reveal some secret sliding doors at the rear of the building. They opened them and led us all through, and none of us could believe our eyes. We were right in the middle of an illegal gambling den.

'It's like another world in here,' I whispered to one of the other stewardesses.

It was dark, smoky and filled with seedy-looking men playing cards for huge sums of money. I was slightly scared, but at the same time strangely fascinated, and before I knew it, one of the men we were with led me up to one of the tables. Soon I was shooting craps with some dodgy-looking local fellows and having a whale of a time. That is, until one of the waitresses from the restaurant came running in, screaming something in Tagalog, which was the official language of the Philippines. I didn't have a clue what she was saying, but I'd never seen people move so fast.

'Quick, the police are here,' one of the men who had brought us shouted. 'We've got to get out of here.'

All of us Pan Am girls were absolutely terrified as we ran out of the back door into the street. Thankfully we escaped without being arrested, but it certainly taught us a lesson about being choosier when it came to our dinner companions.

One country that was in complete turmoil in the 1960s was Vietnam. The war had been going on since the late 1950s, and the US had waded into it in the early 1960s, as they were worried that communists would gain control of Vietnam and they wanted to prevent communist rule from spreading to other countries around the world. By the mid-sixties it seemed to have escalated, and by the end of the decade the US had over half a million troops over there. It was a brutal war: the US dropped more bombs during Vietnam than they did during the Second World War, so unsurprisingly there was a huge loss of life. By the end of the war it's estimated over 58,000 American soldiers had been killed and hundreds of thousands left wounded or disabled, not to mention the millions of Vietnamese who had lost their lives.

Pam Am continued to fly into Vietnam during the war, and on the way over we would sometimes have a layover in Guam, an island in the Pacific between Wake Island and the Asian coast. It belongs to America, although it was captured briefly by the Japanese during the Second World War. It was so remote, it was mainly just jungle. In fact it was so isolated that during the 1960s they were still finding Japanese soldiers from the Second World War alive in the jungle because nobody had been able to reach them to tell them that the war was over and Japan had surrendered.

There were no hotels on the island, so we would stay in apartments in a town called Agana. When it rained, the tropical showers were so heavy it was like someone was tipping buckets of water on you, and all the cars would have to stop because there was no visibility.

One afternoon I was sat on the balcony of our apartment when I saw a fleet of large, dark-grey planes swoop down over us.

'What on earth are they?' I gasped.

'They're B52 bombers,' said Brenda, who was working on the same flight as me. 'They will be on their way back from Vietnam.'

There was a large American air force base on Guam and at around five o'clock every day, we would look up into the sky and see these planes coming back after dropping their bombs. They were so dark and foreboding, with their turned-down, ominous wings. They looked like death, and it always sent a chill through me. I felt uneasy seeing them coming back, knowing what they had been doing. Each B52 carried up to a hundred bombs and

I couldn't help but think about the innocent civilians they had been dropped on. Growing up in wartime, I knew how it felt to live with the constant fear that your lives and homes would be obliterated.

Pan Am continued to fly into Saigon during the Vietnam War, but it was always nerve-wracking, as we knew it was a risk. This was brought home to us all in 1965, when an Air France stewardess was shot and killed by a sniper as she opened the front door of the plane just after landing. Her murder sent shockwaves through the entire industry, and Pan Am immediately upped its security at Tan Son Nhut Airport in Saigon. From then on, one of the male cockpit crew would open the airplane door when we landed in Vietnam. The pilots also changed the way they landed, to minimise the risk of being shot at. We would stay at altitude for as long as possible and then suddenly drop down very sharply and quickly onto the runway. It was stomach-lurching, and we had to make sure all of the passengers and crew were strapped in very tightly. They would also take off at the maximum climb, but even despite all these precautions, bullet holes were often found on the planes' exterior during the war years.

We never had layovers in Vietnam during the war. In fact it was deemed too dangerous to even leave the airport, as the road leading to it was always littered with landmines, which had to be cleared each morning. We always had a few hours to kill before we flew straight out again, so we would go to the little café overlooking the runway and have an orange juice or a slice of papaya while the cleaners came on board the aircraft. But even this was a big risk, as the cleaners were all Vietnamese, and no one was really sure whose side they were on. So there would be a Pan Am operations staff member following each cleaner around, even into the toilet, to make sure that they didn't tamper with anything on the plane. It was always such an uneasy atmosphere, and I never properly relaxed until we were safely out of there and back at altitude.

Pan Am was one of the airlines which had a contract with the military to transport soldiers to and from the war, and sometimes I worked on the flights which flew the soldiers in and out of Vietnam. We would deadhead to Travis Air Force Base, where we would pick up the plane and then fly to one of the military bases, like Cam Ranh Bay or Danang. The thing that always struck me was how young these soldiers were. I would look at their baby faces and feel so sad. They were drafted from the age of eighteen and the average age of the American soldiers fighting in Vietnam was nineteen. All males between eighteen and twenty-six had to register. Some volunteered to go to war, to avoid the uncertainty of whether they were going to be called up, while hundreds of young men fled to Canada to avoid being drafted at all.

I would sometimes see these new recruits at the airport on the way to my flight briefing, saying goodbye to their families, sobbing like the young boys they really were. But once they were on the airplane with the other guys, they put on a brave face. There was no first class on these military flights, but they enjoyed the fact that they were on a nice plane, and we made sure it was a lovely experience for them and gave them the same service we would give any other Pan Am passenger.

They would try to be cheeky to the stewardesses in a nice way, and they enjoyed pulling our legs.

'I'll have a couple of beers, dear,' one of the soldiers would always ask me, even though they knew we weren't permitted to serve them alcohol on these flights.

'How about a Coke cocktail or lemonade on the rocks?' I would joke.

But as we got closer to Vietnam, you could feel the mood in the plane change. It would suddenly hit these young men that they were going to war, and you could have cut the sombre atmosphere with a knife. All I could do was stay upbeat and try to help keep their spirits up.

'Don't worry, I will see you on the way back,' I told them. 'Then you can have as many beers as you want.' But in reality we all knew that many of them would not be coming back alive.

Pan Am also operated 'rest and recuperation' flights during the war, where they would take a plane of soldiers to Sydney, Hong Kong, Tokyo or Bangkok for five days, for them to have time away from the war and to help boost morale. Every soldier was entitled to one of these breaks during his service and we would give them first-class standard food and serve alcohol on these flights.

After being in the jungle for months on end, these men thought they were in heaven when they got on the plane, and they were so appreciative. They would always be happy to see civilisation, after living in the jungle without flushing toilets, running water and electricity. I'm sure they were also glad to see women, so I dread to think what they got up to on these trips! I can imagine that they got pretty wild. Later on in the war, the R and R destinations were expanded to include Hawaii and Japan, and some servicemen were even allowed to be joined by their wives.

They each had to serve ten months' military service, and on the return flights, it was a completely different atmosphere. Some of the soldiers would even remember me from the outward journey, which was always sweet. It was a really relaxed, happy atmosphere. I couldn't imagine the traumas these men had been through and the horrors they had seen, but none of them talked about what had happened. Instead, they all seemed euphoric that they were going home, and they were all very chirpy and excited. They told me about their families and friends and how they couldn't wait to see them.

I remember one soldier who was in tears when he got on the plane – thankfully they were tears of happiness and relief. 'When we pulled up to the airport in the bus and I saw the blue ball of the Pan Am plane and you gals in your uniforms, I knew I was already home,' he said.

It made me feel very proud that we were doing the nation a service and doing our bit to help during the war. I knew there was a field hospital in Cam Ranh Bay for injured American soldiers, so I would always save any leftover milk or ice cream from the flights and give them to military operations to pass on to the patients, and they always told us how much they appreciated that.

The war was also directly affecting some of my stewardess friends. In May 1966 Brenda Lea married John Morris, whom she had met at the Marine Corps Ball, when I'd been invited down there by Raymond Sellick. I was their bridesmaid, and it was a lovely day in San Diego. But a few months after the wedding, John was sent to Vietnam, so Brenda moved in with me. I knew it was so hard for them being apart and I could see how worried Brenda was about her new husband. The only time she got to see him was when she was working on a flight that landed in Saigon. She would make contact with other marines going over there on flights.

'If you could pass this message on to Lieutenant Morris, I would be so grateful,' she would ask them, and they would tell him when Brenda would next be flying in, so he could meet her at the airport.

I remember working on one of those flights with Brenda, and she couldn't wait to see him. She had brought him over his favourite crackers and Swiss muesli. Her face lit up when the plane doors opened and she saw John waiting there in his uniform at the bottom of the ramp.

They only had an hour to go and get a coffee and sit together hand in hand in the café and chat. Brenda was elated to see him, but when we had to leave again, the tears flowed.

'Oh, Betty, I miss him so much,' she sobbed. 'I'm constantly worried about him.'

'He'll be OK,' I told her. 'I'm sure of it.'

John served eight months as a captain in the US Marine Corps and thankfully he was one of the lucky ones who came home safely, although 70 per cent of his company were killed or wounded in the eight months he commanded them. Of course it was difficult for him to forget that. He left the Marine Corps when he came back in 1967, but I know those losses still stay with him today, all these years later.

Seeing as I had introduced him to his future wife, John was determined I would be a good match for his cousin, a man called Harreld Martin, who was training to be an officer in the air force. So, in March 1966, I went to visit him in Indiana, where he was based. As he was related to John, I knew I would be safe with him and he was a sweet man.

Harreld was a bit on the chunky side and, if I'm being honest, he wasn't my usual type of person. He seemed to dwell on the negative side of life more than the positive, like me, and was quite a serious soul, but he was gentle and kind and we got on well. He took me to meet his family in Kentucky and introduced me to his parents, who were both teachers and seemed very nice

One night we were sitting on the swing on his parents' porch kissing when he turned to me with a very serious look on his face.

'You know, I'm going to die before I'm forty, Betty,' he told me, taking my hand.

'Don't be so silly,' I told him. 'Of course you're not.'

But Harreld was convinced of it and told me so many times. A few months later he was drafted to serve in Vietnam. We wrote to each other for a while, but as the months passed, we lost touch.

Sadly, Harreld's premonition came true. He was serving in Danang and was asleep in his quarters one night when they were bombed in their beds. Poor Harreld was only twenty-six when he died.

But the soldiers that did survive in Vietnam weren't even coming home to a hero's welcome after risking their lives on the frontline. By 1965 a huge wave of anti-war feeling was sweeping the country. Thousands of people were marching in protest against the war and demanding that the men be brought back. Their main argument was that the US should not be sacrificing so many of their soldiers' lives for a country that was on the other side of the world. Their feeling was that the US should never have become involved in the war in the first place and should have let the Vietnamese sort it out for themselves.

Returning soldiers were too scared to wear their uniforms out in public, as they were called 'baby killers' and spat at in the street. There were stories of men being attacked or having their car tyres slashed. Unfortunately they all had the same haircut, which was called 'whitewalls' because of the shaved sides, so whether they were wearing their uniforms or not, people instantly knew they were military and they were shunned because of it. I felt really sorry for these soldiers and the fact that they were being given such a hard time.

I must admit, looking back, that I was very shallow and didn't give the war a huge amount of thought. Maybe I shouldn't have been on those planes taking the troops to war. At the time it was part of my job and I just got on with it, but in hindsight, perhaps I should have asked more questions.

As part of the massive backlash against the war, hippies started appearing all over San Francisco. I would walk through town and see these 'flower children', as they were called, sitting cross-legged in Union Square or in some of the parks, playing their instruments. They brought with them a whole new wave of fashion that was totally different from everything that had gone before. The women wore outlandishly long skirts, flowery dresses or tie-dye clothes in psychedelic colours, while the men sported bell-bottom jeans and necklaces. Both men and women had long, straggly hair and wore headbands or flowers in their hair. Although I was never a hippy myself, I quite liked seeing them around and hearing their music.

It was mainly the hippies, with what they called their 'flower power', who protested at the anti-war demonstrations which, in San Francisco, were centred around Berkeley University. But even though they were all about peace and love and they carried placards saying, 'Stop the war' and 'Make love, not war', these demonstrations often got quite heated and rowdy. Protestors would sometimes clash with police who were on horseback or carrying truncheons, such was the strength of the anti-war feeling in the country.

Society was definitely changing. Suddenly young people had a voice, and were making it heard and expressing themselves in different ways. I thought the hippies and the flower children were sweet, but I didn't like the drugs that often came with them. Drugs were another way young people could rebel and, for the first time, they were out in the open and people were experimenting with substances like marijuana and LSD, which remarkably wasn't illegal for most of the 1960s. I would see people out on the street who looked drunk, with glazed eyes, but then I would smell the strong scent and realise they were smoking pot. To be honest, it scared me and I didn't like walking past them. I didn't even smoke, never mind take drugs. I was always way too cowardly.

Another thing that the hippies made fashionable was free love and open sexuality. San Francisco was the centre of the hippy revolution and it all culminated in the Haight-Ashbury district in the summer of 1967 – the Summer of Love – when hundreds of thousands of hippies descended on that area. I'm sure that, whatever your age, most people know the song 'If You Are Going to San Francisco Be Sure to Wear Some Flowers in Your Hair' which was written about that time.

I wasn't sure about the free love thing either. It was all a bit much for me, and I was a bit of a scaredy cat. I would rather have lunch with the ladies in Union Square than go down to Haight-Ashbury and sit on the kerb, singing and smoking stuff, like the hippies all did.

But things were definitely changing and society was becoming more accepting. People felt able to be openly gay for the first time and the hippy movement brought all sorts of nationalities together. I didn't know it then, but the war was also going to have a massive effect on my own life. It was going to bring me a husband.

Chapter Fifteen

Here Comes the Bride

The woman swept around the room, swishing her long, tas-selled skirt, her armful of bangles jangling away. I held my breath as she made a beeline for our table.

'Uh-oh, Betty, I think she's heading for you,' whispered Mimi.

When it came to the spirit world and the supernatural, I had always been a big believer and now I was about to get a glimpse into my future. Sure enough, the lady flounced over to me, bent down and grabbed my hand.

'Hmm, very interesting,' she said, her dark-brown eyes peering out at me from beneath her headscarf. 'What's your name, dear?'

'It's Betty,' I said, swallowing nervously.

'Well, Betty, your palm tells me that good things are heading your way,' she smiled. 'I see a handsome man coming into your life.'

'Ooh, that sounds exciting,' I laughed.

It was September 1966 and I was in a restaurant in London called the Brush and Palette. We had heard about Madam

Giselle from some of the Japanese crew girls, who'd said she was a renowned palm reader who came around the restaurant while you ate and predicted your future. It sounded like fun and I was always up for a spot of fortune telling, to check that there were no plane crashes on the cards!

Like me, the Japanese stewardesses were really interested in the spirit world and the supernatural, and it was quite fashionable in the 1960s. A few months earlier Mimi and I had been to see a lady in London who read auras. She had told me that I had a lovely strong aura and that I would always be safe in an airplane, which was a relief.

But now I was very interested in hearing what Madam Giselle had to say. She examined my palm extremely closely and started to smile.

'Oh, this man is definitely"the one",' she said.

I listened intently as she told me that he was going to be North American or Canadian, a lawyer, and his family would be from a German or Scandinavian background.

'It won't be long before you two are walking down the aisle,' she said.

'Good heavens,' I said, pressing a pound note into her hand before she moved on to the next table.

'He sounds nice, Betty,' said Wendy, another stewardess.

'I wish,' I laughed. 'I'd better keep my eyes and ears open for this fellow.'

It was just a bit of fun, but I was twenty-seven now and the truth was that although I was in no rush to walk down the aisle, I felt ready to meet someone special. I went on the odd date with Graham Kretchman when I was at home in San Francisco, and poor Harreld Martin was the only other person I had dated recently. But there hadn't been anyone serious, no one who had really caught my interest, for a while. I think Graham would have liked to get more serious, but my feelings for him weren't that strong and I was trying to cool things off.

Ironically, although I hadn't found a husband of my own, I was very good at finding them for other people. I had earned myself a reputation as a bit of a matchmaker after introducing so many of my friends to their other halves. I'd been a bridesmaid a grand total of seventeen times so far and I loved a good wedding, even though my own still seemed a long way off. But I certainly wasn't bitter or in a rush to settle for second best, and I enjoyed matchmaking.

My view was, if you knew nice people, then what better thing to do than introduce them? I was always tuned in to who would be right for whom.

Dawn Hester had recently got married to a fellow I had introduced her to and I had been their bridesmaid. Bill McGee was a teacher I had met on the airplane when he was flying to Bangkok to work for a year, and we had sent airmail letters to each other while he was away. He was a really nice chap, and when he came back to Boston and Dawn was based there, I thought it would be a good idea for them to look each other up.

'Do you mind?' Dawn had asked me.

'Of course not,' I'd said. 'We're just friends.'

Bill was handsome, with a great sense of humour, but we'd never had the opportunity to become more than pen pals and I just had a feeling that he and Dawn would be a good match for each other. My instincts proved right and I was so pleased when they started dating. Within months, Bill had proposed and they were planning their wedding. It makes me very proud that couples like Dawn and Bill and Brenda and John are still together today, and they are still some of my dearest friends.

But, unbeknown to me, someone was doing a little match-making on my behalf.

Pat McHenry, one of the marines I was friendly with, was about to be sent to Vietnam and one of his colleagues, a man called Kent Riegel, had just returned from the war and was stationed at Treasure Island. Kent had never lived in the San Francisco area before and didn't know anyone, but he was ready to go on a few dates after serving six months in Vietnam. Pat knew I wasn't seeing Raymond Sellick anymore, so he thought that perhaps I would be up for going out with him.

'There's a fine young lady I want you to meet,' he had told Kent. 'I'll give you her number.'

I didn't know Pat had passed on my details to him. All I knew was that someone called Kent Riegel kept calling me at home. But whenever he had rung, I had always been away on a trip, so he'd spoken to my roommate, Holly.

By now, myself, Pauline and three other Pan Am stewardesses, Jill, Muriel and Holly, had moved to a bigger apartment in Pacific Heights.

'I don't know anyone called Kent Riegel,' I told Holly. 'That sounds like a made-up name to me.'

'Whoever he is, he's desperate to go out with you, as he's been calling for three weeks,' she said. 'Well, he's desperate to go out with *someone*.'

Holly laughed as she told me how this Kent Riegel fellow had asked her out.

'Well, if Betty's not there, what are you doing tomorrow night?' he'd said to her.

'What I'm definitely *not* doing is going out with you,' she'd told him.

He had been well and truly put in his place, and I didn't think

Kent Riegel would be bothering me again. But a couple of weeks later, I was at home when the phone rang.

'Is that Betty Eden?' said a man's voice. 'This is Kent Riegel. I've been trying to get hold of you.'

'Oh, it's you,' I said. 'You're certainly very persistent.'

He explained how Pat had given him my number and suggested he got in touch. Pat was a nice guy and I knew he wouldn't give my details out to any old creep, so I thought, 'What have I got to lose?' I agreed to go out with Kent, and a couple of nights later he called for me at the apartment.

Kent told me later that when I first opened the door, the sun was just setting and it was shining through my hair, so he thought I looked like an angel with a halo! My first impressions of Kent were good. He was wearing a smart tweed jacket, a shirt and tie and grey trousers. He had a lovely smile and a little gap between his two front teeth, which was very endearing.

'Oh, he's nice,' I thought.

He took me to a restaurant called Scoma's at Fisherman's Wharf in San Francisco, and we talked and talked for hours. He asked me all about my job, my travels and my family in England.

'You'll never guess what happened to me last week,' I told him. 'I was in London and I ended up going to this restaurant and getting my palm read.'

I told him all about what Madam Giselle had said – how she had predicted that I was going to marry an American lawyer from a German or Scandinavian background. Up until that point, we'd been chatting away so easily, but then it was like something had killed the conversation. What I didn't know was that Kent's grandparents were German and he was a lawyer. I thought all marines walked through the jungle with a gun. I didn't realise he was a trained lawyer and that was what he'd been doing for the troops in Vietnam.

Here was Kent, just arrived in swinging San Francisco, ready to date anything in a skirt after six months in the jungle in Vietnam, and here I was, one of his first dates since he'd got back, describing him as the man I was going to marry. No wonder the poor man looked like a rabbit caught in the head-lights! He told me many months later that he'd debated whether he should go to the toilet, climb out of the window and never come back again.

But despite the fact that he must have felt like running for his life, Kent was a real gentleman. He took me home and kissed me on the cheek, and I went inside with a big, soppy smile on my face.

'I think I've just met someone really special,' I told Holly.

But then the weeks passed and I didn't hear a dickie bird from Kent. I was so disappointed, as I had really liked him. He had a great sense of humour and for most of the night we'd had so much to talk about.

'Oh well, you win some, you lose some,' I told myself sadly.

But then, three weeks later, Kent finally called and asked if I would go to the Marine Corps Ball with him.

'It's nice to hear from you after all this time,' I told him.

I went all out and made a real effort. I bought a lovely evening gown – a white satin strapless dress – teased my hair into a beehive and put a hairpiece I'd had made in Japan on the top. Kent was in his marine uniform, and he looked so hand-some.

We had a wonderful time, and he invited me up to a cabin near Lake Tahoe for a skiing weekend with some other marines and their friends. I was very nervous, as I wasn't a skier, but I was even more nervous when I found out the person I was shar-ing a room with was a very attractive girl called Dee Riley, who Kent had been on a few dates with before me. Thankfully she was seeing another marine friend of his now, so she was out of the picture.

From then on, Kent and I started dating and within a few months I knew that he was someone special. I was more interested in him than I had been in any other man I had met before, and he had all the qualities I liked. He was considerate, intelligent, funny and a true gentleman. We'd had very different upbringings – he came from a small, rural Pennsylvanian village and was the youngest of four children. He'd paid his own way through university by working at the same time.

I liked Kent so much, I quickly knew I didn't want to date anyone else, so I told Graham I wasn't going to see him any more.

'It won't last with this fellow,' he told me. 'He'll break your heart.'

'Well, it's a chance I'm prepared to take,' I told him.

Now that things had become more serious, I knew it was time to let Mum and Dad know. I was a bit worried about telling them about Kent, as he was American, and I knew that at the back of their minds, they would be thinking that if this worked out, I would definitely be staying in the US for good. I had never made the decision to stay in America permanently, but I didn't really know anyone in England any more. Of course I still missed my family, and that fact would never change.

'I've met someone special and I'd like to introduce you to him,' I told them.

'I'm so pleased for you,' Mum said.

In April 1967 I had my month off work, so I decided to go back to the UK with Kent, so he could meet Mum and Dad. It was really important to me that my parents liked him, and I was very nervous. But I need not have worried. My dad loved him from the beginning, and I could tell Mum thought he was the cat's whiskers. It was such a relief.

In fact Dad's exact words were: 'He's very nice, dear. Not at all American!'

After that, we borrowed Dad's car for a week and drove around Devon and Cornwall. We always had separate rooms, of course – it was still considered a real no-no for an unmarried couple to share the same room. People were even funny about Kent being American. We checked into one B&B and the owner gave us the frosty treatment when she heard Kent's accent. An English girl travelling around with an American man was still considered a bit scandalous.

By October 1967, we had been dating almost a year, and I knew by then that I was in love with Kent. So much so, we had even become intimate. His mum and dad's sixtieth wedding anniversary was that same month, and Kent invited me to come with him and meet all of his family. It all went well and his family seemed to like me, but while I was there, I realised something terrible.

'My period's a week late,' I whispered to Kent when we were alone later that night. 'I'm really worried.'

'Oh, Lord, please don't let you be pregnant,' he said.

We were both absolutely terrified, as having a child out of wedlock was still such a scandal in those days. I was so ashamed, I didn't tell a soul, and as soon as we got home, I went to see the doctor.

'My time of the month is a little late,' I mumbled, too embarrassed to come right out and say that I thought I was pregnant.

There were no such things as pregnancy tests or scans in those days, so he just poked and prodded my stomach.

'There's nothing there that shouldn't be,' he said sternly. 'Would you like me to prescribe you some birth-control pills?'

'Oh ... er ... no, thank you,' I said, my cheeks blushing red. 'I don't usually do that.'

The contraceptive pill had first become available in the early 1960s, and although it had signified a lot more freedom for women, it wasn't really talked about amongst me and my friends. If an unmarried woman said she was on the Pill, everyone would assume she was a bit loose. Once you were married, it was seen as OK to ask the doctor for the Pill.

I found the whole experience mortifying and scary, and I was so relieved when my period arrived a week later. All I can think is that it must have been the stress of meeting Kent's family that had delayed it. But it certainly taught Kent and me a lesson, and we were a lot more careful from then on.

A couple of times, when the rest of the girls were away, Kent stayed overnight at my apartment. Once, he'd slept over and early the next morning I heard the buzzer ring. When I looked out of the window to see who it was, I almost had heart failure.

'It's Auntie Belle,' I yelled to Kent. 'You've got to get out quick.'

Of all the people to drop by unannounced, Auntie Belle would have been the most horrified by the fact that I'd had a man to stay overnight. Poor Kent quickly got dressed and hurriedly dashed down the stairs, while Auntie Belle came up in the lift. Thankfully we got away with it!

Soon it was Christmas 1967, and on Christmas Eve, Kent and I decided to spend the evening together. I had the apartment to myself, so I made Kent his favourite dinner of steak, and afterwards we sat by the tree with a glass of wine.

'Why don't we open one gift each?' said Kent.

'Oh no,' I cried. 'We never do that in our family; you've got to wait until Christmas Day to open your presents.'

But Kent kept going on and on about it, so in the end I gave in.

'Oh, alright then,' I sighed. 'Just one little one each.'

'I'll go get yours first,' he said, going over to the Christmas tree and bringing back a small, beautifully wrapped package. I couldn't believe it when he suddenly got down on one knee and opened the box to reveal a gorgeous diamond solitaire ring.

'I love you, Betty Ann,' he said. 'And I would be very honoured if you would marry me.'

I was so shocked, and it was so unexpected, that I did what I always do in times of extreme stress. I ran to the toilet and promptly threw up!

Thankfully Kent knew about my delicate constitution and thought it was funny.

'Is that a yes then?' he asked when I came back ten minutes later.

'Oh,' I smiled. 'Sorry, yes, it's a yes!'

Although I had never been in a rush to get married, I knew I loved Kent. Unlike all the other proposals I'd had before, this felt right.

That night we were due to go to a party at Sandra and Jim's house. All of the Pan Am girls were there with their husbands and they all screamed with delight when I showed them my sparkly new ring. I was the last of the group to get married and they were so pleased for me.

The first thing I had wanted to do was phone my parents, but because of the time difference, it would have been the middle of the night, so we had to wait until Christmas morning to break the news. At that time, direct dialling international calls without needing an operator to put you through had just become available. So Kent had researched the process and, armed with a long, complicated sequence of numbers, he started to dial, while I sat next to him on the couch and listened in.

There was a long pause while the call went through and we waited nervously. Finally someone picked up the phone.

'Hello, this is Kent Riegel, Betty's boyfriend in San Francisco,' he said. 'I wanted to tell you that I've just proposed to your daughter. I love her deeply and I promise to care for her for the rest of our lives, and I wonder if I could have your blessing to get married?'

We both waited with bated breath to hear my dad's response.

'What?' said a strange voice on the other end of the line. 'Who on earth is this?'

'This is Kent Riegel in San Francisco and I'm trying to call England,' Kent said. 'Who are you?'

'My name's Roy and I'm in Kansas, and I don't know anyone called Betty,' the man said.

'Oh, sorry,' said Kent. 'Wrong number.'

Poor Kent had given his big speech to the wrong person! Finally he got through to my dad and repeated it all over again.

'Yes, please,' said Dad. 'Thank you.'

I was absolutely horrified that he'd said 'please' and 'thank you' – as if he was glad to get rid of me, or he'd just asked Kent to pass him the butter!

Then it was my turn to talk to him.

'I'm really excited, Dad. I didn't know anything about this,' I told him, and I could hear Mum squealing in the background.

'That's lovely news, dear,' she said.

Kent wanted to get married straight away, but I managed to persuade him to wait until March 1968. My supervisor arranged a free ticket for Mum and Dad to come over for the big day, which was at the chapel on Treasure Island Naval Station, followed by a reception at the Bachelor Officers' Quarters, which overlooks San Francisco Bay and the city. We invited 120 guests for hors d'oeuvres and Champagne, including Auntie Belle, Uncle C. D. and Shirley, and my bridesmaids were all stewardesses – Sandra, Hazel, Angie and Dawn.

My parents had a great time, especially Dad, who got a bit tipsy. He was drinking Champagne and getting really wobbly because he wasn't used to it.

'Don't be drinking so much,' Mum told him.

'It's not my fault, these waiters keep filling my glass,' he slurred.

'Well, don't drink it, silly, then they won't have to fill it up,' said Mum.

It was Kent's job to book the honeymoon, but because I'd already been to so many places with Pan Am, he didn't have a clue where to take me. At that time, the film *The Night of the Iguana*, which starred Richard Burton and Ava Gardner, was very popular. It was set in Puerto Vallarta, Mexico, which looked really beautiful in the movie, so he thought it would be nice to go there.

We spent the first night at a hotel at the airport in LA. As I opened my suitcase, which I had entrusted to Hazel, my maid of honour, for safekeeping, I discovered that all my clothes, including the negligee I'd bought especially for my wedding night, were covered in paper flower petals.

'It's an English tradition,' I explained to a puzzled-looking Kent. 'Don't worry, I'll sort it out in time for "lights out"!'

As it turned out, we were staying at the same hotel that my parents were staying in, so we had breakfast with them the next morning, before they caught their flight back to London. I could tell Kent was a bit bemused by it all.

'I didn't think I'd be having breakfast with my new parents-in-law the day after our wedding night,' he joked. 'Is this another English tradition? Is there something you're not telling me? They're not coming to Mexico, are they?'

We flew to Mexico on a Comet, which was the world's first commercial jet and was made and designed in England. We couldn't book a hotel because we were 'space available' on the flight, as it was a free ticket, and unfortunately we ended up staying in a horrible, run-down motel.

'What a hovel,' I said when I saw the dirty, tatty room, with its two grubby single beds. Even worse, as we discovered later, it was opposite a bar, so there was loud music playing all night and trucks coming and going.

'I'm sorry, Betty,' said Kent. 'This wasn't the exotic honeymoon destination that I'd planned.'

I knew it wasn't his fault, but I'd wanted everything to be perfect and instead I spent the night sitting on the bed, crying.

Thankfully things only got better. The next morning we got a flight to Mexico City, then on to Acapulco. We ate all the local food and we were very proud of the fact that we didn't get ill the whole time we were gone. The first night we got back to San Francisco, we bought two Mexican TV dinners. TV dinners were an amazing new invention in the late 1960s – a ready-made meal on a foil platter, which you put in the oven for half an hour. But although we'd survived the food on honeymoon, we both got as sick as dogs from our TV dinners.

Now, finally, I was Mrs Riegel, and Kent and I moved into a rented apartment together. It was only going to be a temporary home though. Kent had always told me that when his marine service finished, he wanted to move to the east coast of America, to be near his parents, who were quite elderly. So, three months after our wedding, his time was up and he got a job as a civilian lawyer with the Judge Advocate General's Office in Virginia.

Even though I was married now, I was determined not to give up my career, like most of my friends had after they'd walked down the aisle. I still loved my job and it was a big part of my life.

'I'd be bored just sat at home all day while you're at work,' I told Kent.

He understood how important it was to me to continue working, and fortunately by now, Pan Am had changed the rules, so you no longer had to retire once you were married. So I spoke to my managers and they agreed to transfer me to the nearest airport to our new home, which was Washington Dulles.

But even though I wasn't giving up work, my life was about to change, as I had to leave San Francisco, which had been my home for eight years. It also meant I would no longer be able to fly on the routes that I loved across the Pacific. There would be no more wonderful adventures in places like Hawaii, Hong Kong, Australia and Moorea. The time had come to say goodbye to my old life.

Chapter Sixteen

A Farewell to Flying

My last flight out of San Francisco is something that I will always remember. It was a twelve-day trip, looping around the South Pacific and visiting all my favourite places.

I was allowed to take Kent with me, which was lovely, as I could show him all the places I had been telling him about. We went to Honolulu, Pago Pago, Fiji, Papeete and then on to Sydney. The rest of the crew made him feel very welcome and he was in his element, especially as he flew first class all the way. It felt a bit strange to have to serve him, but he tried to be very professional and made an effort not to distract me from my work.

'Don't worry, I'm not going to be a difficult passenger or give you any problems,' he joked.

True to his word, Kent ate everything in sight and really savoured every single moment, as he had never experienced anything like it before.

I must admit, it was a strange feeling, knowing that it was going to be my final working flight in the Pacific. On our trip out

of Sydney, Bucky McGaigan, who was one of my favourite captains, was flying the plane. He was a lovely guy in his fifties who
reminded me of my Uncle Ted. He knew it was my last flight, so
he let me sit behind him in the cockpit for take-off.

'Well, Betty,' he said. 'Let me give you a little farewell tour.'

Much to my surprise, as we were taking off, he did a big
swoop around Sydney Harbour, so I could see all the sights and
film it on the new Super 8 camera that I'd recently bought in
Tokyo. It made me feel so special that the captain of a 707 full of
passengers was doing this just for me, and it was such a great
way to bow out.

When we were at altitude, I went out of the cockpit to see
Kent. 'What was that strange thing we did just after take-off?' he
asked.

'That was my leaving present from the captain,' I smiled.

Later, on another flight, Bucky let Kent sit in the cockpit and
observe a landing, which was contrary to the rules at the time
and definitely wouldn't be allowed today, but needless to say, it
was a huge thrill for Kent.

In August 1968 it was time to say goodbye to San Francisco.
I loved the city and I was so sad to be leaving my friends behind.
We were all like sisters, but our lives had moved on, and I was
quite proud of the fact that I was the only one out of the origi-
nal group of trainees whom I'd kept in touch with that was still
flying. Hazel had three little boys, Sandra had two girls and
Angie had a daughter by then. Under Pam Am regulations, you
had to resign when you were pregnant, so they had all stopped
flying. Mimi, Florence and Jo were all still in Honolulu and,
sadly, I knew I wouldn't see them as much when I lived on the
east coast.

'Why don't you give up work now you're married?' Hazel
asked.

'I think I'd get bored just being a housewife, and Kent and I don't want children straight away,' I told her.

We found a two-bedroom garden apartment to rent in Falls Church, Virginia. Neither of us had much furniture and, in fact, the only large item we owned was Kent's beloved Mustang convertible, which Pan Am kindly agreed to fly to New York in the hold for the discounted rate of $100, otherwise it would have taken him a week to drive it across the country. We flew on the same flight for the bargain employee's rate of $10 each.

As we landed at JFK Airport, as Idlewild was renamed after President Kennedy's death, my mind was reeling. I was back to where I had started – this was the very first place that I had landed from the UK to begin my training with Pan Am, and it felt like I had come full circle. I remembered how exciting and so full of promise New York had seemed, and for the first time, I realised how far I'd come. I was no longer a naive young trainee. I was an experienced purser and, as Washington Dulles was a much smaller and newer base than San Francisco, I was considered to be quite senior. Now I was the slick professional the young trainees came to for guidance and advice.

Out of my new base, I mainly flew European routes, so the benefit was I got to see Mum and Dad quite a bit. I knew now that I had married Kent, America was going to be my permanent home, but even after all those years, I still missed my parents. Whenever I left, Mum would always pack me off with a case full of all my favourite things that I couldn't buy in America, like Bird's custard powder, McVitie's Chocolate Digestives, Tetley tea bags, Bisto and, my favourite thing of all, a packet of Wall's pork sausages.

Under strict US immigration laws, you were not allowed to bring meat products into the country, so I came up with the most ingenious of hiding places. I would keep the sausages in my handbag, then, just before we landed, I'd stuff one down each finger of my pair of rubber gloves! I was always terrified of being caught as I walked through customs and immigration with a guilty look on my face, but the thought of those fat, juicy British bangers and mash for dinner was always too much of a lure to put a stop to my illegal smuggling.

A few weeks after I started work at Dulles, I was promoted to check purser. It meant I would go on flights and observe newly qualified stewardesses and pursers and write a report on them.

'What's it like being the boss?' asked Kent.

'It's strange because it seems like only yesterday that it was happening to me,' I told him. But now I was the one in charge.

The one thing my new job made me realise is that there is definitely a different atmosphere on a flight when there's a check purser on board. Everybody is on their toes and watching their backs, as they don't want a bad write-up on their record. I must admit, I did find this new responsibility tricky, as I'm the type of person who wants to be everyone's friend, so I tried not to be too critical and always tried to stress the positives.

Another part of my new job was helping Pan Am recruit stewardesses. Again, it felt odd, as it didn't seem like two minutes since Dawn and I were going through the selection process at Heathrow. Pan Am put an advert in the newspaper, then I would go to the Washington offices and interview any girls who turned up.

One important part of my brief was to specifically try to hire some girls from minority groups. In 1964 a landmark Civil Rights Act had been passed which outlawed discriminating against someone because of their sex, race or religion for the first time. Pan Am had hired its first black stewardess in 1965, and I had only ever worked with one African-American girl.

The 1960s were a tumultuous time for race relations. All

throughout my career, tensions had been bubbling around the United States, as people campaigned for equal rights at protests and demonstrations, the most famous one being the 1963 march in Washington DC, where the black Civil Rights activist Martin Luther King had given his famous 'I have a dream' speech.

But sadly, literally days after our wedding, on 4 April 1968, Martin Luther King was shot and killed while he stood on a hotel balcony in Tennessee. As a result of his assassination, there had been race riots in more than a hundred cities across the country. Consequently, race was a highly controversial issue, and companies like Pan Am actively had to be seen as being more inclusive.

On my first day as a recruiter, I think I was more nervous than the applicants, as I didn't know what to expect. I was given a little office of my own and the candidates were brought in one at a time. If I liked any of the girls, I would refer them to the area manager and they would have to go through another interview.

Thankfully there was nowhere near the same number of girls that there had been that day at Heathrow when I had gone through the selection process. In fact there were less than fifty. As each girl came in, I would have to weigh and measure them. I would also look at them carefully to check their deportment, and then I would interview them. I was mainly looking for girls with a good attitude – I wanted to hire people who genuinely cared for others.

The first young lady who came in seemed pleasant enough, but I could tell straight away from looking at her that she was over the required weight limit. I knew how humiliating it must be to not get a job because you were too big, so I tried to be as tactful as possible and let her down gently.

'I'm afraid I can't put you through this time,' I told her, as she stepped off the scales. 'But perhaps try to lose a few pounds and watch out for the adverts and come back and try again.'

'Oh, OK,' she said.

I really didn't like saying no to people, but I had to accept that the strict rules about appearance were part of the job and it had always been that way for me and my peers too.

Even though my duties had changed, life with Pan Am was still as eventful as ever. One day I was working at Washington Dulles when a flight came in from San Salvador and the purser came to see me in a flap.

'I don't know what to do,' she said. 'There was an unaccompanied minor travelling with us, but there's no one here to meet her.'

The little girl was around eight years old, and the poor thing looked terrified. None of us spoke much Spanish, so we couldn't even reassure her. When children were travelling alone, they wore tags around their necks and the purser on the flight looked after them. The purser had been calling the number on the paperwork belonging to the relative who was supposed to meet her, but there was no answer.

'Don't worry,' I said. 'I'll take her home with me and we'll try to contact her family again tomorrow.'

Kent's face was a picture when I walked through the door with my new friend.

'This is Maria,' I said. 'And she's going to be staying with us tonight.'

'Oh ... er ... lovely,' he said, not sure what was going on.

Despite the fact that she had been abandoned at the airport, Maria seemed quite happy as she tucked into some roast chicken with us, and even though I only spoke a little bit of Spanish, we managed to get by. Thankfully, by the time I took her back to work the next day, they had managed to trace her relatives, who came up with the pitiful excuse that they had been delayed on their way to the airport. I often look back on that story and think how times have changed. There's no way I would have been allowed to take Maria back home with me these days, and the poor thing would probably have been taken into care.

Kent and I wanted children of our own eventually, but we decided to wait until we had been married a year. Seemingly, we waited exactly a year and a day! The night after our first anniversary, we went to a party and when we came home, we turned on our black and white television set to watch the footage of the Apollo 9 rocket blasting off into space. It was a major breakthrough for space travel, as the mission was testing out the spacecraft that would eventually enable man to land on the moon.

It was a historic night in more ways than one. It was also the night that I conceived our first child.

By the time the first man walked on the moon, on 20 July 1969, I was four months pregnant. It was so exciting, sitting in bed with Kent, watching that incredible moment when Neil Armstrong put his left foot forwards and proclaimed: 'That's one small step for man, one giant leap for mankind.'

'I can't believe a man has actually walked on the moon,' I sighed.

Suddenly the world seemed full of so many possibilities. Such was the excitement that Pan Am announced it would be accepting reservations for its first passenger flights to the moon. It's rumoured that it was just a bit of a joke at first, but the response was so overwhelming that the company started what it called the First Moon Flights Club. Every person who put their name down on the list was issued with a free card with their name and a number on and it was signed by the vice president. By the time the list was closed in 1971, it was rumoured there were 93,000 people on it, and apparently it's still stored in the airline's archives somewhere.

But going to the moon was the last thing on my mind. I was thirty by now, so had come to motherhood relatively late compared to my friends. But it had me taken until now to feel ready to have a family.

But, true to form, the minute I found out I was pregnant, I was as sick as a dog. My view was that pregnancy wasn't an illness and I was determined not to let it affect my work, but it was impossible when I was throwing up day and night.

When I was six weeks pregnant, I managed to make it through a flight to London. But then a manager rang me at the crew hotel in the middle of the night.

'We need you to supervise an all-first-class flight to New York,' he said.

I hadn't told anyone I was pregnant yet, as I knew it would mean that I would have to resign. But I felt so awful, I knew I would have to come clean.

'I'm so sorry, but I don't think I can do it,' I said. 'I'm pregnant and I feel dreadful.'

'Miss Eden [even though I was now married, under the Pan Am culture, I would always be referred to as a "miss"], may I remind you that this call is being recorded,' the manager told me. 'So you might want to keep your news to yourself for now.'

'I know,' I said. 'And I know I'll have to resign eventually, but I just don't think I can do this flight because I keep throwing up.'

I was so sick, they gave me permission to deadhead back to Washington instead. I felt too ill to realise it at the time, but that was my last ever flight as a Pan Am employee. After I returned,

I was put on desk duty and did the pre-flight briefings instead. In accordance with the rules, I resigned when I was seven months pregnant.

Of course I was excited about having a baby, but I was sad to be giving up my career, especially as there were exciting times ahead in the aviation industry. A few months after I left, 747s came into service at Pan Am. They became known as jumbo jets and brought with them hundreds more passengers, brand-new uniforms and a whole new era of flying that, sadly, I would no longer be part of.

At that time, every stewardesses had to retire when she had children. But later on, in the early 1970s, the Supreme Court ruled that it was illegal for a company to discriminate, so Pan Am had to offer us our old jobs back. I knew it wouldn't work for me with young children, but some ex-stewardesses did return to work, especially if they had older children or were now divorced.

When I was six months pregnant, Kent got a job as the general counsel for the Department of Agriculture in Maryland, so we moved to Annapolis. For the first three years I'd worked at Pan Am, $300 had been taken out of my wage each month to pay for my uniform. When that had finally been paid off, I'd got used to not having that money, so I'd started putting the $300 into a savings account. By now, I had over $3,000 in the bank, which I used as the deposit on our first house – a brand-new three-bedroom detached. I felt so proud that my hard work had helped buy us a home.

Our son, John Kent, was born in December 1969. One night, when he was six months old, I was stood in the garden holding him while Kent planted some roses. It was around the same time as the Pan Am flights would leave for Europe, and as I looked up, I saw a plane taking off. But on this particular night, the clouds were rolling in and the sky looked very dark and foreboding, like it was going to storm.

'I'm so glad I'm not up there tonight.' I said to Kent.

I looked at him, working away in our new garden, trying to make it beautiful for our little family, and I looked at John Kent, snuggling into my shoulder, all sleepy and sweet-smelling after his bath. Then I glanced down at myself. I hadn't had my hair done in weeks, I was wearing a pair of old shorts and a plain top and I was burping John Kent, so he was probably about to be sick on my shoulder. But I realised then that I wouldn't swap this for anything. Yes, I used to fly around the world to glamorous locations, my clothes were dry-cleaned for me, I stayed in five-star hotels and ate gourmet meals in the best restaurants. That was my life then, but this was my life now. I was no longer a stewardess and the perks and the glamour that went with the job had long gone. I was so lucky to have been part of that exclusive club, and I'd had the time of my life. But I was a wife and a mother now, and I finally felt ready for that, so I had no regrets.

Forty-odd years have passed now since that moment, but old habits die hard. I constantly find myself looking up at planes in the sky and wondering where they are going. Even the sight of a jet trail makes me all nostalgic, and I can still recall the feeling of being part of that select community up in the air.

I'm a terrible flyer these days. I find it so boring, just sitting there, not doing anything. A few years ago, I was on a flight and I could tell the attendants were really struggling, so I went to the back galley to see if I could help.

'I used to be a Pan Am stewardess,' I told them. 'Would you like a hand?' So, much to Kent's amusement, I ended up pouring coffee for the passengers.

But things are so different now. Stewardesses are no more: everyone is a flight attendant or cabin crew, which is more politically correct, and sadly there's not the same level of service. It's all about cramming as many people as possible onto a plane, and no one has time to get to know the passengers or chat. My favourite part of the flight when I was a purser was always straight after we were airborne, when I would sit on the arm of the last seat in economy class, right at the back of the plane, and look down the long corridor of people. Then I would think to myself: 'This is my world and these are my guests and I'm going to try to make this a wonderful experience for them.' I treated Pan Am passengers as if they were guests in my own living room, and I took great pride in that fact.

Of course it wasn't all fun; it was hard work too. On long flights we would be on our feet for thirteen hours. It was hard and I felt like chewed-up string by the time we arrived at our destination, especially as, in the early years, I had probably been up late at a party the night before. But sadly what we had is no more – the excitement and the glamour of flying have long gone. To be on a plane in the 1960s felt like being a guest at an exclusive party, and it was a real privilege to be there.

I was only flying for nine years, but my whole life is based on my Pan Am experience. It was a real finishing school for life, in all sorts of different areas, and it's made me who I am now. It was an amazing career, and the best part was seeing all those wonderful places and meeting so many great people. Even now most of my close friends are ex-stewardesses because they're the people I have most in common with.

I feel so privileged that, unlike other girls my age growing up in the sixties, I didn't just have a job to pass the time until I got married – I had a career that I loved. Pan Am stewardesses were the envy of women the world over and I even came to be a mini-celebrity in my home town. I was financially independent and travelled the world without needing a man by my side.

Now, at the age of seventy-three, that feels like another life. I often wonder how things would have turned out if I hadn't gone for the Pan Am interview with Dawn that day. I don't dwell on it, but the only sad part for me is that if I'd stayed in England, I would have been able to see Mum and Dad more. The only downside of the job was that it took me away from my family and I missed out on the day-to-day contact with my parents. Dad passed away twenty-two years ago, at the age of seventy-seven, after having heart problems for a number of years. Thankfully I was able to fly back to England and see him before he died.

Mum is still the remarkable, strong, determined woman she always was. She's ninety-eight now and lives in South Gloucestershire, close to my brother Geoff and his family. I talk to her every day on the phone and fly over to visit her, and we worked out the other day that she has flown over the Atlantic at least sixty times. Not bad for someone who hadn't been on a plane until she was in her fifties.

Unfortunately Pan Am no longer exists, but I savour every single memory of my time with the company. When I look at my photographs, I can't believe I did all of that. I cherish every single memory of my wonderful adventures up in the air, and I feel so very lucky that I was given this most incredible opportunity. I will never ever forget it.

Acknowledgements

This whole book process started after my dear husband Kent watched the Pan Am TV series and contacted our local paper, the *Wilmington News Journal*, to ask if they would like to do a story about a real Pan Am stewardess from the 1960s. Unbeknown to us at the time, this kick-started a chain of events which have led to this book, and I would like to pay tribute to everyone involved in that journey.

From Betsy Price, the lovely journalist who wrote the article in the *News Journal*, and Jennifer Corbett, who took the photos, to my talented and warm new friend and ghost writer, Heather Bishop, who came across my story and believed it had the potential to be something more than a newspaper article. I would also like to thank my literary agent, Rowan Lawton, who has guided me through all of the intricacies of publishing with patience and good humour, and my editor, Carly Cook at Simon & Schuster. All of these ladies have helped contribute to what has been the thrill of a lifetime, and the most incredibly exciting opportunity for me.

Finally, I would like to thank my wonderful family. My brother Geoff and his lovely wife Pauline, who devotedly care for our mum, Ruby, in the UK, as she approaches her ninety-ninth birthday. And last, but by no means least, my husband Kent and our sons, John Kent Junior and Geoff, who have been with me every step of the way, cheering from the sidelines.

About the Author

Betty Riegel was born in March 1939 at Thorpe Coombe Maternity Hospital in Walthamstow. At the age of twenty-one, she was one of seventeen British girls chosen out of a thousand applicants by Pan American Airlines to be a stewardess. Leaving her parents and brother thousands of miles away back in the UK, she flew to New York for six weeks of intensive training. She served with Pan Am for nine years and was based in New York, San Francisco and Washington DC, where she had many exciting adventures travelling around the world.

In 1975, drawing on a lifetime's experience of travel, Betty qualified as a travel consultant, which she still does. Since then, she's helped to run 'Fear of Flying' courses with other ex-Pan Am employees and is an associate member of World Wings, the Pan Am veterans' group.

Pan American Airlines ceased operating in December 1991, after declaring bankruptcy.

Betty now lives in Centreville, Delaware, USA, with her husband Kent, their sons, John Kent Junior and Geoff, and their rescue dog, Abby. At the age of seventy-three, she is fulfilling a lifelong ambition to obtain a degree and is in her third year at the University of Delaware.

Appendix

Qualifications for Probationary Flight Service Employment
Pan American World Airways – Atlantic Division

1. Age: 21 to (and including) 27 at time of employment.
2. Height: 5'2" to 5'8" (1.58 to 1.73 metres).
3. Weight: 110 to 135 pounds (50 to 61 kilograms), well proportioned.
4. Marital Status: Single.
5. High School Graduate or equivalent (two years' college preferred).
6. Must be fluent in English and one of the following languages: French, Italian, German, Portuguese, Dutch, Swedish, Danish, Norwegian, Finnish, Turkish, Arabic, Hindustani or Greek.
7. Must be citizen of the United States or be able to obtain an Immigration Visa to the U.S.
8. Must be able to obtain and maintain passport, visas and resident status, and be able to travel freely and perform duties as assigned while in all countries to which the Company flies.
9. Must be in excellent health and able to pass flight physical (medical) examination. Vision must be 20/50 in each

eye correctable to 20/20. Eyeglasses or contact lenses not permitted.

10. Must have good posture and appearance.
11. Must be of good moral character.
12. Must have pleasant speaking voice and habitually use good English.
13. Must have pleasing personality, tact and diplomacy, and possess a genuine liking for people. Previous stewardess experience helpful.
14. Must be willing, adaptable and prepared for hard work.
15. Must be able to swim.
16. Although domicile normally is New York, applicant must be willing to accept an overseas assignment of up to three years' duration, should the need arise.

This book is to be returned on or before
the last date stamped below.